James Bates and J. R. Parkinson

BUSINESS ECONOMICS

Third Edition

Revised for this edition by
JOHN BATES, BRIAN CHIPLIN
& MIKE WRIGHT

Basil Blackwell · Oxford

© Basil Blackwell Publisher Limited 1963, 1969, 1982

First published 1963
Second edition 1969
Reprinted 1971, 1978
Third edition revised by John Bates, Brian Chiplin and
Mike Wright 1982

Basil Blackwell Publisher Limited
108 Cowley Road, Oxford OX4 1JF, England

British Library Cataloguing in Publication Data

Bates, James
    Business economics. – Rev. ed.
    1. Managerial economics
    I. Title II. Parkinson, J. R.
    III. Bates, John IV. Chiplin, Brian
    V. Wright, Mike
    330'.024658   HD58.5

    ISBN 0-631-13146-9
    ISBN 0-631-13147-7 Pbk

Typesetting by Unicus Graphics Ltd, Horsham.
Printed and bound in Great Britain by Billings, Worcester.

Contents

Tables

Figures

Preface to the Third Edition

We found the prospect of writing a third edition of *Business Economics* daunting and we were not able to bring ourselves to do it. Yet we felt that a textbook that had run for 20 years on two editions might justify a further effort to bring it up-to-date. Faced with this dilemma we found an answer in the energy, expertise and enthusiasm of our colleagues, the new authors, who have taken the burden off our shoulders. Mr John Bates has prepared chapters 2 and 3; Mr Brian Chiplin chapters 1, 4, 5, 6 and 11; and Mr Mike Wright chapters 7, 8, 9 and 10. All of them are at the University of Nottingham. In extending our thanks to them we derive a perhaps undeserved satisfaction in realizing that what we set out to do so long ago has gained a new lease of life in a completely new setting.

In the Preface to the first edition of *Business Economics* we wrote:

Those who have attempted to teach short courses in economics to students in industrial administration will appreciate how necessary it is to be selective in choosing material. Economics as it is taught is concerned largely with the economy as a whole and its organization and management; the theory of the firm is scarcely more than a step in this process; and much of what is taught in economics seems to have small relevance to the problems of those in business – particularly those in small business. A knowledge of the factors making for a high level of demand, an efficient exchange of commodities in international trade and the organization of world finance are sometimes relevant to the success of large businesses and can be considered by expert economic sections in relation to the general policy of the firm; but the small firm can seldom rise to these refinements and to a young general manager economics often seems to be either obvious in elementary exposition inapplicable to real-life situations in its more sophisticated forms, or just plainly irrelevant. It is not easy to defend economics against these criticisms by arguing that the best form of education for management is general education, and that relevance is a secondary matter. Education for management covers a wide field and some, at least, of the matter imparted must be of use in a narrow technical sense in addition to contributing to general education.

In this book we have attempted to extract from the general body of economic thought some parts that seem to us to be particularly relevant to taking decisions in business. We do not, of course, think that we have covered every aspect of economics with relevance to business decisions; and we have deliberately abstained from treating some subjects of importance, for example, wages and industrial relations.

The theme of the book is that while the economic situation is always changing, and the businessman is therefore operating in an uncertain world, it is nevertheless possible to take business decisions in a systematic fashion, and by using appropriate techniques and ways of thought to reduce the uncertainties involved.

Although *Business Economics* has been almost completely rewritten, what we wrote 20 years ago about our aims still remains valid in this up-to-date treatment of the subject.

JAMES BATES   J. R. PARKINSON
Belfast   *Nottingham*

1

The Rules of the Game

Business economics is concerned with the factors that operate in determining business decisions and with the effects of those decisions. It provides a useful framework of analysis through which the implications of any particular decision can be traced. It can therefore suggest whether the course of action proposed is likely to result in the achievement of the objectives. The operation of a business essentially involves three key elements: the generation of a plan; the actions taken to put the plan into effect; and an assessment of the success of the actions in meeting the plan. For any business, these three elements will be complex and will involve considerations of production, sales and marketing, and finance, which are all interrelated. In order to generate plans that are likely to be successful, it is important to have an understanding of these major factors.

Consequently, in this book we examine first, the principles involved in production; aspects of the market; and finance (chapters 2–7). This provides a basis for the discussion of assessing performance (chapter 8); investment (chapter 9); control (chapter 10); and corporate strategy (chapter 11). The chapters have been arranged in this way as an aid to exposition. Although corporate strategy (the plan) should come first in the determination of actual business decisions, the complex factors involved cannot be fully understood without a basic analysis of the key areas of the operations of a business. We also place considerable emphasis on assessment of performance both in terms of financial and accounting data and in relation to control. It seems to us essential that any treatment of business economics should pay due attention to performance indicators and any manager should have at least a working knowledge of the main issues.

In the book we concentrate on the general principles of business operations while seeking to relate the concepts closely to real-world illustrations. The book is designed not as an exercise in abstract economic reasoning, but rather as a guide to the practical advantages of analysing decisions in economic terms. We emphasize that business problems cannot be solved with economic analysis alone, but we would like to suggest that a familiarity with economic principles is important if a business is to achieve success in the long term. There are many examples of businesses that have been started on the basis of a good idea, only to founder on the neglect of economic factors. The collapse of the Laker business early in 1982 illustrates no more than the surface of this phenomenon.

The principles we expound in this text are of relevance to all types of business enterprise. They apply equally to the large state-owned enterprise, the large private-sector firm, the small owner-managed business, partnership, worker co-operative and 'one-man band'. The precise circumstances, the range of decisions and the objectives pursued will differ from case to case, but all enterprises are affected by general economic and market forces whether they are 'free' or controlled by the state. In order to set the decisions in context, we consider in this chapter the broad 'rules of the game' under which businesses operate.

THE OBJECTIVES OF THE BUSINESS

If a business is to formulate a plan, the first necessity is to determine the objective that the plan is designed to achieve. These objectives may vary according to the type of business, its organizational structure and the type of markets in which it operates. Thus, for example, the objectives of a workers' co-operative are likely to be different from those of a firm that is owned by a single entrepreneur. Whether, in fact, market forces will lead to the same outcome independent of the original objectives is a matter of some contention.[1] In both these cases there is a clear relationship between ownership and control of the business. But in the larger businesses in a country such as Britain, the owners may be totally distinct from those who have day-to-day control (the managers).

This divorce between ownership and control and its effects has been central to much of the discussion of business economics. In large-scale private enterprises, the controls that owners can impose on managers are fairly limited in practice. Thus, for example, the annual general meeting of most companies tends to be rather short and attendance by shareholders sparse.[2] The facts that the ownership of a typical large company is diffused and that any one shareholder has a limited impact both serve to reduce the element of control. The institutional shareholders (insurance companies, pension funds, unit trusts, banks, etc.) now own a substantial proportion of the ordinary shares in UK companies, but traditionally they have been rather reluctant to interfere in the day-to-day management of the companies in which they have a stake. One important threat to managerial autonomy that remains is that the company might be taken over by another enterprise, and it is frequently presumed that managers wish to preserve their independence. However, as we note in chapter 11, there are good reasons why a company might wish to become part of a larger enterprise and, in addition, it does not seem as if poor performance is necessarily penalized by a takeover bid.[3]

There is a further important point in relation to objectives: except for some small firms, most companies are not run by a single person. The objectives of a business will, therefore, be determined as some combination of the differing objectives of the individuals concerned, and the more individuals there are, the more difficult will be the process of formulating the agreed objectives for the organization as a whole. The outcome is similar, therefore to a coalition among managers.[4]

In most treatments of business economics, the role of profit is regarded as central to the aims of the business. The enterprise will not survive if it is unable to make a profit for any length of time; the necessary finance for both working and physical capital (see chapter 7) will be forthcoming only if the firm can demonstrate that it has a profitable future. There is no denying that profit is a major factor in business decisions, but there is some dispute between business economists as to whether firms predominantly seek, or are forced to seek, the maximization of these profits, or whether the need to earn some minimum level of profit acts as a constraint on other objectives that the firm might wish to pursue. For our purposes, it is not necessary to come down firmly on one side or the other but merely to recognize that profit will be important to businessmen in reaching their decisions. Profit is, however, a complex concept, which is frequently misunderstood. It is therefore appropriate in this section to reflect on the nature and purpose of profits.

Put at its simplest, profit arises when there is a surplus of revenue over costs in a period of trading. In a limited sense this is a definition, but it does not say anything about how or why profits arise, or about their function and relation to other economic concepts. Moreover, the concept of profit is open to dispute over the meaning of the terms 'cost' and 'revenue'. As we shall discuss in detail in chapter 7, there is a crucial difference between the business economist and the accountant over the valid items to be included in calculating profit, particularly on the cost side.

For generations, theoretical economists have sought a consistent definition of profits. Wages, rent and interest may be looked on as a reward for the corresponding factors of production, labour, land and capital, but it has always proved difficult to isolate a specific factor of production to which profit may be said to accrue as a reward.

Several different theories have been advanced, and perhaps the best known of these is that profits are a reward for bearing risk and uncertainty.[5] There is no need to bear those risks of fire and other accidental damage to, or loss of, plant and stocks that can be covered by insurance, and they are not related to profit. But most of the risks of manufacture and trading are not insurable. Every businessman undertakes some risk when he manufactures a product in anticipation of demand, and the more specialized is a form of business activity, the more risk and uncertainty there may be. The successful salvage of gold from the wreck of HMS *Edinburgh* in 1981 is a good example of a high-risk activity which in the end resulted in substantial rewards. The reduction of risk may be one of the main motives for a policy of diversification, which we discuss in chapter 11. Anything new involves the risk that the public will not buy it, and the failure rate of new products is high. Certain trades are more susceptible to sudden swings in demand and are, therefore, likely to be more risky. Technological change can render whole sections of industry obsolete.

If profit is thought of purely as a reward for risk, however, it will not coincide with what most people would think of in a general way as profit. Certain wage-earning occupations, such as coal mining, diving in the North Sea, etc., carry physical risks, and increasingly many jobs carry the risk of redundancy. Nevertheless, it is rarely suggested that an appropriate part of the wages of such employment should be thought of as 'profit'. Even if the risk theory does not provide a complete explanation, there is little doubt that it would be difficult to justify economic risk-taking without some prospect of gain or profit, which in capitalistic countries would accrue to the entrepreneur and the providers of share capital.

Another theory regards profit as a reward for innovation and enterprise, for seeing the possibilities latent in various fields of action and in new technological development.[6] To some extent this view is a variant of the risk theory, but reward for risk is not a necessary part of the profit from innovations. The theory may also be looked on as a variant of that concerned with imperfections of the market or 'market failure', because it stresses that profit may come from the exploitation of a temporary advantage. This temporary advantage may arise by chance from unexpected events, which may vastly increase anticipated profits or turn them into losses ('windfall' gains or losses). For example, large changes in profits can occur through variations in the exchange rate, and the Laker Airways collapse in 1982 illustrates the problems that a substantial fall of the pound against the dollar causes when fixed payments have to be made in dollars.

On the other hand, temporary advantage may arise from the superior ability of some firms to recognize or create profitable opportunities. In this case, profit can be regarded as a reward to entrepreneurial ability. When innovations of technique or marketing, or indeed in any other aspect of business organization, are made, there will be a period when the successful innovator can make substantial profits. As long as there are no particular barriers preventing other firms from following the example, these profits will eventually be reduced and shared out by the forces of competition. For example, even where there is some barrier created by a patent on an invention, the latest research would indicate that imitation is fairly rapid and extensive.[7] Since innovation is almost always taking place, profit is always earned somewhere in the economy, and thus profit is linked to change and growth.

The economic literature distinguishes between 'normal' profit and 'super-normal' profit (or, in the case of sub-normal profit, losses). Normal profit is defined in opportunity cost terms (see chapter 2) usually in relation to capital, where it is recognized that the capital involved in any particular enterprise has an alternative use. If it is to be employed in any particular sector it must earn a profit at least as great as that which could be earned elsewhere with due allowance for any differences in risk. If an activity yields a return lower than this normal profit, it would be expected that some businesses will cease trading in that sector and use their capital elsewhere; although it should be noted that capital is not necessarily mobile between uses and there may be barriers to exit. We look at the problems of adjusting to declining demand in chapter 11. Similarly, if firms in a particular sector are earning above-normal profits, one would expect the entry of new participants. In a perfectly competitive economy (see chapter 6), in the long run the equilibrium would occur when no abnormal profits or losses were being made by any firm; i.e., all firms would be making only sufficient to keep them in that business. This is part of the difference between the accountant's and the economist's view of profit. The concept of normal profit (i.e., no more than is required to maintain an activity) is useful for the understanding of the operation of a business.

In the light of the previous discussion, it can be seen that super-normal profit can derive from at least three sources:[8] divergence from conditions of perfect competition and the importance of monopoly elements in a market; windfall gains; and reward to entrepreneurial ability. Once these distinctions are recognized it can be seen that it is misleading to regard above-normal profit as necessarily bad. If it arises as the result of innovation and the spotting of opportunities, it is an essential element in the dynamic re-shaping of an economy.

Some of what is normally called profit in everyday life is part of the reward to the various factors of production, such as rents on property owned by the business or interest paid on capital borrowed (a proportion of the dividend on ordinary share capital is likely to be profit). One factor of production — management, a specialized form of labour — may also receive its reward partly in the form of profit. The sole owner, who manages as well as owns the business, achieves a surplus of receipts over costs, some of which is, in a sense, his managerial income and some of which is pure profit or return to enterprise. But what matters to him is that he earns something for running the firm, whether it be for entrepreneurial ability or risk-bearing, and he calls this his profit.

With the increasing difficulty in modern business life of identifying the entrepreneur, particularly in large corporations, it becomes harder to state which factor of production receives its reward in the form of profit. If, as is often the case, a business is run by professional managers on fixed salaries who use the capital of other people, the answer may well be that it is not possible to ascribe anything called profit to the firm as an institution. Some of the surplus will accrue to managers in the form of extra-high wages or 'perks'; some will be paid to shareholders as interest and a reward for the risks that they bear; the rest will be put by for future expansion.

Profit is different from other kinds of income because it is not contractual, like wages and rent or fixed interest; it is a residual item accruing as a result of producing in anticipation of demand: the businessman may be able to estimate profit fairly accurately, but he rarely receives it from anyone else as a contractual obligation: the rare cases in which he appears to do so, as in certain contracts agreeing a particular profit margin irrespective of cost, are really to be regarded as payment for services. Since profit is a residual, it runs the risk of being negative, and is liable to fluctuate with changes in business conditions. Thus the element of uncertainty distinguishes profits from other components of the value added by the productive process.

There is a lot to be said for the common-sense notion that profit is a reward for the successful conduct of a business. Several things contribute to this, and theories of profit draw attention to some of them; it is not really necessary to go any further. For present purposes profits may be defined as the monetary proceeds from and incentive to successful business activity. This definition is not water-tight and it evades rather than solves the theoretical difficulties, but it is a convenient categorization of this complex source of income.

The aims of businessmen are varied, and the money to be obtained from a business is only one reason for being in it; non-financial consi-derations are more important than is often imagined. An important reason for setting up a business has always been the desire for personal independence. But the way of small business is hard; it is not easy to get established, and it is difficult to expand.[9] Larger firms may benefit from economies of scale, which enable them to buy more cheaply, to use methods of production that are economical only for long runs, and to push sales with all the resources of a specialized section of the firm. Personal supervision often does not suffice to offset these advantages, and many small proprietors get a smaller income from their businesses than they would be able to earn in alternative occu-pations. Many small shopkeepers, in particular, are likely to be in this position. Such people must be regarded as maximizing the net advantages of their occupation – in this case the value of indepen-dence sustained by a modest income – rather than as struggling to maximize monetary earnings in isolation. It would be misleading to judge their success or failure by the profit-making criterion alone.

It is increasingly being recognized that an active small-firms sector is an important aspect of a successful market economy. It is note-worthy, for example, that the proportion of people employed in small firms is lower in Britain than in any of the major industrial economies with whom we compete.[10] Successful small firms offer the opportunity for expansion, but growth requires effort; it involves worry and risk; the rewards are cut by taxation; if present profitability is sufficient to provide for an acceptable and customary standard of living in line with the family position and aspirations of neighbours, there may be no desire on the part of the proprietor of a business to expand further. However, in order for an economy to be capable of adjusting to change, it is important that the successful elements in the small-firm sector should be encouraged to grow and that industrial policy should not impose unnecessary restrictions on the ability of small firms to expand.

The reasons for business expansion are not always economic. The tycoon bent on expansion may be more concerned with the prestige, political influence, personal realization and power conferred by control of a large business. At this stage in the development of an enterprise, profits may be sacrificed to expansion. Business is also creative; nursing and teaching are not the only occupations in which a sense of vocation may appear to be more important than pecuniary considerations. There are many dedicated businessmen who rank the satisfaction to be obtained in business with that obtained from practising in the professions. It is no longer realistic to depict the major part of the business sector as being run by some imaginary race of entrepreneurs owning their own firms and personally retaining the profits.

Even large businesses do not concentrate on maximizing profits to the exclusion of other objectives, and they are unlikely to put considerations of growth on one side. Professor Baumol, writing from his business experience,[11] points to management's preoccupation with growth and the rate of growth of output that can be sustained given the availability and cost of capital and the risks inherent in expansion. Many businesses may attempt to maximize growth rather than profits. On the other hand, many businesses may be content with satisficing behaviour[12] rather than with the maximization of some objective. Satisficing behaviour may be said to occur when businessmen aim at satisfactory performance in terms of some criteria such as profit, growth or, on a different level, contribution to the community. Thus, performance is assessed in terms of some level of aspiration that itself is determined by past experience and future expectations. What is satisfactory will also be influenced by the ease with which the target is met. Thus if achievement is simple it is likely that the target will be raised upwards.

Growth and maximization of profits may not be incompatible. Profits may be both the means to and the consequence of growth; it is not suggested that growth is possible without profits or that profits are ever entirely sacrificed for growth. Even when maximization of profits is the objective, it may sometimes be necessary to limit profits in the short run in the interests of expanding them in the future.

In practice, businesses must have regard to the public interest as well as to the interest of their shareholders, and this may mean some sacrifice of profit. Many business decisions involve moral as well as monetary judgements, and such decisions are often difficult to make because a balance has to be struck between different interests. Maximization of profit is unlikely to override all other considerations. A business with monopoly power is likely to exploit its position to some degree, whether through increased profits or excess costs; but, irrespective of fears of encouraging new competitors or of regulation by the government, a company may deliberately refrain from exploiting its market power to the full, preferring to follow some concept of a fair or reasonable price. For similar reasons, a firm's policy in relation, for example, to redundancy may be more generous than would be dictated solely by considerations of self-interest.

The above discussion has provided a brief introduction to some of the issues involved. Within the firms themselves there may be many objectives that the individual managers are trying to pursue, but for planning and decision-making purposes it is essential that, through whatever process, some clear corporate aim is derived. Economists have tended to stress the importance of profit largely because, at the end of the day, what matters is the bottom line — whether the business is making enough profit to keep shareholders happy and to generate funds for re-investment and possible expansion. As we have tried to show, profits generate important signals in the market and indicate where funds can be put to good use. High profits do not necessarily mean that the public is being unduly exploited.

STRUCTURE, CONDUCT AND PERFORMANCE

One approach to understanding the operations and effects of business which has proved useful in a number of areas has been to investigate the three related concepts of structure, conduct and performance. Such an approach, implicitly at least, underlies many of the deliberations of the Monopolies Commission in Britain in its investigations of industry.[13] Using this scheme, the performance of a company in terms of profitability, efficiency and so on is seen as depending on the particular market structure within which the firm operates. The important dimensions of structure cover such issues as the number and relative size of rival producers in the market, the extent to which there are barriers preventing other firms from entering the market, and the degree to which the products of one company are differentiated from those of another. This structure will itself be influenced by technological factors such as the existence of economies of scale and the type of production processes involved.

Structure is linked to the performance of firms as it affects pricing, marketing, finance, research and development, etc. The actual conduct of a business will depend to a large extent on the objectives that are being pursued by the firm. It is generally presumed that the type of market structure in which the firm finds itself will influence both the range of objectives that it follows and the conduct it adopts. Thus, it is generally presumed that a monopolist will have greater discretion over the firm's conduct and that this in turn may result in a higher price than would occur in more competitive conditions.

In this book, as already indicated, we shall examine the main aspects of business operations and consider the measurement of performance. Also, as we shall stress in chapter 11, the generation of a suitable corporate strategy depends on a clear understanding of the market position of the firm and its strengths and weaknesses. This is why we shall examine in this section some aspects of the general market structure in Britain, which will serve to place the discussion of the remainder of the book in context.

In assessing the industrial structure of a country, economists have found it helpful to use some measures of industrial concentration, that is to say, the extent to which production or marketing lies in a few hands. In broad terms, these measures can relate either to aggregate concentration or to market concentration. The former refers to the relative importance of the largest 50 or 100 (or other arbitrary number) of firms in terms of employment, output or assets. It gives some measure of the centralization of economic power within an economy. In Britain, for manufacturing industry as a whole, the large firms have been becoming more important since the early 1900s. Thus, for example, the 100 largest firms accounted for about 16 per cent of value added in manufacturing in 1909, and for over 40 per cent by the late 1970s.[14] Of course, the identity of the large firms was not necessarily the same; some died through merger, nationalization (in the sense of disappearing from the private sector) or bankruptcy, and some dropped out of the top 100 to be replaced by others. Nevertheless, the figures do indicate that a considerable amount of economic power is possessed by a small number of large firms.

The market concentration ratio refers to the share of an individual market, in terms of sales, output or employment, of the largest three firms (or other small number) operating in that market. In calculating the market concentration ratio there are important problems of defining the market, which we consider in chapter 4. But, taking the figures as they stand, the postwar trends in market concentration in Britain can be broken down into three periods.[15] Prior to 1958 concentration increased but at a moderate rate, but between 1958 and 1968 there was a marked acceleration. Thus, the average share of the five largest enterprises in sales of individual products rose from just over 55 per cent in 1958 to just over 63 per cent in 1968.[16] After 1968, however, there has been a deceleration in the rate of increase.

It would not serve the purposes of this chapter to embark on a detailed analysis of the causes of these trends. It should be noted, however, that a substantial proportion of the increase in market concentration during the 1960s can be put down to the waves of mergers during that period. To assess the contribution of mergers to the change in concentration is difficult, but the broad result suggested by most studies is that about 50 per cent of the increase in concentration resulted from merger activity.[17] What is clear from the studies is that many sectors of British industry are dominated by a small number of large firms. It also seems that the degree of concentration at the firm level is rather higher in Britain than in other parts of Western Europe.[18] But it has to be recognized that the concentration ratios generally refer to domestic production only and neglect the role of imports, which is substantial in some markets.

These comments on industrial structure would imply that in many markets in Britain some firms will operate with considerable market power. This point has to be borne in mind when examining the options and strategies open to the business, which we consider in subsequent chapters.

GOVERNMENT AND BUSINESS

The government is directly involved with business through the nationalized industries. These industries account for some 13 per cent of gross domestic product, about 10 per cent of employment and about 20 per cent of investment.[19] They operate in the energy sector (gas, electricity, coal, oil and atomic energy), transport and communications (British Rail, National Bus Company, British Airways, postal services and telecommunications) and manufacturing (British Steel, British Leyland, etc.). These sectors are clearly of importance to the economy as a whole and to the successful performance of other producers.

Some disquiet has been expressed about the performance of these state industries and the fact that some of them are now running with substantial losses. The present Conservative Government has initiated a policy of de-nationalization of some of these activities, although so far with only limited success. In addition, under the Competition Act 1980, the power was introduced to allow the Monopolies Commission to conduct an 'efficiency audit' of the parts of the nationalized industries referred to it, and reports have been published on the Post Office (Inner London Letter Post), British Rail (London and South Eastern Commuter Services), the Central Electricity Generating Board and the Severn Trent Water Authority. The National Coal Board is the latest major nationalized industry to be referred (March 1982). The reports have reviewed the performance of the enterprises and made some critical comments, particularly on labour productivity with respect to British Rail and the Post Office.

Besides this direct involvement with industry, the government plays a substantial role through many aspects of its operations: competition policy (see chapter 6); taxation provisions; labour legislation; regional policy; and prices and incomes policies (when operative), among many others.[20] There is a vast array of legislation that affects the day-to-day operations of businesses and of which businessmen must be aware. To consider these issues in this book would make it of inordinate length. Our neglect of these factors should not, therefore, be taken as indication of their lack of importance, but rather of our decision to concentrate on the general economic principles involved in running a business.

BUSINESS ECONOMICS AND MANAGEMENT

The growing awareness in recent years of the need for systematic management has led to the development of a number of approaches designed to instil in managers an appreciation of the ways in which business problems can be tackled. This is most commonly done through the employment of a series of devices leading to the production of check lists which help managers to identify the major problem areas of a modern business.

The job of a manager may be divided into a number of elements, which can be summarized as: planning, forecasting, co-ordination, organization and administration of the resources at his disposal; decision-making, command (or the initiation and supervision of action by the communication of decisions and information); the fostering of good human relations and control. The efficient execution of these functions requires a great deal of expertise in a number of fields, and it is not surprising that the manager needs guidance in his task.

Management by objectives and long-range planning are two of the drills devised to assist the manager. Both of them proceed by listing a number of steps that assist in the statement and achievement of objectives; they point, for example, to the need to identify market opportunities, company strengths and weaknesses, and to the need for profit. Management by objectives next proceeds through establishing objectives for individuals in the organization in order that delegation can be efficiently carried out. A number of other techniques, such as value analysis, critical path analysis, and PERT (Programme Evaluation and Review Technique), are also available to assist the manager in some of the more detailed tasks of the organization. Sophisticated financial modelling packages are now available for even the smaller micro-computers, which allow the businessmen to assess instantly the effects of varying the assumptions about the likely future course of the business on cash flow, profitability and so on.

Systems analysis is another such approach which, in its more advanced forms, presents both the need and the opportunity for sophisticated analysis. The basic philosophy of systems analysis is that all operations have to be seen as part of an overall system, which must be comprehended and co-ordinated if an optimal solution is to be achieved. Thus, a business organization may be seen as part of a system in which *management* co-ordinates *labour, materials* and *machines*, in order to produce *goods*, which are sold to *consumers* in *markets* in which there are *competitors*, and in which the actions of *governments* may have an important effect. The components of the system are in italics; systems analysis identifies, analyses and suggests courses of action suitable to the elements. It is similar in concept to the input–output analysis of the economist, which identifies and analyses interactions between different sectors of an economy.

Such approaches are extremely convenient to the manager in that they identify many of the problem areas; their main shortcoming is that, in themselves, they neither suggest methods of analysis nor lead to operational solutions. Analysis, and the solutions that it suggests, requires a conceptual framework, which in turn implies a theoretical (or model-building) approach to problems. The check list or cookery book approach to problems works well when the major constituents of a problem remain the same in all circumstances. There are, however, few businesses in which such conditions regularly apply, and the ability to think through a problem from first principles is essential for a manager in a changing world. These first principles – economics, quantitative methods, human relations and organization theory – are the disciplines of modern management.

QUANTITATIVE TECHNIQUES

Some familiarity with quantitative methods is essential for the understanding of business problems as outlined in the previous section. We do not seek to provide an explanation of such techniques in this book, but we do demonstrate the practical application of business economics through the use of some simple quantitative analysis. In the parts of the book where such techniques are referred to we provide a brief introduction to the main principles involved, but this should not be taken as a substitute for more detailed study. On several occasions we refer to the empirical testing of particular economic relationships, and it may be helpful to those who are not familiar with the statistical methods used if we provide a brief outline here.

The main technique we shall use is that of linear regression. In simple terms, regression seeks to establish a linear relationship between a variable of interest and the factors that might be thought to influence that variable. Thus, for example, as in chapter 4, we might be interested in the quantity of some particular product that is sold on a market. We would expect this quantity to be determined by the price of the product and the income of consumers, among other things. Linear regression postulates that this relationship between quantity (the dependent variable) and price and income (the explanatory or independent variables) takes the form of a straight line (drawn in three-dimensional space).

To explore this, we obtain data on the three variables and seek to establish the relationship. The detailed calculations involved need not concern us here, as there is now widespread access to computer programs which will perform the appropriate calculations on either large or small computers. We would not expect our observations to follow a straight line exactly, and errors will occur, but on average we would expect them to even out, if we got things right. There are other assumptions about the error which need not detain us here.

Putting these arguments together, we obtain a relationship between quantity, price and income that could be expressed in an equation of the following form:

$$Q = a + bP + cY + u$$

where Q is the quantity demanded; P and Y are price and income respectively; u is the error; and a, b and c are the coefficients of our equation. Coefficient a is the constant, and it shows the quantity that would be bought it price and income were both 0. To take a hypothetical example, suppose our computer printout reveals the following (and assumed correct) relationship:

$$Q = 100 - 2P + 0.1Y.$$

Then, if P and Y are both 0, the quantity bought would be 100. The coefficients b and c show how the level of price and income affects the quantity demanded. For example, the coefficient b reveals the effect of price when we assume that income can be taken as a given constant. Correspondingly, c shows the effect of a particular level of income while holding constant the price to the consumer. Thus, if price were 10 and income 100, the quantity demanded would be 90 (i.e., 100 – 20 + 10).

But, the equation can at best be regarded as only an approximation, and the next question to ask is how well it actually fits the data. One commonly used statistic is referred to as 'R-squared'. This statistic shows the proportion of the variation in our dependent variable that can be explained by our independent variables. Its value ranges from 0, meaning of no explanatory power, to 1, explaining everything! Thus, if our R-squared were 0.8, we would have explained 80 per cent of the variation in Q by price and income – probably not too bad an explanation. Some other statistics relate to the coefficients themselves, and it is common to report either the t-value or the standard error of the coefficient (a measure of the extent to which the coefficient might be affected by chance). The t-value is obtained simply by dividing the coefficient by its standard error. Normally we are interested in seeing whether the estimated value of the coefficient is significantly different from 0, and as a rough rule of thumb we can say that it is if the t-value is 2 or more (i.e. if the coefficient is twice its standard error). This means that we are inclined to believe that the coefficient attached, in this case, to price or income reveals something of a causal relationship. Using this t-test we can, therefore, judge whether price and income appear to affect the quantity demanded.

Many relationships in economics do not fit simple straight lines, but even in this case all is not lost. One common procedure, particularly for estimating demand as in chapter 6, is to take the logarithms of all the variables. By this means a relationship that is non-linear (or curved) in absolute values may be transformed into a linear relationship when measured in logs. In this case our equation would be of the form:

$$\log Q = a' + b' \log P + c' \log Y + u'.$$

This equation can be estimated in the same way as the one above, but using the logarithms of the values of the variables. It so happens that the coefficients measure the proportionate effects of changes in the variables; this gives us an important concept known as 'elasticity', which we shall discuss in detail in chapter 4.

The above discussion is intended as nothing more than an elementary review of the principles involved in regression analysis. As such it may help those who have not studied statistics to understand the few simple equations we use in later chapters.[21]

NOTES

1 For a discussion of some of the issues see B. Chiplin and J. Coyne, 'Some economic issues of a workers' co-operative economy', in A. Clayre (ed.), *The Political Economy of Co-operation and Participation: a Third Sector* (Oxford University Press, 1980).

2 See K. Midgley, 'How much control do shareholders exercise?', *Lloyds Bank Review* (October 1974). According to Midgley's research, the average length of an AGM was 23 minutes, and only a quarter of 1 per cent of shareholders attended the AGM.

3 See, e.g., A. Singh, 'Takeovers, economic natural selection and the theory of the firm', *Economic Journal*, 85 (1975).

4 R. M. Cyert and J. G. March, *A Behavioural Theory of the Firm* (Englewood Cliffs, NJ, Prentice-Hall, 1963).

5 Frank H. Knight, *Risk, Uncertainty and Profit*, Reprints of Scarce Works no. 16 (London School of Economics and Political Science, 1933).

6 See S. C. Littlechild, 'Misleading calculations of the social costs of monopoly power', *Economic Journal*, 91 (1981).

7 See E. Mansfield, M. Schwartz and S. Wagner, 'Imitation costs and patents: an empirical study', *Economic Journal*, 91 (1981).

8 See Littlechild, 'Misleading calculations', p. 357.

9 For a discussion of the importance and problems of the small firm, see M. Binks and J. Coyne, *The Economics of Entrepreneurial Birth*, Hobart Paper (London, Institute of Economic Affairs, 1982).

10 Ibid.

11 W. G. Baumol, *Business Behaviour, Value and Growth* (New York, Harcourt, Brace & World, 1967).

12 H. A. Simon, 'Decision-making in economics', *American Economic Review*, 49 (1959).

13 For a brief review of the legislation in this area see chapter 6.

14 See S. J. Prais, *The Evolution of Giant Firms in Britain* (Cambridge University Press, 1976), and P. E. Hart and R. Clarke, *Concentration in British Industry 1935–1975* (Cambridge University Press, 1980).

15 Hart and Clarke, *Concentration in British Industry*, p. 6.

16 Ibid., p. 7.

17 See, for example, *A Review of Monopolies and Mergers Policy: A Consultative Document*, Cmnd 7198 (London, HMSO, 1978).

18   K. D. George and T. S. Ward, *The Structure of Industry in the EEC: An International Comparison* (Cambridge University Press, 1975).
19   R. W. S. Pryke, *The Nationalised Industries* (Oxford, Martin Robertson, 1981).
20   For a review of some of the more recent developments see A. R. Prest and D. J. Coppock (eds), *The U.K. Economy: A Manual of Applied Economics*, 8th edn (London, Weidenfeld & Nicolson, 1980).
21   For a more detailed but readable treatment of the principles involved see J. Stewart, *Understanding Econometrics* (London, Hutchinson, 1976).

2

Production and Costs

Production is the organized activity of transforming resources into finished products in the form of goods and services; the objective of production is to satisfy the demand for such transformed resources. Coal and iron are of little use to anyone until they are mined and worked on to produce steel for motor vehicles, bridges, ships and other goods.

To be specific, the productive process consists of taking materials, and adding value to them by applying factors of production in the form of labour, machinery and all of the other services of modern industrial organization. The addition of value means that goods are sufficiently different at the end of the productive process to justify charging a higher price for them; the rewards of production go to those factors (including capital and management) that add the value. Any activity that results in such added value constitutes production: while we tend to think of production as being confined to manufacturing, strictly speaking, the processes of marketing and transport are also a part of production. For practical purposes, however, it is convenient to think of production in terms of the two main categories of manufacturing and distribution; our concern here is manufacturing.

The *net output* of an enterprise consists of the *value added* to materials and bought-in components by the processes of production; looking at it from the point of view of rewards to the factors that make up the productive process, it constitutes a fund from which charges are met, in the form of wages and salaries, rents, taxes, depreciation, advertising, etc.

The composition of costs and net output differs considerably from industry to industry; and even within the same industry and among firms with essentially similar processes, differences between firms may be great. Physical and technological characteristics differentiate firms from each other, and there are also differences in the efficiency of utilization of factors and processes that affect cost structures.

Table 2.1 Production and costs in UK industry, 1978

Industry	Sales (£m)	Cost of materials and fuels (% of sales)	Net output (% of sales)	Wages and salaries (% of net output)
Food, drink and tobacco	27,482	72.6	27.4	33.8
Chemicals and allied industries	21,542	70.0	30.0	30.4
Metal manufactures	10,419	68.1	31.9	59.7
Engineering and allied industries	52,423	53.6	46.6	52.8
Textiles	11,247	58.4	41.6	54.3
Other manufacturing	23,792	50.4	49.6	45.9
Mining and quarrying	4,134	26.4	73.6	48.4
Construction	20,032	56.2	43.8	58.1
Gas, electricity and water	9,627	47.7	52.3	29.5
All industries	180,697	58.5	41.5	47.2

Source: Annual Abstract of Statistics (London, HMSO, 1981).

The main items of expenditure in most businesses consist of payments for materials and bought-in components; the main costs of *production proper* (or net output) are wages and salaries. These are shown for the main manufacturing industry groups in the UK in table 2.1, which illustrates the diversity of conditions. Wages are a relatively small proportion of net output in the 'Food, drink and tobacco' group, where a large part of net output is accounted for by advertising, selling expenses and depreciation, and in gas, electricity and water, where capital charges are uppermost; at the other extreme, wages account for a high proportion of net output in metal manufacture and construction. Net output as a percentage of sales is low in food, drink and tobacco and high in mining. Managers in industries in which net output is low in relation to the cost of bought-in materials and fuel often feel they have little control over costs because they depend so heavily on their suppliers. In fact, when alternative sources of supply are available, they are less dependent than might appear, because they can shop around; it follows that their ability to buy cheaply and effectively is one of the major tests of their efficiency.

More detailed statistics, available from the *Census of Production*, tell us something about the costs of the productive processes but little about the processes themselves. These differ considerably from trade to trade; some industries, such as light engineering, require much intricate and relatively expensive machinery; others, such as shipbuilding, require heavy and expensive machinery; some industries need many skilled workers to operate their machines; others, like the motor industry, with many automatic processes, require much unskilled and semi-skilled labour, though the advent of electronic 'robots' may be changing this; either way, the motor industry spends considerable sums on machinery. The clothing industry is different from all of these industries: it requires little machinery, most of it relatively inexpensive, and a large amount of semi-skilled labour; premises in the industry are usually small and an insignificant item in costs. In this industry the main costs are materials and labour.

If this diversity of conditions is taken to its extreme, every firm is different, but there are some basic principles that help the economist and the businessman to sort out the meaning and efficiency of the productive process in general terms, without the need to consider each individual technique. In one sense, the techniques themselves do not matter; what matters is the most efficient use of them, and this is both a technological and an economic problem.

PRODUCTION AND BUSINESS DECISIONS

In the productive process costs are incurred in payment for factors of production and resources, and the businessman has to solve two main problems. The first is to find the combinations and types of factors that will produce his output at least cost; the second is to find the most profitable or economical output at which to produce, and the proportions in which to produce the components of this output. To put it at its simplest, he has to think in terms of costs and scale of production. In this section we will discuss only the choice of inputs to produce a given output at least cost.

In the short run (defined as the period during which at least one factor of production is fixed in quantity), the production problem is to make the best use of available productive facilities; there is usually a variety of ways in which they can be employed profitably.

As time goes on, there may be various opportunities of modifying capital equipment; these may range from the addition of comparatively small pieces of capital equipment in order to balance productive facilities, to a far-reaching and fundamental change in productive methods.

It is unusual to find that there is only one method of producing goods or services. In the production of electricity, for example, generators may be driven by water power, diesel engines, gas turbines or steam turbines, and in the case of the last the steam may be produced either by conventional fuel or through the use of nuclear power. The proportions of capital and running costs involved in the use of each of these methods differ appreciably. The construction of a dam usually involves large capital expenditure, but once it is completed the cost of keeping the turbines in operation is small. The capital cost of generating electricity by gas turbines, on the other hand, is much lower and the operating costs, in the form of fuel, much higher, than for hydroelectricity.

The choice between these alternative methods of generation will depend on the precise circumstances encountered, but, for example, if interest rates are high and the cost of fuel low, the choice will be tilted against hydroelectricity and nuclear power and in favour of conventional stations.

Similarly, it is possible to construct roads using either modern machinery and limited numbers of men, or by primitive methods involving the employment of large numbers of men. In underdeveloped countries, where wages are low and the cost of road-making machinery relatively high, the choice often lies in favour of an intensive use of manpower.

Thus, the choice of productive methods is always affected by relative prices of factors of production or inputs.

In order to examine the problem in more detail, let us consider a hypothetical example in which a company is about to enter the road-making business. A number of different production techniques are known to exist. One of them, labelled as technique A in table 2.2, will enable 1 km of road to be built in one year by employing 2 men and 5 units of capital of type A. (Not having a ready measure of the quantity of capital, the company has chosen to measure capital by its price, each 'unit' costing £10,000 to hire for a period of one year.) The company does not yet possess any road-making equipment, and is thus free to choose whichever technique it wishes.

Figure 2.1 depicts the different combinations of inputs that can be used in order to make 10 km of road. The point A (20 men and 50 units of capital) is derived by assuming that production technique A is used and that it can be applied unchanged when the production level increases to 10 km per year. Points B, C, D and E

Table 2.2 Inputs of capital and labour required for a kilometre per year of class '1' road

Technique	Quantity of capital employed	Number of men employed
A	5	2
B	3	4
C	2	8
D	1	10
E	0	25

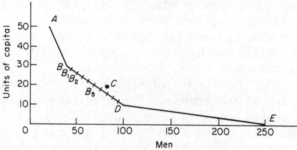

Figure 2.1 Input combinations to make 10 km of road.

are similarly derived. The point B_1 is derived by assuming that 9 km are built by technique B and 1 km by technique D: B_2 is obtained by assuming 8 km are built by technique B and 2 km by technique D.

Even without any knowledge of the price of labour, it is immediately apparent that technique C can be disregarded, since appropriate combinations of techniques B and D use fewer inputs than technique C does: for example, at point B_5 fewer men are used than by technique C for the same amount of capital.

If the costs of inputs are fully known, then it is possible to select the technique that will achieve any given level of output at minimum cost. Figure 2.2 depicts the information graphically if a man receives £6,000 for a year's work. The dotted line represents the possible combinations of inputs that can be obtained for £120,000, and because of this is described as an equi-cost curve. If the money is allocated entirely to capital, 12 units of capital can be hired: alternatively, 20 men can be employed. If the money is divided equally

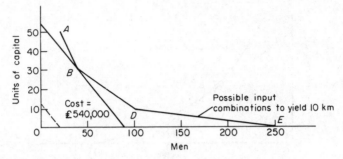

Figure 2.2   Least-cost method of building 10 km of road.

between capital and men, then 6 units of capital and 10 men can be hired. More generally, anything on the straight line is possible by suitably varying the proportion of money to be allocated to the two factors of production.

As is seen, the dotted line, which represents an expenditure of £120,000, does not enable enough inputs to be hired to enable 10 km of road to be built. For that to be possible, it is necessary to spend more (move further away from the origin): the expenditure line of £540,000, which once again has a slope of – 6,000/10,000 to represent the relative costs of labour to capital, enables 10 km to be built. Point *B* represents the minimum cost method of building 10 km of road.

The presentation given here of the optimal combination of inputs differs slightly from the usual textbook presentation. Most textbooks assume an infinite number of techniques of production to be possible, thus obtaining a curve of the type depicted in figure 2.3. The minimum cost method of achieving any level of output occurs at *P*, the point on this curve that is a tangent to an equi-cost curve (see dotted line on the graph).

The one reason for the usual textbook approach is that at equilibrium, point *P*, we have equal slopes for the equi-cost line and the 'equi-product' curve (i.e., the curve specifying the different input combinations that can yield a given output). From this the conclusion is drawn that, in equilibrium, the relative *productivities* of factor inputs are equal to the ratio of *prices* paid for those factors. This conclusion is reached on the assumption of a large number of possible techniques of production close to the optimum one, an assumption that is not needed in our subsequent discussion.

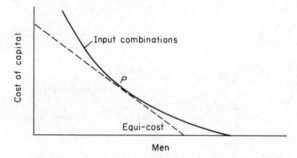

Figure 2.3   Input combinations to make a given quantity of output.

SHORT-RUN COSTS AND RETURNS

Our concern is to depict the way in which costs vary as output is changed. To do this it is necessary to consider separately two different situations. In this section discussion will be restricted to the situation in which at least one factor of production is fixed in quantity: this factor is often the quantity of plant and machinery. While most decisions taken within a firm relate to what to do with the equipment currently available, decisions about what, if any, plant and machinery to install for the future are obviously important: discussion of these decisions, or more specifically the impact that investment decisions might have on costs, will be delayed until the next section.

The distinction between these two types of decision is recognized by economists who signify the periods of time as being short-run and long-run respectively. As noted earlier, the period of time over which at least one factor of production is fixed in quantity is defined as the short run. This time period differs from industry to industry and depends on the techniques and methods of production: in the rubber plantation industry, where it takes several years for a tree to come into full production, the production period is long (as it is for electricity, where it might take several years to build a power station); in the clothing industry the period is relatively short, provided that the premises are large enough to accommodate extra or new machines, or that there are nearby premises that are suitable for clothing manufacture. The long run is defined as the time period over which all factors of production may be varied in quantity.

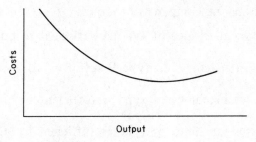

Figure 2.4   Average total cost.

It is argued that, when one factor (or more) is fixed in quantity, average costs vary with output in a way similar to that shown in figure 2.4. At low levels of output, costs are relatively high because certain 'fixed costs' are spread over only a few units of output: as output expands, these costs are spread over more units of output, thus bringing average fixed costs down. In addition, however, there are certain variable costs incurred in production: while unit variable costs may initially decrease as output is expanded, ultimately they will certainly increase, eventually causing average total cost to increase.

Let us first define a few terms, and then see how the argument is developed.

Fixed costs	those costs that do not vary with output
Fixed unavoidable costs	costs that do not vary with output and cannot be avoided even if production ceases entirely (e.g., rates, repayment of interest on bonds and bank borrowing)
Fixed avoidable costs	costs that do not vary with the level of output, but are avoidable if production ceases (e.g., heating and lighting in the factory)
Variable costs	those costs that vary with the level of output
Incremental cost	the addition to total cost made by increasing output
Marginal cost	the addition to total cost of producing one more unit of output

The argument can most easily be seen by means of an example. Imagine a road-making company as follows:

(a) it possesses machines of type A sufficient to build 8 km per year;

it possesses machines of type B sufficient to build 13 km per year;

it possesses machines of type C sufficient to build 3 km per year;

it possesses machines of type D sufficient to build 8 km per year.

These machines have already been purchased (and re-sale, though possible, is thought to be an unattractive economic proposition);

(b) its fixed costs are £600,000 per year, only £18,000 of which would be avoided if production were to cease;

(c) its labour costs are £6,000 per man-year.

Table 2.3   *Returns for each process*

Process used	Maximum output (km)	Labour used per km	Incremental and marginal output (km per man)
A	8	2	1/2
B	13	4	1/4
C	3	8	1/8
D	8	10	1/10
E	unlimited	25	1/25

Table 2.4   *Average and marginal costs (£'000)*

Total output (km)	Total fixed cost	Marginal cost per km	Total variable cost	Total cost	Average (total) cost
8	600	12	96	696	87
21	600	24	408	1,008	48
24	600	48	552	1,152	48
32	600	60	1,032	1,632	51
33	600	150	1,182	1,782	54

Information on each process is summarized in table 2.3. Given that the machinery has already been bought, the only consideration in determining which process to use is the quantity of the variable factor that is used. In our example, the first 8 km of road would all be built using process A, since this process uses the minimum amount of labour; the next process to be used would be B; after that one would proceed to use C, D and E in that order. We may note that capital of type C would not be recommended for purchase (as can be seen from figure 2.1), but that once it has been acquired it would be used before capital of type D because of the lower variable costs incurred when using it.

From knowledge of the processes used in achieving any output level, we can record the costs of these different levels of production. The information is given in table 2.4 for certain selected output levels.

Figures 2.5 and 2.6 depict the information recorded in tables 2.3 and 2.4 of returns per man and costs per kilometre. Note that average fixed costs decrease continuously as output is increased. The curve is a rectangular hyperbola, and it decreases considerably as output is expanded at low levels of output. Average variable costs increase: in our example they increase steadily after 8 km of road have been built, but the more usual situation is that average variable costs may well decline for a while before ultimately increasing, because there are economies to be gained through specialization. In a moment we will have more to write about specialization. For the time being, we note that we have derived a U-shaped average total cost curve by noting the behaviour of average fixed costs and average variable costs.

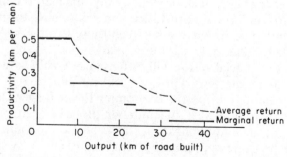

Figure 2.5   Average and marginal output (returns).

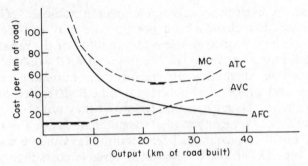

Figure 2.6   Average fixed and variable costs. MC, marginal cost; ATC, average total cost; AVC, average variable cost; AFC, average fixed cost.

The fact that the average variable cost (eventually) increases is because of the operation of the Law of Diminishing Returns. More specifically, the Law of Diminishing Returns states that *marginal* returns to the variable factors eventually diminish. The usual reason given for this is that the fixed factor (frequently capital) eventually gets spread 'too thinly' over the variable factors as more variable factors are employed.

Finally, let us note that we have omitted to record the effects that can arise from specialization. In drawing figure 2.5, we recorded average and marginal returns (which in our case are measured in kilometres of road built) as though a process were 'divisible'. Not only was it possible to build 1 km of road by employing 2 men (yielding an average return of 0.5 km per man), but by implication it was possible to have $\frac{1}{2}$ km of road by employing 1 man. In practice this is unlikely. If only one man were to be employed, he would not be able to enjoy the advantages of specialization. For example, when two men are employed, one might drive a machine that laid the road surface and the other load the machine: when only one man is employed, he would have to undertake both tasks, and would have to spend much non-productive time in moving between those two tasks. As such, he might be able to build only $\frac{1}{4}$ km in a year.

Economies of specialization will differ considerably between industries. In road-making few types of task are undertaken, and there may be only limited scope for economies through specialization. In vehicle assembly, however, the number of tasks is numerous, and economies through specialization may be considerable: thus, if output is to be decreased in such a firm, many men may be asked to work 'short time'.

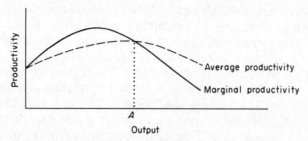

Figure 2.7   Average and marginal returns, allowing for economics of specialization.

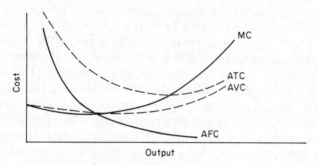

Figure 2.8   Average and marginal costs, allowing for economics of specialization. MC, marginal cost; ATC, average total cost; AVC, average variable cost; AFC, average fixed cost.

It becomes possible to take advantage of specialization as one moves from very low output levels to higher levels of output. As these higher levels of output are reached, marginal productivity increases and marginal cost decreases. Figures 2.7 and 2.8 represent the typical relationships. Note that average productivity is at its highest when marginal productivity = average productivity. At lower levels of output the marginal productivity is higher than average productivity, thus causing the average to increase as output is expanded. Beyond point A, marginal productivity is below average productivity, and this pulls the average down.

Now that the nature of short-run costs has been described, let us see how the businessman uses them to take decisions about how much to produce.

First, the ease with which information on fixed and variable costs was presented in our road-making example should not mislead us into thinking that the dichotomy between fixed and variable costs is always obvious. The cost of machinery is treated by economists as a fixed cost, one element of which is depreciation. In fact, depreciation through wear and tear sometimes may be reduced by stopping production, even though the element of depreciation through obsolescence continues, which part is therefore properly regarded as a fixed cost. The justification for treating the whole of the cost as a fixed cost is partly one of practical convenience, for it is not easy to assess the decrease in a machine's life brought about by using it more heavily. Similarly, some of the 'variable' factors are less easily varied than is sometimes supposed. Labour cannot always be shed easily apart from natural 'wastage', and even where it can be shed it is often only at the expense of redundancy or other compensation payments.

As an example, let us take a firm in a competitive industry which produces goods considered to be virtually identical to a number of other producers, and as a result is a 'price-taker'; in other words, it feels compelled to accept the price set by the market. (This is clearly a simplifying assumption: other cases are examined in later chapters.) Faced with price p_1 and the cost curves shown in figure 2.9, the firm would wish to produce quantity q_1 of goods. The reason for this is that for quantities less than q_1 the marginal costs of production would be less than the price at which the product could be sold, while for quantities greater than q_1 the marginal costs of production would be higher than the price at which the product could be sold. At point q_1 the last unit produced cost the same amount to produce as it gained in additional revenue. If, however, the unit price of the

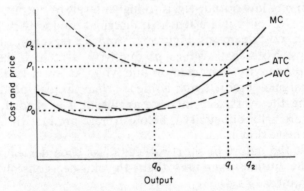

Figure 2.9   Output decision for price-taker. MC, marginal cost; ATC, average total cost; AVC, average variable cost.

product were to increase to p_2, the firm would find it profitable to expand production until quantity q_2 were produced. From this it is apparent that the nature of the marginal cost curve is predominant in determining the quantity of goods produced.

If the unit price were to fall, it is claimed that production would still take place provided price exceeded the minimum point of the average variable cost curve: the minimum of the average variable cost curve occurs at q_0, where marginal cost cuts the curve. It is to be noted that the firm is only covering variable costs, and is making no contribution to fixed costs, the reason being, so it is argued, that fixed costs are incurred even if production ceases. This story is told in many economics textbooks, and is true only under two assumptions. The first of these assumptions is that none of the fixed costs is avoidable, for if it is the business would want the revenue from production to meet variable costs plus avoidable fixed costs. The second assumption is that *either* there are no additional costs involved in stopping production, *or* that prospects of earning future profits are considered remote. For example, if price fell below p_0, the minimum point of the average variable cost curve, companies would *not* cease production and issue redundancy notices to all their employees if they thought there were reasonable prospects of prices increasing above p_0 after a short period of time. For the businessman, indeed, expectations of future market conditions are of considerable importance, and he has opportunities, such as increasing the levels of stocks of finished products, that may lessen some of the losses that might otherwise seem to be implied by figure 2.9.

This discussion has focused upon the principal ways in which businessmen use cost information to determine output levels. It is apparent, however, that considerations other than those represented in figure 2.9 are of relevance to the final decision that is made, and that figure 2.9 therefore gives merely an imprecise, though important, indication of what to do.

RETURNS TO SCALE

In the long run when plant can be altered, the situation is rather different. Figure 2.6 accurately portrays the costs for the amount of plant being considered for that illustration. But the firm is free to increase or decrease the amount (and composition) of its plant in any way that it chooses. There would be a large number of possible plants that it might choose, five of which have been represented in

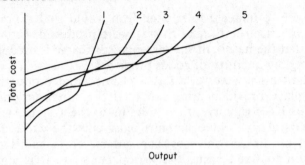

Figure 2.10   *Total costs for five possible plants.*

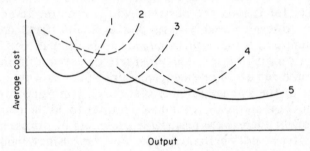

Figure 2.11   *Average costs for five possible plants. Minimum cost method of producing a given output is depicted by a solid line.*

figure 2.10. Plant 1 is a relatively small plant, suitable for the production of small quantities of output. The other plants depicted are bigger, with plant 5 being costly at low levels of output but well suited for larger output levels. The average costs for the five plants represented are given in figure 2.11.

If the businessman knew which output level to aim for, he could satisfactorily choose which plant to have. Thus, for no output level is plant 2 the most appropriate, since there is always at least one plant that can produce a given output at lower average cost. Where a particular plant is the minimum cost method of producing a given output level, it has been depicted by a solid line.

In practice, there will be many more than five plants that could be built. Average costs for different output levels would move in a less jerky way than in figure 2.11. Figure 2.12 is one possibility. Beyond an output of q_1 we have average cost remaining constant as output is increased. This is known as a case of *constant returns to scale.* With an

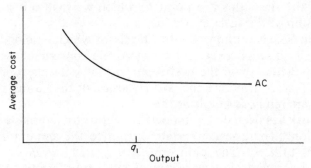

Figure 2.12   *Nature of long-term average costs (many different possible plants).*

output of less than q_1 average costs decrease as output is increased, representing a range exhibiting *increasing returns to scale*. A third possibility, called *decreasing returns to scale*, in which average cost rises as output is increased, is not depicted in figure 2.12.

Constant returns to scale are likely to occur in cases where it is possible to duplicate all services as output expands. The road-making example of table 2.2 was, by implication, a constant returns to scale example, each kilometre of road requiring the same inputs as each previous kilometre built.

Constant returns to scale are perhaps rare in real life. The main reason usually given for this is that certain productive services are indivisible and come in fairly large discrete units. A machine may be able to turn out, say, 1,000 parts per day, and, if it is to be used efficiently, the other factors (labour and materials) will be so employed that the machine is utilized to that capacity. If output is to be increased by the use of the same methods of production, it is economical to do so only if a further 1,000 parts are required – if only 500 parts are required, there is underemployment of the fixed factor (the machine) and decreasing returns to scale are the consequence. Much machinery in use nowadays is of this type; it is expensive to produce, and a machine with an output of 1,000 units may be sometimes little cheaper than one capable of producing many times as much (small machines are usually much more expensive in relation to their output).

In terms of the hypothesis of constant returns to scale, it is not always possible to increase all productive services in a given proportion. It is often argued that the most important of these indivisible services is management, which sets a limit to the size and rate of growth of the firm: this is a point to which we shall return later in our discussion of the scale of production.

These, in rough outline, are the terms in which economics textbooks usually discuss costs, and they provide convenient theoretical abstractions which serve the useful purpose of isolating some of the important factors affecting the cost structure of the business. Things in real life are rarely as simple as this.

Much work has been done on how in practice to determine production functions. These seek to relate output to the amount of labour and capital utilized. The pioneering study was carried out in the 1920s by Cobb and Douglas,[1] who fitted a function to time series data of the form

$$P = f(L, C)$$

where P = the index of manufacturing output;
L = the index of employment in manufacturing industry;
C = the index of fixed capital in manufacturing industry.

The numerical value of the function for American manufacturing industry from 1899 to 1922 was

$$P = 1.01 \, L^{0.75} \, C^{0.25} \, (R^2 = 0.9409).$$

The coefficient of determination (R^2) means that 94 per cent of the variations in the dependent variable (P) were accounted for by variations in the independent variables $(L$ and $C)$.

The exponents of the two inputs, labour (0.75) and capital (0.25), add up to unity (i.e., 1). Consequently, the production function exhibits constant returns to scale. If both labour and capital inputs were doubled, output would double.

Although this function was originally calculated for manufacturing industry as a whole, it has been successfully employed, with modifications, for the measurement of production functions within firms and for comparisons between firms.

The main value of the work of Cobb and Douglas lay in its pioneering nature, and there have been many further developments of their work. For example, J. S. Bain,[2] in a study of 20 US industries, assessed the magnitude of economies of scale, drawing a distinction between economies to be found in large plants and those to be found in large firms. In the UK J. Johnston[3] studied 6 industries and also assessed the work reported in 31 other studies. He concluded (p. 193) that:

The empirical results on long-run costs seem to us to confirm the widespread existence of economies of scale. The evidence on diseconomies is much less certain for, while there is in some studies a suggestion of an upturn at the top end of the size scale, it is usually small in magnitude and well within the range of variation displayed by the data.

Let us consider the causes of economies of scale. Distinction may be drawn between technical and managerial economies of scale: technical economies refer to the plant or product line, and are concerned with the process of production; managerial economies refer to the business unit, and its economic administration.

TECHNICAL ECONOMIES OF SCALE

Technical economies of scale arise for a number of reasons. One way of looking at them is as simple arithmetical economies arising from the spreading of overheads over greater output. Underlying this process is the *indivisibility* of factors of production: many industrial processes need expensive equipment which cannot be produced economically, or which for technological reasons will not function, for small outputs. If it is to justify its cost, such equipment should be used to full capacity, and all related operations must be so arranged that it is in fact so used. For example, if three main processes of production are required to manufacture a given product, it is possible to find out for each process the average output per process: thus, there may be a purely hand process, which produces 60 units per hour per man (this may be, for example, the delivery of bought-out billets of steel to the second process); a second semi-automatic process of, say, rough machining, may be able to produce 400 units per machine-hour; and a third purely automatic process may produce finished goods from the roughly machined billets at the rate of 1,000 units per machine-hour. The most efficient use of the whole combined process will require that the machines operating the last two parts of the process should be fully utilized: this can be done only if an output equivalent to the least common multiple of all the processes (6,000 units per hour) is achieved, requiring the use of 100 men in the first operation, 15 machines (with their operators) in the second operation, and 6 of the last type of machine. Such an output is necessary because the machine for the last process cannot be divided to produce small enough units of output to allow the use of smaller quantities of the other factors.

As technology advances, the size of many plants needs to grow. In the steel industry, for example, the most efficient size of blast furnace is very large, and it has been claimed that this dictates to some extent the size of steel works. We should note, however, that where flexibility is important certain parts of the steel industry have increasingly adopted relatively small-scale techniques, as is to be witnessed in the increased use of electric arc furnaces.

There are also what are sometimes referred to as 'economies of skill', or of specialization and the division of labour, which result from the fact that it is possible with large-scale production to assign each individual to the tasks for which he is best fitted, in the knowledge that his performance will improve by concentrating on them and by repetition.

At the plant level, too, there may be economies in the use of materials and utilization of by-products; the size of minimum stock requirements tends to fall as the scale of production increases; it is often cheaper to buy and sell in large quantities than small, because up to a point it is administratively no more difficult to deal with large than small quantities.

Attempts have been made to quantify economies of scale in practice and to develop empirical rules related to the theoretical considerations. The starting point is the relation between the volume of a container and the area of the material needed to manufacture it. In the case of a cube of length of side r, the volume is given by r^3 and the area of the material needed to contain it is $6r^2$. It is easy to demonstrate that large cubes need less material per unit capacity than small ones. For two cubes of dimensions r_1 and r_2, the ratio of the surface areas is:

$$\frac{S_1}{S_2} = \left(\frac{r_1}{r_2}\right)^2.$$

The corresponding ratio of the volumes is:

$$\frac{V_1}{V_2} = \left(\frac{r_1}{r_3}\right)^3.$$

From which it follows that:

$$\frac{S_1}{S_2} = \left(\frac{V_1}{V_2}\right)^{2/3}.$$

Thus, if we double the volume of the cube we shall need to increase the amount of material needed to form it in the proportion of $2^{2/3} = 1.59$. In other words, doubling the volume can be achieved with a 59 per cent increase in material.

It is from reflections of this kind that the '6/10 rule' (approximated to 2/3) has been derived. At first sight such a rule may seem trivial and confined to one small aspect of production processes, but this is far from the case, and many industrial processes are affected by relations between area and volume. Blast furnaces are essentially boxes containing the ingredients needed to produce iron, and the reduction of surface area per unit volume that comes with increase in size has the added advantage that heat losses are reduced. Tankers, too, are essentially large boxes containing oil, and the area of the surface is important in relation to the surrounding environment – in this case the sea – because it affects the resistance of the ship to passage through the water in a rather complicated way related to powers of the vessel's principal dimensions. Chemical processes in the main are reactions carried out in vessels.

Another reason for attaching some importance to the '6/10 rule' is that the form of the relationship postulated (though not the value of 6/10) may be useful in describing empirically determined relationships between size and cost. A number of attempts to develop such descriptions have been made.

S. P. Alpert[4] related the horsepower needed in milling operations to the amount of material to be removed and found that a useful approximation was $HP = kU^{0.75}$, where U measured the cubic inches of metal removed. S. C. Schuman, among others, has worked on similar problems relating to the chemical industry; in one investigation he examined the statistical relationship between capital costs (C) involved in producing a large variety of chemicals and the amount produced measured in pounds weight (S). The statistical relationship that emerged as a good fit to the data was

$$C = 0.126 \, S^{0.70}.$$

Some distrust may be felt about the validity of a relationship applying to a collection of heterogeneous chemicals produced by different methods; nevertheless, there may be common underlying factors governing capital costs.

The relationship outlined above can also be expressed in terms of capital costs per unit of product (K) by dividing both sides of the equation by S. In this form we have

$$K = 0.126 \, S^{-0.3}.$$

This shows that the cost per pound of product falls when output is increased. The capital cost per unit may not decrease indefinitely.

Beyond a certain point the increase in scale may require that certain parts of the plant be strengthened in some way. For example, in house building it is usually claimed that a two-storey house provides accommodation at a cheaper cost per cubic metre than a bungalow. Beyond three storeys, however, the traditional brick house would need additional strengthening in the walls and in the foundations, and thus there may be limits to the economies of scale as far as building with bricks is concerned.

Another aspect of the relationship between costs and scale of production is that expressed by learning curves. It is common experience that practice, while not always making perfect, results in improvements up to a point. The learning process has relevance to batch production, particularly of expensive units such as ships or aircraft. It is recognized by shipyards that producing, say, a score of fairly similar ships reduces shipyard costs quite substantially by the time the end of the run is reached.[5] For aircraft production more detailed investigations have been made in order to see whether the reduction in labour costs can be said to conform to a learning curve.[6]

One such curve relates the labour input of the nth unit of production to the labour input of the first unit produced. If L is the labour input to the first unit and r the learning factor, the labour inputs to the second, fourth, eighth and nth aircraft (where $n = 2^P$) respectively are:

$$Lr, Lr^2, Lr^3 \ldots Lr^P.$$

The learning factor, r, has often been found to lie within the range 0.7–0.9, indicating that each doubling of accumulated output reduces costs by between 30 and 10 per cent. A review article that provides a good introduction to learning and experiencing curves has been written by the Department of Prices and Consumer Protection, UK.[7] Learning curves are of use in indicating, on the basis of past experience, how costs may vary with the expected length of run; they also provide some basis, when combined with other data, for determining price–output relationships, manpower requirements, etc. For many types of production, labour costs account for a substantial part of total costs. In aircraft production labour costs may account for about 25 per cent of non-launching costs for the first unit produced and fall to about 10 per cent for a long run; learning costs are clearly important in such cases. Such savings are useful, but on small runs they tend to be dwarfed by the costs of launching the aircraft.

It has been seen that there are a number of ways in which technical economies of scale arise. For many businessmen it is undoubtedly true that further technical economies of scale are possible. It is true that they may not continue indefinitely, but once full economies of scale have been utilized there is usually no reason why the plant cannot be duplicated, thus giving rise to constant returns to scale beyond that point.

MANAGERIAL ECONOMIES OF SCALE

Technical economies of scale are important, but they are not the only consideration in the choice of the size of business unit, which may have several plants. There are economies or diseconomies of scale, which we have labelled *managerial*, that may refer to whole series of plants. There are a number of different factors that come under this umbrella title of 'managerial economies', and they include marketing services, research, finance, risk-bearing and general management.

For many of these factors it is not difficult to point to economies of scale that may be quite large for low levels of output. Thus Pratten,[8] who has done much work on economies of scale in UK industries and some on industries in other European countries, writes: 'The firm with the larger sales can achieve economies by spreading certain marketing and management costs.'

Financial factors may also be important. As is demonstrated in chapter 7 below, the large firm has advantages over the small firm in this field: it has access to capital markets and usually has substantial resources of its own, while the small firm frequently finds that, partly for institutional reasons, it cannot raise all the funds that it may need. Once a firm has succeeded in growing beyond a certain point (which is frequently though not invariably associated with its becoming a public company), these particular difficulties become less important, but it may on occasions still find it difficult to obtain further funds. The opportunities for obtaining funds are therefore markedly different for firms of differing size. When funds are available for both large firms and small, it is customary for the small loan to attract a higher interest charge, if only because the 'handling' charge associated with all loans is spread over a larger amount for the bigger loan: since the small firm usually borrows less than the large firm, the interest rate on its borrowing is usually higher.

Given the existence of so many factors for which there are economies of scale, the question is asked: what limits the size of a firm? Two answers are given. One is that the market may set a limit to the scale at which a firm may operate; the other is that there may ultimately arise diseconomies of scale concerned with management. About the first there is little dispute that, for a given product, a firm may well be limited by its market: if a market is small, or highly specialized, like the market for 'quality' motor cars, technical and managerial economies of scale may not be realizable, because a firm could not sell an output that would achieve such economies. The problem with this explanation, however, is that the firm is not constrained to make just one product. The 'quality' car manufacturer could make other cars, or other vehicles such as tractors or buses. In order to assess the attractiveness of such diversification we will be obliged to discuss whether there are any problems of managing such a firm.

In one respect, there are potential gains in diversifying. Risks are spread. Furthermore, if a number of products are made in the same product range, the firm often receives early intimation of any shift in tastes by the public. The one important structural decision for such multi-product firms is how much to delegate. Delegation enables the individual plant or unit to take decisions quickly, and the decisions can be taken by those who have considerable experience of the product concerned. In contrast, some decisions are best taken centrally. Economies of finance may make it advantageous for the firm as a whole to acquire finance on behalf of all its plants, and this would enable specialist financial experts to be employed. If the firm is to centralize some of its activities, then it will be forced to draw up some procedural rules — for example, that the borrowing by each firm may be limited to certain 'small' projects or a certain overall sum, and beyond that a case has to be made to top management within the firm. The disadvantage with such procedural rules is obvious: to achieve economies that are available centrally may restrict the freedom of individual plants, which will slow down the speed of decision-taking.

Pratten, in his book, wrote that 'Economies of scale . . . generally apply to producing a constant range of products on a larger scale. . . . Where differences in scale are attributable to differences in the range of products made, there are no simple rules such as "the bigger the better".' Economists are often puzzled as to why there seem to be limits to economies of scale. One answer is to suggest that some firms are less efficient than is theoretically possible — called 'X-inefficiency'. Thus, Silberston[9] writes:

[An] important proviso concerns the varying X-inefficiency of different firms. . . . in practice the efficiency of firms varies widely. This is especially so if efficiency is taken in its broadest sense, to include such factors as success in product design and marketing; and it helps to explain why many small firms do better than large rivals who are better placed to take advantage of economies of scale.

Other researchers are coming to the view that it is not just that firms sometimes fail to achieve potential economies, but that economies may be limited — even, perhaps, that there may be certain diseconomies of scale. Coyne[10] specifically looks at different management structures, and suggests that economies of scale are not as large as traditional economists used to argue; furthermore, that many firms are finding it advantageous to allow many plants to act independently of plants producing other products.

Diseconomies of scale are said to exist in the area of labour relations, where Eisele[11] found that in general large firms are more likely to suffer strike action by their employees. There was one notable exception, however, relating to unit and small-batch production, in which firms of about 600 employees (medium size) had the worst strike record. It would seem that firms have to concern themselves not only with communications systems for managers, but with keeping the whole workforce 'informed'.

Overall, our conclusion is that there are often significant managerial economies of scale to add to technical economies, but there may be certain managerial problems of co-ordination encountered beyond a certain stage. Perhaps with good management these potential problems can be lessened, but it seems unwise to assume that they could never occur, whatever the scale.

NOTES

1 P. H. Douglas, *The Theory of Wages* (London, Macmillan, 1924).
2 J. S. Bain, *Barriers to New Competition* (Cambridge, Mass., Harvard University Press, 1956).
3 J. Johnston, *Statistical Cost Analysis* (New York, McGraw-Hill, 1960).
4 S. P. Alpert, *Journal of Industrial Economics*, 7 (1959).
5 See J. R. Parkinson, *The Economics of Shipbuilding in the UK* (Cambridge University Press, 1960), p. 146.
6 S. G. Sturmey, 'Cost curves and pricing in aircraft production', *Economic Journal*, 74 (1964).
7 *A Review of Monopolies and Mergers Policy*, Cmnd 7198 (London, HMSO, 1978), Appendix C, pp. 77–96.
8 C. F. Pratten, *Economies of Scale in Manufacturing Industry*, University of Cambridge, Department of Applied Economics, Occasional Paper 28 (1971).

9   A. Silberston, 'Economies of scale in theory and practice', *Economic Journal*, 82 (1972).
10 J. Coyne, 'Smaller-scale enterprise: a corporate trend', *The Director* (January 1982).
11 C. F. Eisele, 'Organization size, technology and frequency of strikes', *Industrial and Labour Relations Review*, 27 (1974).

3

Production Decisions

In the long run, new technology contributes more to the efficiency of business than any other factor. But, given the existing technology, the application of economic analysis to the affairs of an enterprise can contribute a great deal. In essence, the concern of production management is the improvement of efficiency and the reduction of costs. Techniques of economic analysis are helpful whenever there is a major element of choice between alternative courses of action and an optimal solution is sought.

METHODS OF PRODUCTION

One of the choices that needs to be made in practice is the method of production. Given available techniques, the choice is essentially an economic one, related to costs and returns and depending on such factors as price and availability of materials, labour and capital and the size of the market.

In practice, production may be carried on in any of three main ways (or a combination of all three), the choice depending largely on the scale of production and length of run that can be achieved. The first of these, job production, is usually small-scale; the second, batch production is usually medium-scale but may also be employed in large-scale production; the third, mass (or flow) production, is almost always as its name implies, large-scale. Large-scale production does not necessarily entail flow methods. It is rare to find a firm that uses one method to the exclusion of the other two, but product lines or part lines are frequently specialized on this basis.

Job production is common in small businesses, but many large concerns produce some of their lines by this method, the essence of which is that the firm manufactures single products (or at the most a few of any one product), usually to the requirements of the customer. This is sometimes referred to as a 'one-off' method of production: it suffers from the disadvantage that few economies of scale can be achieved (save for multi-purpose plant, building and staff) and unit costs are usually relatively high; where individual requirements have to be met, however, no other method is possible. Examples of this kind of production are to be found in the manufacture of special-purpose machinery, bespoke tailoring and similar trades.

Batch production is the typical method of manufacture in British industry. It consists, as the name implies, of the manufacture of a batch or 'lot' of products at one time, but is distinguished from flow production in that the process is not continuous. The manufacture of several different products for stock, as in the shoe trade and the clothing trade, or to fairly regular orders, as for components for the motor vehicle industry and the radio industry, are particularly suited to batch production. Some of the advantages of large-scale production are achieved − for example, regular use of machinery, plant, skilled staff and so on, and the consequent ironing-out of indivisibilities and the spreading of fixed costs − but complete specialization of inputs is not possible. This is the type of production that is most difficult to control; it is more difficult the larger the variety of products, and efficient production makes big demands on management. It requires good quality control, well devised stock control and efficient programming.

Mass or flow production is frequently found side by side with batch production, but it depends for its success on large-scale operation. In general, the word 'flow' is preferable to 'mass' in this context: mass production is often regarded, by both economists and businessmen, as synonymous with large-scale production, but it is not necessary for flow methods to be used to achieve large-scale production, which may well be feasible for the production of large batches. Single-purpose plant and machines of large output capacity and high cost, like the automatic and semi-automatic machinery in modern motor car factories, are usually employed in flow production methods, and large outputs are needed to justify their installation. Products are usually highly standardized and they usually go through identical sequences of operations. Industries like oil refining, cement manufacture and flour milling have to be operated on a large scale and by flow methods in order to be efficient.

The advantages of large-scale production can usually be summed up as the advantages of specialization of function, standardization of product and full-capacity use of large indivisible factors. The main danger of flow production in particular is over-specialization and susceptibility to economic fluctuations: closing a motor car factory is an expensive business and may be disastrous, but a reduction of output to (say) 50 per cent of capacity may have almost equally serious effects.

Two typical problems associated with both batch and flow production are those of variety and length of run. A limitation of large-scale production is that specialization usually means standardization, because small changes in routine have to be ruled out. Further, the more complex is the mass-produced article, the more components it will usually have and the more the components themselves must be standardized, with the result that even minor differences in finished products are extremely difficult and costly to introduce.

From the point of view of the market, standardization has both its good and its bad sides. Standardization makes choice easier, but there is a limit to the amount of uniformity that consumers will tolerate; in practice, many large-scale producers have decided that the consumer will buy more of their produce if some variety is introduced. Product differentiation and advertising are the consequences of this, and they can be taken to extremes, from the point of view of the consumer, who may become cynical about the whole process, and also, and more relevant to the present discussion, from the point of view of the producer. The cost of variety in the last resort is the loss of benefits of standardization and specialization. In modern large-scale industry the tendency is for more and more reduction of variety where it costs most − in the large-scale production lines − and its introduction where it costs least − in the least specialized and the smallest-scale parts of the operation, such as the trimming processes of motor car manufacture. Usually, the nearer to the finished product, the better suited is the process for the introduction of variety. Standardized products may make for duller living; they almost always make for cheaper living.

The 'length of run' problem is closely associated with the scale of production. At the extreme, the largest mass production units require the longest feasible production runs and fullest utilization of fixed factors, maintained if possible until all of the high-cost high-output plant can be written off. But even where full-time long runs are not possible, it is still desirable to use fixed factors as fully as possible, and the longest possible production runs are needed. Some motor car manufacturers aim for a model that will run for several years with only minor modifications from year to year: the Volvo and British Leyland's Mini have been conspicuous successes in this sense. The problem also applies to batch production, in which economies of scale resulting from long runs must be balanced against the cost of holding stocks, and the final answer may demand a complicated operations research solution.

SHIFT-WORKING

One way of achieving the maximum possible length of run in relation to capital is by shift-working.

The main advantage of shift-working is that it economizes on capital; its main disadvantage is that it increases the cost of labour. The saving of capital arises because buildings and machines may be used for 24 hours a day rather than for 8 or 16, and for 7 days a week rather than for 5 or 6. This reduces the cost of capital to a limited degree because less capital is required to produce a given output if it is used intensively rather than intermittently. Thus, if machinery is never idle it will be used 168 hours a week rather than the 40 that might be normal with single-shift working. Interest charges on capital and buildings will be cut to a quarter in relation to the output produced. Interest is the only charge that will be cut in such a striking manner; there may be small reductions in insurance costs per unit of output (although in total there is likely to be an increase), and charges for depreciation or obsolescence are also likely to fall much less markedly. No hard and fast rule can be laid down. Depreciation is to some extent the result of using a machine and to some extent the result of general ageing. Even without use machinery deteriorates: it may rust or perish; it may become out of date or obsolescent; Stephenson's Rocket is a museum piece, even though it could still haul a coach.

Some orders of magnitude may be assigned to the costs of operating capital in the United Kingdom industry:

Depreciation and obsolescence	10
Interest charges or equivalent	10
Raw materials	50
Labour	30
	100

The figures given are illustrative; they give an average view of industry as a whole but do not represent the situation in any specific industry or firm. A little arithmetic on the basis of the above figures demonstrates the effect of working two or three rather than one shift per day, while leaving the number of days worked per week unaltered. Since interest charges do not increase when output is increased, costs per unit of output on the second shift will fall immediately by 10; there may also be some reduction in the cost per unit of depreciation and obsolescence; a reduction of between 2 and 4 may be taken to represent this. Thus, costs on the second shift fall by about 12–14 per unit of output. A similar cost reduction may be achieved when working the third shift. It may be seen that interest charges are the principal saving achieved by shift-working.

The savings in capital cost will almost certainly be offset in part by the need to offer some incentive for shift-working. Additional payments for shift-work vary; for an evening shift for the housewife no additional payment may be needed above ordinary rates of payment, but second and third shifts are normally likely to involve additional payments equivalent to a quarter or third of earnings on the day shift, even if the times of the shifts are adjusted to minimize inconvenience. The actual increase in labour costs is often higher than this; it is not always easy to maintain standards or provide adequate supervision on the night shift. Thus, an addition of one-third to labour costs per unit of output is not an unreasonable estimate of the increase that would result. In the arithmetic example, the savings in capital costs per unit of output would be slightly greater than the increase in labour costs, but there would not be much in it.

One of the effects of shift-working is to reduce the ratio of capital to labour costs, because more labour is used when working two or three shifts with the same amount of capital. The effect is to open up new technological possibilities appropriate to a situation in which there is an economic incentive to substitute capital for labour.

Shift-working is favoured when:

(a) capital costs are high: this may be because a process uses a comparatively large quantity of capital in relation to output, because the cost of capital equipment is high relatively to, say, other countries, or because interest rates are high;

(b) depreciation is not closely linked to the output that is produced and is mainly the result of the ageing process: this, for example, is true of buildings, but not of high-speed cutting tools;

(c) obsolescence is a material danger and as much as possible has to be got out of the capital used before it is out of date;

(d) labour costs are low: this may be true when wages are low or because in a capital-intensive process very few men may be required;

(e) trade unions and their members do not require a substantial increase in wages for shift-working;

(f) more intensive use of capital opens up new technological possibilities.

In practice, the reasons for working shifts are often technological rather than economic. The industries in which shift-working is predominant are generally those working continuous processes such as metal manufacturing and chemical industries, or those that find it necessary to work at night, such as cinemas, newspaper printing, electricity generation and transport. But there are a number of other industries in which shift-working is important for economic reasons: the jute manufacturing industry is one; coal mining, where large sums must be invested in opening and developing pits, is another. Other industries, such as the motor car industry, may work shifts when demand is at a seasonal peak, and occasionally a few machines or departments may work continuously because they use exceptionally expensive equipment.

In underdeveloped countries, where capital is scarce and therefore expensive, and where some forms of labour are cheap, there are strong reasons for shift-working. In the major industrial countries there is little reason to suppose that shift-working is ever likely to predominate. Higher real earnings make men more reluctant to work shifts and encourage them to exact a higher price for doing so. There is no reason to suppose that capital costs per unit of output will rise as time goes on, and some reason for supposing that they will fall. Shift-working is thus likely to be confined to processes where it is unavoidable for technological reasons and to those exceptional industries or processes that require large amounts of capital.

OVERTIME WORKING

Shift-working predominates in a small number of industries, and its introduction is usually planned in advance (i.e., *ex ante*). In contrast, smaller variations in the level of intensity of work are achieved by variations in the amount of overtime that is worked.

Payments to labour for overtime working vary according to the day of the week and sometimes even the time of day, but frequently amount to 1.5 times the basic hourly rate of pay for one-shift working. Given such a figure, it might be supposed that overtime could never be planned in advance, but undertaken only when demand is unexpectedly high; for, taking the costs presented in the previous section on shift-working, the additional labour costs would add 15 per cent to total costs, a figure that may not be equalled by the saving on depreciation and interest payments. It might therefore appear to be cheaper to employ more machinery and more men on the basic week than to use overtime. Such reasoning is however false, because it ignores the fact that unexpectedly low levels of demand might then typically involve an employer in significant additional costs. In an establishment in which no overtime is worked, an unanticipated reduction in demand can be met by increased stocks of finished products, by working the basic week but producing less, by working 'short time', or by making employees redundant. None of these measures is costless, and in some circumstances it may be cheaper to *plan* for a certain amount of overtime working, and for unanticipated reductions in demand to be met by a reduction in the amount of overtime worked. The two crucial types of factor to consider are the (un)predictability and variability of demand, and the magnitude of the different costs. Overtime working will be favoured when:

(a) demand varies seasonally;
(b) demand fluctuates considerably but with little warning;
(c) demand currently exceeds capacity during the 'basic' week, but this is thought to be temporary;
(d) stock-holding costs are large;
(e) employees will not accept reduced wages for working less than the 'basic' week;
(f) taxes (for example, national insurance contributions) are significant and payments are not lessened by reductions in the number of hours worked;
(g) redundancy payments are large;
(h) capital costs are high relative to labour costs – see points (a)–(d) listed under the 'shift-working' section.

This list consists principally of factors that will cause overtime to be planned *ex ante*. But the third item – demand being unexpectely high – is a factor that is of an *ex post* kind, and shows that a certain amount of the overtime that is worked arises in an unplanned way. Recent literature has broadened the area of interest to consider generally why capital should often be idle for much of the day, and the interested reader may find the writings of Marris[1] and Winston[2] to be instructive.

LINEAR PROGRAMMING

Linear programming is used in business principally to solve the product mix problem: given limited resources, which products should be made, and how much of each should be produced?

Linear programming problems arise in business when three conditions apply:

(a) a linear function is to be optimized;
(b) inputs are proportional to outputs;
(c) there are limitations on the availability of certain resources.

Although the techniques of linear programming can be modified to handle cases in which not all these conditions apply, we will first restrict our attention to an example that meets these conditions fully.

The example is as follows. A certain farmer wishes to determine the quantities of different crops to grow. Suppose the details of resources available to him, and anticipated revenues for each crop, are as follows. He possesses 80 acres and employs five men, one of whom is the tractor driver.

The farmer believes four weeks in September to be the busiest part of the year, and during that period each ton of sugar beet harvested requires 32 man-hours, 5 acres and 20 hours of tractor-plus-driver; the net revenue per ton excluding fixed costs is expected to be £80. Similar information is given in table 3.1 for potato inputs.

Availability of labour resources is as follows. Each man works a standard week of 50 hours; so that for the four men a total of 800 hours would be available during the four-weekly period.

Table 3.1   *Input requirements per ton of crop over a four-week period*

Input	Sugar beet	Potatoes	Availability
Labour (man-hours)	32	80	800
Land (acres)	5	7	80
Tractor + driver (hours)	20	4	200
Net revenue per ton excluding fixed costs (£)	160	40	

This example clearly satisfies the conditions stipulated above, so it is a linear programming problem. As there are only two activities, it is possible to represent the problem graphically, with the number of tons of sugar being on one axis, and the number of tons of potatoes on the other. Figure 3.1 denotes the restrictions imposed by the limited resources available. The line L denotes the maximum combination of output of sugar and potatoes given the amount of labour time available. If all 800 man-hours were devoted to sugar beet, only 25 tons could be grown (since each ton requires 32 man-hours): alternatively, 10 tons of potatoes could be grown. But any combination of sugar and potatoes on the straight line joining these two points is also feasible as far as the labour constraint is concerned. In the same way, lines A and T represent the acreage and tractor constraints respectively. If we consider all three constraints together we are limited to the shaded portion of the graph, for we must be on or below each of the three lines: thus we can grow no more than 10 tons of sugar beet because of the tractor constraint.

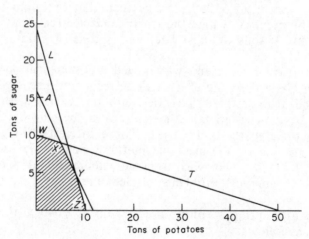

Figure 3.1   Production limits.

Figure 3.1 has shown what is feasible. From among the possibilities that are feasible we wish to choose the combination that yields the greatest net revenue. In figure 3.2. an equi-revenue line of £800 is depicted by the dashed line. It is clearly possible to achieve this level of net revenue, but higher levels are also possible: the furthest that an attainable equi-revenue curve can be drawn from the origin and not go beyond point X in figure 3.1 is the thick solid line, giving

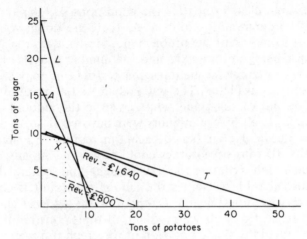

Figure 3.2   Determination of crop outputs.

a net revenue of £1,640. It can be seen that optimum revenue is achieved at point X, where the tractor and acreage inputs are fully utilized, and 9 tons of sugar beet and 5 tons of potatoes are produced.

This particular problem was solved by graphical means. For problems where there are at least three resources restricted in availability and at least three 'activities' (for our example, three crops that can be grown), graphical means cannot be employed. In such cases algebraic methods are used. Those interested in gaining an insight into one of the algebraic methods commonly used should read on. But those who wish to avoid algebra should skip to p. 55 where other practical problems of deciding what to produce are discussed.

Before attempting a solution it is helpful to state the problem formally, as follows:

Maximize

$$160B + 40P$$

subject to

$$32B + 80P \leqslant 800 \text{ (labour)}$$

$$5B + 7P \leqslant 80 \text{ (acreage)}$$

$$20B + 4P \leqslant 200 \text{ (tractor)}$$

The first line is the net revenue, which we wish to maximize, and the other equations are the constraints on the resource: B and P denote the number of tons of beet and potatoes grown respectively. For the labour constraint the left-hand side represents the time spent on the harvesting of beet and potatoes; the right-hand side represents the total time available, which cannot be exceeded.

The first stage in any solution is to eliminate the inequalities by introducing 'slack' variables. If we let L denote the amount of unused labour, A denote the amount of unused acres and T denote the amount of unused tractor time, we can write the problem as

Maximize

$$160B + 40P$$

subject to

$$32B + 80P + L \qquad\quad = 800 \qquad\qquad (1)$$

$$5B + 7P \quad\; + A \;\; = \;\; 80 \qquad\qquad (2)$$

$$20B + 4P \qquad\quad + T = 200 \qquad\qquad (3)$$

with $B, P, L, A, T \geqslant 0$. The equations (1), (2) and (3) must at all times be satisfied: subject to these requirements, we wish to maximize net revenue. The method we will use is known as the 'Simplex' method, which examines which of the points W, X, Y or Z in figure 3.1 leads to the maximum revenue. Readers with superb intuition will be able to see why we can safely restrict our attention to such points. They have two important factors: they are all feasible, and they are all 'basic', by which we mean that the number of non-zero activities (including slack variables as well as beet and potatoes) is equal to the number of equations that have to be satisfied.

As a starting-point, let us decide to make the amount of beet production as large as possible. From equation (1) we would be limited to 25 tons, but equations (2) and (3) would limit us to 16 and 10 tons respectively. We therefore are limited to 10 tons (from equation (3)). A reference to figure 3.1 shows that we will be considering point W, which involves spare labour and spare acres.

In order to examine the characteristics of this point we need to express our equations in terms of the relationships between the variables that have been *included* in our trial solution and those that have been (temporarily at least) *excluded*. The limitation on beet production came from the third equation, and from this we can express B (the number of tons of beet) in the following way:

$$B = 10 - \tfrac{1}{5}P - \tfrac{1}{20}T. \tag{3}'$$

In order to express the spare labour in terms of excluded variables we can use equation (1) but substitute for the value of B in equation (3). Thus:

$$L = 800 - 32(10 - \tfrac{1}{5}P - \tfrac{1}{20}T) - 80P$$

$$= 480 - 73.6P + 1.6T. \tag{1}'$$

Similarly,

$$A = 80 - 5(10 - \tfrac{1}{5}P - \tfrac{1}{20}T) - 7P$$

$$= 30 - 6P + 0.25T. \tag{2}'$$

Finally,

$$\text{net revenue} = 160(10 - \tfrac{1}{5}P - \tfrac{1}{20}T) + 40P$$

$$= 1600 + 8P - 8T.$$

This final equation is most important. Remembering that P and T are set at level 0, it tells us that revenue is currently 1,600, but would be increased by the introduction of P (potatoes): in contrast, the introduction of T (spare tractors) would reduce revenue, as can be seen from the negative sign.

We are now ready to examine a different solution. The introduction of P has been suggested. Since each unit by which P is introduced will increase net revenue by 8 units, we clearly wish to introduce P by as much as possible. Referring back to equations (1)$'$, (2)$'$ and (3)$'$ will enable us to see how much is possible. From (3)$'$ we see that P can be as large as 50 ($10 \div \tfrac{1}{5}$) before B drops to 0: we cannot increase P beyond this or B would become negative, which is not feasible. But examination of equation (2)$'$ further limits the value of P (to 5), and it is clear that P will replace A first.

Rewriting equation (2)$'$,

$$P = 5 - \tfrac{1}{6}A + \tfrac{1}{24}T. \tag{2}''$$

Substituting for P in equations (1)$'$ and (3)$'$, we get:

$$B = 10 - \tfrac{1}{5}(5 - \tfrac{1}{6}A + \tfrac{1}{24}T) - \tfrac{1}{20}T$$

$$= 9 + \tfrac{1}{30}A - \tfrac{7}{120}T \tag{3}''$$

$$L = 480 - 73.6(5 - \tfrac{1}{6}A + \tfrac{1}{24}T) + 1.6T$$

$$= 112 + 12.26A - 1.46T \tag{1}''$$

net revenue $= 1600 + 8(5 - \frac{1}{6}A + \frac{1}{24}T) - 8T$

$= 1640 - 1.3A - 7.6T.$

Given that the coefficients of A and T in the net revenue equations are negative, we know that net revenue cannot be improved by introducing A or T. The highest net revenue is indeed the 1,640 of this solution, which involves growing 9 tons of sugar beet and 5 tons of potatoes. (If there has been a positive coefficient, then it would have been necessary to introduce that variable, and proceed as before.)

The coefficients of the final net revenue equation tell us something more. The $- 7.6$ for T tells us that one hour spare of the tractor availability will reduce revenue by 7.6. The corollary is that an extra hour of tractor time, if it could be made available, would yield an *extra* 7.6 of revenue. This 'shadow price', as it is called, is very informative. The farmer may well be tempted to have the tractor working more than the basic week: given the amount of spare labour in the system, he may well attempt to introduce some form of shift-work, with the tractor being driven by other men for some hours of the week.

Before we get carried away by the implications of the shadow prices, it is as well to remember that the problem posed is almost certainly over-simplified. The farmer will have a choice from among many more than two crops. Furthermore, there will be other restrictions. For crop rotation reasons the farmer may wish not to have more than a third of his acreage devoted to any one crop, or he may have three fields, the largest of which is 30 acres. Such extra restrictions can easily be handled. For example, if the largest field is 30 acres and it is desired to have beet in only one field, the restriction

$$5B \leqslant 30$$

will ensure this.

This examination of linear programming has been restricted to a simple discussion incorporating the traditional assumptions. The desirability of relaxing constraints is pursued in a number of texts under the title of 'parametric programming', and economists may well choose to look at the book by Dorfman, Samuelson and Solow,[3] or the book by Vandermeulen.[4] If the price received for the products depends on the quantity produced (so that the revenue function is no longer linear), a part of the Simplex technique is still utilized, though the calculations involved become much more cumbersome: for details, see the book by Dorfman, Samuelson and Solow.

Generally, linear programming problems in business are solved by computers. The human input, indeed, is much more concerned with checking whether any restrictions have been omitted or whether the assumptions made are likely to be reasonably valid. One particular feature of the linear programming solution needs stressing. If there are just three restrictions, then no more than three activities will be chosen. For the farmer, therefore, the linear programming solution is that no more than three crops should be grown. Given any assumptions made about crop prices and crop yields, the technique will certainly yield the maximum net revenue. But it will take no account of risk. A producer therefore, may choose to take the 'solution' of the linear programming calculation as a starting-point upon which he will add his own modifications.

The justification for using linear programming techniques arises from a combination of two facts. First, many problems can be put in a linear programming framework, as is illustrated by the opening chapter of a book by Chung.[5] Second, the solutions obtained are much better than those derived from experience or rule of thumb. An interesting study by J. K. Wyatt compared the utilization of recovered metal in making up alloys to specification when decisions were taken on the basis of experience with those suggested by linear programming. It appeared that linear programming increased the use of recovered metal by 5 per cent and produced a worthwhile financial saving. At the same time, the process of deciding on alloy specification was greatly simplified by being reduced to a routine and systematic procedure.[6]

STOCK CONTROL

Most businesses hold stocks of both finished products and raw materials. The purpose of holding stocks is to bridge the interval between the availability of a new supply of an article and an immediate requirement for it. But the average level of stocks must be related to the benefits to be derived from holding stocks balanced against the costs of holding them.

The cost of holding stocks is often higher than is realized. It is not unusual for one-third or even one-half of the assets of a manufacturing business to be in the form of stocks or work in progress, and exceptionally the proportion may be much higher, as in the tobacco industry. The cost of holding stocks includes the interest charged on money borrowed for the purpose (or the loss of profit involved in tying up the company's capital in financing them), warehouse and insurance charges, the cost of supervision and the risks that stocks will become obsolete or prove to be unsaleable. In some types of production the costs of holding stocks and the associated risks are so great that production is undertaken only to order; this is always the case when a product has to be tailored to the needs of specific customers, as with many capital goods. Although the cost of holding stocks of finished products is high, the cost of running out of stock may also be considerable if the customer decides to take his business elsewhere.

Running out of raw materials and components is also expensive: it almost always causes a costly cessation of production. But this does not mean that excessive stocks should be held, and it is necessary to establish some systematic way of verifying when stock levels are adequate but not excessive. Some compromise has to be effected between the size of orders and costs of holding stocks. Generally speaking, large quantities of goods can be purchased more cheaply than small quantities, and this points in the direction of ordering in large amounts; on the other hand, at any given rate of consumption, the larger the orders placed the larger will be the average level of stock held. On certain assumptions it is possible to determine the optimum size of an order having regard to these conflicting considerations.

Consider a system in which production takes place evenly throughout the year, and deliveries of raw materials are made just as stocks become exhausted. Let q (which is to be determined) be the number of items in each order. The number of items in stock is depicted in figure 3.3. The two costs to be considered are the order costs and stock-holding costs. Many of the order costs are unaffected by the size of order; for example, there is a need to check which items have been delivered, and there is frequently a delivery charge, which varies very little with the size or the total value of the order. In consequence, it is customary to assume that total order costs depend solely on the number of orders placed per year. Stock-holding costs depend either on the maximum number of units held in stock or, more frequently, on the average number of units held in stock. If the cost per order is C_3, the cost per item held in stock is C_1 per year and the number of items used each year is U, total costs (TC) are given by

$$TC = C_3 \frac{U}{q} + C_1 \frac{q}{2}.$$

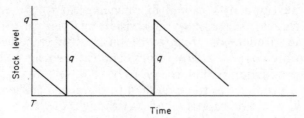

Figure 3.3   Number of items in stock.

Total costs are minimized when

$$\frac{d(TC)}{dq} = 0$$

or when

$$-\frac{C_3 U}{q^2} + \frac{C_1}{2} = 0$$

or when

$$q^2 = \frac{2C_3 U}{C_1}$$

or when

$$q = \sqrt{\left(\frac{2C_3 U}{C_1}\right)}.$$

This result is called the economic lot-size, after Harris.[7] Though the assumptions upon which the analysis has been based are somewhat heroic, the result is robust to a number of variations in those assumptions, as we shall see when other problems are considered. Part of the reason is due to the shape of the total cost curve, as is depicted in figure 3.4.

One of the heroic assumptions of the previous analysis was certainty — certainty about both the rate of use of the material and about its delivery time. When either or both of these are uncertain a further complication arises. Suppose that the system of stock control used is to order a fresh supply of some component whenever stocks fall below some level. How should this level be fixed? In most cases, some time will elapse before the order can be delivered, and it will be necessary to have sufficient stock on hand to ensure that supplies of

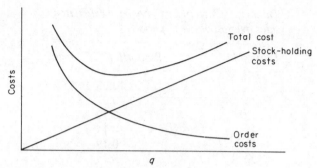

Figure 3.4   Costs for different sizes ordered.

the components can be maintained until the new supplies arrive. Thus, the level to which stocks can fall before a new order is placed must be related to the level of consumption that is anticipated and the time needed to make delivery (the lead time). Both of these may fluctuate. It is often possible to appraise the extent of such variations from past experience, and to allow for alterations.

A simple statistical model illustrates the considerations involved. Consider a retailer who sells 500 pocket calculators of a particular make each year, for which costs (C_3) are £40 per order and £1 per year for each calculator held in stock (cost C_1). Using the economic lot-size formula,

$$q = \sqrt{\left(\frac{2.40.500}{1}\right)} = 200.$$

An order is placed when stock falls to a level S (to be determined); each order is promptly delivered two weeks later. Suppose that the cost of each lost sale (C_2) is £2.20 to the retailer, and that past experience shows a pattern of sales over a two-week period as given in table 3.2. Let us consider the expected cost of lost sales incurred by placing the order at different possible stock levels (table 3.3). The differences in the figures in column (3) represent the reduction in the cost of lost sales made by increasing the value of S by 1: thus, if 21 items are held instead of 20, the sales lost will on the average be worth £(1.222 − 0.506) or £0.616. These savings are to be contrasted with the additional stock-holding cost incurred. At the *worst*, each addition to S involves holding an additional item in stock until the re-order level is next encountered, which in our example is 200/500 of a year (given the annual sales of 500 and the order quantity of 200).

Table 3.2 Pattern of pocket calculator sales over a two-week period

Units sold	Proportion of times
15	0.03
16	0.07
17	0.12
18	0.14
19	0.19
20	0.17
21	0.13
22	0.08
23	0.06
24	0.01

Table 3.3   Expected cost of lost sales incurred

(1) Possible stock level, S	(2) Expected no. of lost sales	(3) Expected lost sales cost $=(2) \times £2.20$
20	$(1 \times 0.13) + (2 \times 0.08)$ $+ (3 \times 0.06) + (4 \times 0.01) =$ 0.51	1.122
21	0.23	0.506
22	0.08	0.176
23	0.01	0.022
24	0	0

Since each additional item in stock costs £1 per year, or £0.40 per cycle, the 'lost sales' saving of £0.616 clearly exceeds any additional stock-holding cost. Whether to hold 22 items or 21 is much more an open issue. The additional item will reduce the loss of sales revenue by $£(0.506 - 0.176) = £0.33$. The additional stock-holding cost will be under £0.04 – in fact, it can be shown to be $0.4[1 - (0.23 - 0.08)]$ $= £0.34$. Whether this extra item will be held will depend as much on the retailer's view about the desirability of maintaining customer goodwill as on anything else.

It may be noticed that the economic lot-size formula was used to derive the order quantity of 200. Given the risk of losing sales every cycle, which in our example is about every ten weeks, some increase in the order quantity is justified, since the extra stock-holding cost will be balanced by reduced order costs and *reduced* expected lost sales costs. The difference made to the order quantity is, however, exceedingly small, and most businesses do not even bother to undertake such a calculation: rather, they would be prepared to increase the order quantity by a few per cent to a round figure.

In practice, questions of stock control will generally be much more complicated than the simple examples considered above. We will mention three features that lead to some revisions to the schemes outlined, though our discussion is far from exhaustive.

First, we have so far considered schemes involving *continuous* review: as soon as stock reached a particular level, another order was placed. Continuous review schemes enable stock-holding costs to be lower, but they usually involve additional inspection or administrative costs. For many products, a *periodic* review may be preferred: the businessman can choose how often the review is undertaken, and the size of the order that is then placed depends on the level of stock found at the review. Periodic reviews work well for products whose rate of use is reasonably steady, or in cases where a large number of items are ordered from the same supplier.

Second, the existence of a number of products often calls for a mixed system. Items that represent an appreciable proportion of the value of components used might be subject to continuous review, whereas other items might be subject to periodic review. Certain items that are used frequently but are of small value might be subjected to the 'two-bin method of control'. Two bins are used to store the parts, and when one is empty a replacement order is put in hand. The effect of such a scheme is that supplies of these parts are assured without it being necessary to pay particular attention to the stock position.

Third, our discussion has concentrated on the ordering of parts rather than on the production of finished products. Production scheduling involves many similarities with the ordering of parts. Stock-holding costs are common to both. If there are no finished products available when a customer wishes to buy, there is the risk of losing sales. The one difference is that the order cost is replaced by a production 'setup' cost. This is clearly a cost of a rather similar kind as far as any mathematical treatment is concerned. The more items that are produced at a time, the less often it will be necessary to stop production in order to set the tools appropriately, and the parallel with the ordering costs should be clear. There are, however, two differences in the analysis. One is that production of a good builds up stocks gradually, the stock position resembling that of figure 3.5. If the rate of production is very similar to the rate of use, then the economic lot-size formula is no longer relevant. The other difference is that production facilities have to be used for a number of products. Without prior planning the plant would find that it would want to make two or more products at the same time on the same piece of machinery.

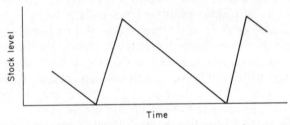

Figure 3.5   Stock level for items produced within the plant.

The kind of planning involved is beyond the scope of this book, but interested readers may find the book by Magee and Boodman[8] helpful. The book discusses a number of production scheduling methods to handle 'known' demands.

A change in the level of demand for a number of products requires a modification of the parameters of any production scheduling scheme. For this reason it is customary to forecast the level of demand, frequently in a simple way as is done by using the methods of 'exponential smoothing', which are described in chapter 10. Our experience has been that businesses may still be partially unprepared for changes in demand. When demand first increases a number of shortages are likely to occur in finished products. Customers (and salesmen too) tend to exert pressure for the shortages to be rectified quickly, and it is natural for production managers to respond. But to respond by bringing forward a new production run is often most unwise, for each stoppage for a new production run implies a loss of total output. At such times a cool reappraisal, plus some overtime working, may be appropriate.

QUEUEING

In business it is frequently difficult to decide the proportions in which productive facilities should be provided. The problem would be simple if there were no uncertainty: but in real life uncertainty is inevitable. Consider a company that employs a number of men to undertake maintenance and repair work on its machines. If many machines require maintenance within a short period of each other it may not be possible to service them quickly unless the team of maintenance men is large; but employing a large team will mean that the men will often be idle. A balance is clearly required here, for too small a maintenance team will mean poor utilization of machines, and too large a team is unnecessarily costly in terms of the wages bill.

When machines cannot be serviced immediately they form a 'queue' awaiting attention — hence the term 'queueing' is given to such problems. There are many techniques for studying the behaviour of queues under different circumstances, and these techniques are concerned with:

(a) the average length of the queue, and hence the average time it takes for a 'customer' (in our example, a machine) to be 'served' (in our example, repaired);
(b) the average utilization of facilities provided to serve the queue (in our example, maintenance staff).

These features can best be illustrated by an example. Suppose that a cigarette-making firm possesses 10 machines for one of the stages of production. Each machine is known to have a $2\frac{1}{2}$ per cent chance of failing in any one hour, in which case it has to be repaired by one of the maintenance men. The time taken to repair the machine varies quite considerably. Ten per cent of machines can be repaired almost instantly, but the other 90 per cent vary between about one and eight hours. Full details are recorded in table 3.4. The present system is that the machines are fully utilized for 50 hours a week (ten hours a day for five days), except when being repaired. The maintenance staff work the same hours as the machine operators, but any machines not repaired by the end of the week are then serviced during the weekend. A machine that is idle costs the company £9 per hour in terms of lost production. A maintenance man is paid £200 for a 50-hour week, and £6 for each hour of overtime worked during the weekend. The company presently employs one man (Mr Brown), though it can call upon another man if Mr Brown is ill: it wishes to know if it would be worthwhile to employ a second man.

The two parts to this problem are the number of machines that may fail in any hour, and the length of time it takes to repair a machine once it has failed. There is a 97.5 per cent chance that a particular machine will not fail in any given hour, and the probability that *none* of the machines fails is 0.975^{10}, which is 0.77633. Calculations of the probabilities of 1, 2, 3, etc., machines failing are recorded in table 3.5. These figures are correct when there are ten machines at risk: were a machine to fail there would be only nine remaining at risk, and the probabilities are amended accordingly.

To assess the problem we will simulate what might happen if one man only were to be employed on maintenance work. The kind of

Table 3.4   *Time taken to repair machines*

Time taken, in hours (to nearest hour)	Probability
0	0.10
1	0.05
2	0.20
3	0.25
4	0.15
5	0.10
6	0.05
7	0.05
8	0.05

Table 3.5   *Total number of machines requiring maintenance in any given hour*

No. of machines	Probability	Cumulative probability
0	0.77633	0.77633
1	0.19906	0.97539
3	0.00157	0.99993
4	0.00007	1.0
5 or more	0	

Table 3.6   Details of machines requiring maintenance for each hour of week 1

(1) Hour	(2) Random 5-digit number	(3) No. of machines failing	(4) Machine failing	(5) Random 3-digit number	(6) No. of hours to repair	(7) Machine being repaired	(8) No. of machines out of action	(9) Maintenance man idle
1	02484	0					0	1
2	88139	1	A	599	3	A	1	
3	31788	0				⎮	1	
4	35873	0				↓	1	
5	63259	0					0	1
6	83680	1	B	985	8	B	1	
7	56131	0				⎮	1	
8	12238	0				⎮	1	
9	68291	0				⎮	1	
10	95093	1	C	002	0	⎮	2	
11	37336	0				⎮	2	
12	63266	0				⎮	2	
13	18632	0				↓	2	
14	79781	1	D	298	2	C, D	1	
15	09184	0				D	1	
16	04060	0					0	1
.								
.								
.								
40	82680	1	K	739	4	K	1	
41	88098	1	L	499	3	⎮	2	
42		0				⎮	2	
43	85250	1	M	885	6	↓	3	
44		0				L	2	
45	99184	2	N, O	255, 637	2, 4	⎮	4	
46		0				↓	4	
47		0				M	3	
48	84906	1	P	602	4	M	4	
49		0				M	4	
50		0				M	4	
Total number of hours							76	13

(No. of hours of overtime = 12)

calculation required for such a simulation is presented in table 3.6. In order to make these calculations, five-digit random numbers were taken to represent how many machines might fail. The numbers used have been taken from a book of statistical tables prepared by H. R. Neave.[9] The random numbers of column (2) are translated into the number of machines failing (column 3) in the way indicated in the left-hand part of table 3.7.

Table 3.7 The assignment of random numbers to the number of machines failing and to the time taken to repair them

Random numbers	No. of machines failing	Random numbers	Hours taken to repair
00000-77632	0	000-099	0
77633-97538	1	100-149	1
97539-99835	2	150-349	2
99836-99992	3	350-599	3
99993-99999	4	600-749	4
		750-849	5
		850-899	6
		900-949	7
		950-999	8

Table 3.8 Average number of machines being repaired or awaiting repair per week

	Average	Range
(1) No. of machine hours lost	85	26-222
(2) No. of hours maintenance man idle	13	0-30
(3) No. of hours of overtime for maintenance man	5	0-18

The calculation recorded for week 1 gave 76 hours of idle machine time, 13 hours when the maintenance man was idle, and 12 hours of overtime. Repeating this calculation for a further 13 weeks gave the figures recorded in table 3.8.

Using the same results as before, a recalculation was performed to determine the effect of adding a second man to the maintenance staff. It was assumed that each machine was attended to by only one man, an assumption that is perhaps a little pessimistic as far as service time is concerned. Table 3.9 records the average cost incurred by each of the systems. The results of the simulation suggest that it is well worth employing the second man.

Two observations on this example are pertinent. First, the calculations that have been undertaken were rather tedious, even though the example is much simpler than the typical queueing problem

Table 3.9   Costs of different numbers of men in the maintenance team

			One man		Two men	
(1)	a	No. of machine hours lost	85		49	
	b	Cost of lost production		£768		£440
(2)	a	No. of hours maintenance men were idle	13		57	
	b	Basic cost of maintenance team		£200		£400
(3)	a	No. of hours of overtime	5		2	
	b	Overtime cost		£31		£11
Total				£999		£851

encountered in industry: furthermore, the level of accuracy required for many industrial problems is such that a larger number of weeks would be simulated. Second, it would be possible for a firm to undertake a real trial-and-error study, by varying the number of men actually employed. Though this has the merit of reliably illustrating what can happen, it is usually a very expensive way of experimenting. The advantage of the 'paper' simulation that has been discussed here is that a large number of variants can be examined. For example, it would be possible to consider both the results for a different number of machines (15, say) or a variation in the number of hours worked; or, indeed, a combination of these two factors could be assessed by a paper (or computer) simulation.

The example given above was solved by a simulation technique. It illustrates quite well the kind of problem encountered, but it is not the only solution technique that can be adopted. Some problems are amenable to more direct statistical/mathematical methods. These mathematical methods enable solutions to be obtained much more quickly, but are reliable only when the two distributions – the interval of time elapsing between customers arriving for service, and the time taken to serve them – correspond to certain theoretical distributions. These conditions are met only infrequently, though the mathematical methods are often used to give approximate solutions – which are useful in indicating areas of the problem worthy of further investigation. This rather technical area of study is not normally regarded as the domain of economists, and will not be pursued here. The interested reader is referred to the book by Churchman, Ackoff and Arnoff.[10]

CONCLUSION

This chapter has considered each of a number of topics independently. This was done in order to illustrate the techniques involved. These techniques are very powerful, and are among those most commonly used in industry. Nonetheless, there are clearly many links between the topics. Management frequently has to pursue the implications in one area of changes in another area. For example, if it takes a long time to prepare machinery for a production change, businesses may employ maintenance men on overtime or special shifts; similarly, production runs might often be relatively large so that production is not lost during the course of the 'basic' week. Another example would be that the number of products made (and how often they are made) would have implications for the availability of resources, and hence for any linear programming specifications: the linear programming and production scheduling calculations cannot be satisfactorily undertaken if done wholly independently. These links enable good management to earn their keep, for there are often many ways of tackling a problem.

NOTES

1 R. Marris, *The Economics of Capital Utilization: A Report on Multiple-shift Work* (Cambridge University Press, 1964).
2 G. C. Winston, 'The theory of capital utilization and idleness', *Journal of Economic Literature*, 12 (December 1974).
3 R. Dorfman, P. A. Samuelson and R. Solow, *Linear Programming and Economic Analysis* (New York, McGraw-Hill, 1958).
4 D. C. Vandermeulen, *Linear Economic Theory* (Englewood Cliffs, NJ, Prentice-Hall, 1971).
5 A. Chung, *Linear Programming* (Indianapolis, Bobbs-Merrill, 1963).
6 J. K. Wyatt, 'Two years of linear programming', *Operational Research Quarterly*, 9 (1958).
7 F. W. Harris, *Operations and Co* (Chicago, 1915).
8 J. F. Magee and D. M. Boodman, *Production Planning and Inventory Control* (New York, McGraw-Hill, 1967).
9 H. R. Neave, *Elementary Statistics Tables* (London, George Allen & Unwin, 1981).
10 C. W. Churchman, R. L. Ackoff and E. L. Arnoff, *Introduction to Operations Research* (Chichester, John Wiley, 1958).

4
The Market

The ultimate success, or otherwise, of a business is determined by its performance in the market. The concept of the market is essentially concerned with the institutional structure within which intending buyers and sellers interact.[1] Market operations cover a wide range of transactions, ranging from selling the output of a business to its customers to buying or (selling) primary commodities, providing finance and hiring labour. Thus, for example, we can talk about the capital market and the labour market, as well as the market for individual commodities. The extent to which actual institutional arrangements are formalized varies enormously. Examples of highly formal arrangements cover those where all transactions take place within a particular location such as the London Stock Exchange. But the existence of a specific location or meeting place is not essential. On the foreign exchange market, for example, known buyers and sellers conduct their business via telephones. At the other extreme, one might place the market for second-hand goods. The term 'market' is, therefore, not restricted to any precise institutional form but covers any arrangement whereby buyers and sellers undertake exchange for their mutual satisfaction.

There are clearly two sides to any market transaction: that of the seller (the supply side), and that of the buyer (the demand side). The previous two chapters have considered the supply side, and in this and the next chapter we turn to a consideration of demand. In the present chapter we examine the passive approach to demand, which builds on the existence of consumer preferences and the assumption, often implicit, that consumers are fully informed as to the price, availability and quality of individual products. Working from these premises is an essential building block towards an understanding of market behaviour through which the firm can improve its performance. In the next chapter we shall consider the more active managerial aspects of demand covering the marketing process and the role of advertising in a world of imperfect information.

THE DETERMINANTS OF DEMAND

To the businessman interested in selling his wares on the market, demand must be more than the simple expression of desires; it must be backed up by the willingness and ability to pay. The relevant concept here is that of effective demand. In practice, the effective demand for any particular product will be determined by a whole complex of variables such as its price, the incomes and tastes of buyers, the prices and availability of substitutes, availability of credit facilities and advertising. All of these find expression in the demand function, which is simply an algebraic representation of this information:

$$Q_x = f(P_x, P_s, Y, C, A, T)$$

where
Q_x = quantity demanded of good x
P_x = price of good x
P_s = price of substitute goods
Y = disposable income
C = credit
A = advertising
T = tastes.

For any particular product there may be other specific factors that are of considerable importance. For example, we shall shortly be considering the demand function for cigarettes, where the publication of 'health scare' reports is clearly likely to be significant. For purposes of analysis it is convenient to simplify the problem by taking each main factor in isolation, assuming that the others remain constant – the *ceteris paribus* assumption frequently adopted in economic analysis. The purpose of this procedure is to identify the potential impact of each factor in turn: there is no logical difficulty in generalizing the argument to include more than one variable at a time. Indeed, when attempting to estimate the demand function for a product or to forecast demand it is essential to take account of all the relevant variables. However, working through them one at a time does enable us to assess, without undue confusion, the factors at work.

OWN-PRICE AND THE DEMAND CURVE

In a discussion of the factors affecting demand, the price of the commodity itself is usually the first to come to mind. The simplest expression of a demand relationship is the demand curve, which portrays the relation between the price of a commodity and the quantity bought in the form of a simple graph derived from a demand schedule as in figure 4.1 and table 4.1. In the table, hypothetical demand schedules for two commodities are shown. Although they are not intended to represent actual figures, they are derived in a way that reflects the findings of two recent studies.[2] In later chapters we shall be using as an example the accounts of the Imperial Group. Since their principal activity remains the manufacture of tobacco products, it seemed appropriate to consider the demand function for cigarettes. The study of the demand for herrings by Charles Allan represents a simple, but very useful, illustration of the methods and problems involved. The reader is encouraged to consult the original source for further information.

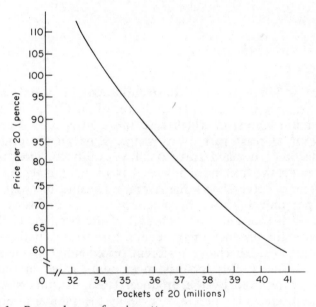

Figure 4.1   Demand curve for cigarettes.

Figure 4.1. shows in graph form the relationship between price and quantity demanded of cigarettes.[3] The price of the commodity is represented on the vertical axis, while the quantity appears on the horizontal axis. Typically, the demand curve will slope downwards from left to right, indicating that, the lower the price, the more of a commodity will be bought. This is not to be taken as a fixed rule,

Table 4.1   Demand schedules for cigarettes and herring

Price* (pence)	Cigarettes packets of 20 per week (millions)	Herring (1,000 lbs per week)
60	40.6	748.7
65	39.6	636.1
70	38.6	547.0
75	37.8	475.3
80	37.0	416.7
85	36.3	368.3
90	35.6	327.9
95	35.0	293.7
100	34.5	264.5
105	33.9	239.5
110	33.4	217.9

* For cigarettes the price is per packet of 20; for herrings it is the price per lb.

since there will be cases of 'conspicuous consumption' goods, or goods where price is taken as an indicator of quality as well as other unusual circumstances, in which case the demand curve may slope upwards over at least part of its range. However, in general the downward-sloping demand curve portrays reality for most practical purposes, and is the form normally used as a tool of analysis.

The demand curve shows the average revenue received by the producer per unit sold on the assumption that the same price is charged to each consumer for each unit of the commodity. In some circumstances the producer may be able to operate a policy of price discrimination, i.e., to charge different prices either to the same or different customers. This topic is considered further in chapter 6. Total revenue received by the producer (total consumers' expenditure on the product) is, therefore, given by the number of units sold multiplied by the price (average revenue) per unit. Total revenue at a price of 80 pence amounts to £29.6 million.

Inspection of table 4.1 reveals one interesting fact. The quantity demanded of herring appears much more responsive than that of cigarettes to a given change in price. Since we have different units of measurement in the quantity dimension, it is important to derive some indicator of responsiveness that is unaffected by the particular units of measurement chosen. The simplest approach is to work in proportionate changes, and this is precisely what the economist's concept of elasticity does. It is important to realize that there is an elasticity measure relating to each of the variables in the demand function. First, therefore, we consider the own-price elasticity of demand.

OWN-PRICE ELASTICITY OF DEMAND

As we have seen, the lower the price the more of a commodity will be bought, but this fact alone is not of much help to the businessman, who wants to know *how much more* will be bought, and whether consumers will spend more or less money on the commodity. Hence, he wants to know what effect a change in price will have on total revenue. Such information is conveyed by the own-price elasticity of demand.

The own-price elasticity of demand represents the proportionate change in quantity demanded resulting from a small change in price; i.e.,

$$e = \frac{\Delta Q/Q}{\Delta P/P}$$

where Δ stands for a small change. Or, in terms of calculus,

$$e = \frac{dQ/Q}{dP/P} = \frac{dQ}{dP} \cdot \frac{P}{Q}.$$

This measure of the elasticity is known as the point elasticity and applies only to small changes around a defined point on the demand curve, although the point may be located anywhere on the curve. Let us try and calculate the own-price elasticity for the two products shown in table 4.1. Here we have information only about discrete changes in price, i.e., steps of 5 pence. Taking any two prices, e.g., 60 and 65 pence, dP is clearly 5, but we will obtain a different answer for the proportionate change in price depending on whether we define P as 60 or 65 pence. When seeking to measure the elasticity over a range of the demand curve in this manner the relevant concept is that of *arc elasticity*. Usually arc elasticity is measured as:

$$e_{arc} = \frac{\Delta Q/\frac{1}{2}(Q_1 + Q_2)}{\Delta P/\frac{1}{2}(P_1 + P_2)}.$$

Assuming a rise in price from 60 to 65 pence for both cigarettes and herrings, the arc elasticities are as follows:

$$\text{Cigarettes: } \frac{(40.6 - 39.6)/0.5(40.6 + 39.6)}{(60 - 65)/0.5(60 + 65)} = -0.3$$

$$\text{Herring: } \frac{(748.7 - 636.1)/0.5(748.7 + 636.1)}{(60 - 65)/0.5(60 + 65)} = -2.0$$

The negative sign for the arc elasticity simply indicates that as price rises demand falls *(ceteris paribus)*. We need to examine this presumption in greater detail in order to understand what is implied. The response of demand for a commodity to a change in its own price involves two steps. The first (the 'income effect') is due to what may be thought of as a change in the real income of the consumer: if money income remains constant and the price of a commodity rises, the real income or purchasing power of the consumer is reduced. The income effect may be either positive or negative: if negative, demand for a commodity falls as its price rises; if it is positive, the demand for a commodity will increase as its price rises. A positive 'income effect' will occur in the case of so-called 'inferior' goods: a large proportion of the income of peasants in the Far East is spent on rice, which is cheap and filling, and there is little money left for other foodstuffs; if the price of rice increases the peasant may become so poor that he cannot afford any of the other foods and will buy even more rice simply in order to fill his stomach. The second step (the 'substitution effect') is due to the substitution that takes place between one commodity and other commodities when the price of the first commodity changes; the substitution effect is always negative in that, abstracting from the change in real income, a change in the price of a good always leads to a change in quantity demanded in the opposite direction. Thus, a rise in the relative price of a commodity leads to a reduction in the demand for it. Usually (for 'normal' goods) the substitution and income effects work in the same direction and the demand for a commodity falls as its price rises. Even for an 'inferior' good it will generally be expected that the substitution effect will dominate the income effect and the same result will occur.[4]

Given that the demand curve is, therefore, normally downward-sloping, it follows that the own-price elasticity of demand will yield a negative value as in the illustrations above. However, it is fairly common practice to ignore the sign and take the absolute value of the elasticity.

Five interesting cases of own-price elasticity may be distinguished: the first two are limiting cases, which it would be difficult to imagine in real life, the third is also rather unlikely, but conceivable; the fourth and fifth are typical of the whole range of possibilities within these limits.

1 *Completely inelastic demand* (e = 0)
This occurs where, regardless of any change in price, there is no change in the quantity demanded, and total revenue changes solely in accordance with, and in direct proportion to, price. A completely inelastic demand curve would be represented diagrammatically as a vertical straight line. Such a case is unlikely to be found in practice, but it is possible to conceive of a very primitive society with one staple food (e.g., rice or bread) where over a wide range of prices the demand for the staple food remained constant.

2 *Completely elastic demand* (e = ∞)
A completely elastic demand, represented diagrammatically by a horizontal straight line, is the case where any increase in price, however small, causes demand for the product to cease entirely. It is unlikely that the demand for any commodity in total would fit this case, but many firms are in practice faced with something like perfectly elastic demand for their product: they produce goods in the knowledge that there is a ruling price for their product in the market which may be fixed by custom, competition or government regulation (e.g., the Common Agricultural Policy of the EEC) to which they must conform if they wish to sell anything. Thus, if they raised their price above the ruling price, no one would buy from them and demand for their product would cease entirely; if they lowered their price they would attract the whole of the market demand (but be unable to satisfy it).

3 *Unitary elasticity of demand* (e = 1)
Here, for any change in price, total revenue remains constant and the quantity demanded changes in the same proportion as the change in price. Again, the precise occurrence of unitary elasticity is likely to be rare, although many observed elasticities may be close to it.

4 *Relatively elastic demand* (1 < e < ∞)
When the proportionate change in the quantity demanded of a product is greater than the proportionate change in price, demand is relatively elastic. An elastic demand is one in which total revenue increases with a fall and decreases with an increase in price. The

amount by which revenue changes is an indication, though not a measure, of the own-price elasticity of demand. Thus, if demand is highly elastic, a small fall in price would produce a large increase in the quantity consumed and correspondingly in total revenue.

5 Relatively inelastic demand $(0 < e < 1)$

Demand is inelastic when the proportionate change in quantity consumed is smaller than the proportionate change in price, and when total revenue decreases with a fall in price and increases with a rise in price. This occurrence is typical of most so-called necessities.

The most straightforward expression of own-price elasticity of demand is in terms of total revenue. If, as a result of a reduction in price, total revenue rises, demand is elastic, and the larger the increase in total revenue the more elastic the demand is; if total revenue falls as price falls, then demand is inelastic. In practice this may, of course, be difficult to determine because some other factors may also affect demand at the same time as the price changes: but it is the change in total revenue that interests the businessman.

The two demand schedules that have been illustrated in table 4.1 both show the property of a constant own-price elasticity of demand over the range of prices we have taken.[5] This property and the actual elasticity are those that were used in the two studies we quoted. For cigarettes the demand is highly own-price inelastic, and hence revenue increases almost in proportion to the change in price as the price of cigarettes rises. Given this fact, it is not surprising that cigarettes have been a popular target for successive chancellors of the Exchequer when they are looking for means of raising tax revenue. (However, there is some suggestion that demand has recently become rather more sensitive to changes in price, at least in the period immediately following a rise in price.) The demand for herrings falls into the elastic range, possibly reflecting the wider variety of substitutes available.

THE IMPORTANCE OF ELASTICITY OF DEMAND

The examples given above are all simplified,[6] but they are useful in that they indicate what economists mean when they talk about elasticity of demand. All businessmen would be expected to know something about the likely effect of price changes on the demand for their product, even though they would rarely express their knowledge in terms of the elasticity of demand; but it is noticeable to the outside observer that several business decisions pay insufficient attention to the elasticity of demand for the product. When costs are rising, it is tempting to try to pass on the cost increases by increasing the price to the consumer, and if demand for the product is relatively inelastic, this measure may well succeed; but when, as for example in the case of rail transport, there are many substitutes and the demand is relatively elastic, increasing prices may well lead to a reduction of total revenue rather than an increase. Because of declining use of off-peak trains, British Rail has, in fact, recently introduced a wide range of low-price special fares.

It is not necessary to labour this point further; most businessmen intuitively know something about the elasticity of demand for the goods that they make, and base their pricing policy on some notion of elasticity. It is desirable to go beyond this and try to form as precise an idea as possible of the degree of elasticity of demand. The concept of own-price elasticity of demand is useful because it is a convenient shorthand way of expressing the effects of price changes on the demand for a commodity, and as such it is relevant to price fixing.

Estimation of the demand curve and measurement of own-price elasticity of demand are by no means easy, but they are feasible, and the more that is known about elasticity of demand, the easier it is to take decisions about pricing and other aspects of business policy.

But, as we have seen, prices are not the only factors that affect demand. The demand curve is an apparently simple device, and price elasticity of demand an indispensable concept; but a great deal underlies both of them. When other factors alter, the demand curve is likely to change, either in shape or location. These changes may arise either from the actions of the firm itself (e.g., a change in advertising expenditure) or from outside causes (such as changes in the income of consumers, the prices of other goods or tastes). A change in income, for example, will usually lead to a shift in the demand curve. Thus if income increases, and the good is not an inferior good, the demand curve will tend to shift rightwards. If the price of a substitute rises, the demand curve will likewise tend to shift to the right. A shift to the left could be caused by a fall in income (for a 'normal' good) or a fall in the price of a substitute. A rightward (leftward) shift indicates that at each price the consumer will now buy more (less) of the product under consideration. It is important to distinguish between movements along a given demand curve (reflected in the own-price elasticity) arising from changes in the price of the product itself and a shift in the curve caused by a change in some other variable in the demand function. It is now time to turn to examine the impact of the other main factors.

As we have seen, the demand for a commodity will be affected by the incomes of the people likely to buy it. At times of general prosperity, when incomes are high and unemployment is low, the demand for particular types of goods (e.g., consumer durables) is likely to be high, but it will fall off rapidly, regardless of price changes, when incomes fall. For such commodities income elasticity of demand, which represents the responsiveness of demand to changes in income, is more important than price elasticity. In the recession that is affecting the United Kingdom and other parts of the world in the early 1980s, it is not therefore surprising that it is producers and distributors of motor vehicles and electrical goods, who based their production plans on rising real incomes, who are having a particularly hard time.

The formula for income elasticity is similar to that for price elasticity:

$$e_Y = \frac{dQ/Q}{dY/Y} = \frac{dQ}{dY} \cdot \frac{Y}{Q}$$

where Y = income. Thus, as has been argued, the income elasticity will be high for most consumer durable goods, which have the character of luxuries. The demand for British exports also tends to be income-elastic, as it depends to a considerable extent on prosperity overseas. On the other hand, the demand for commodities such as cigarettes is likely to be highly income-inelastic, which is confirmed in the study by Witt and Pass,[7] who found the income elasticity to be 0.13.

Income elasticity of demand is frequently more important than own-price elasticity in determining the volume of goods sold. The relationship between demand and income variations is not always straightforward: much will depend on the suddenness or permanence of a change in income, and there is frequently a lag between changes in income and changes in demand; the demand for many goods is not readily postponable when incomes fall: it takes time to plan changes; some commitments, such as credit repayments, may remain fixed;

and old consumption habits tend to die hard, particularly if the change in income is expected to be only temporary.

SUBSTITUTES AND THE CROSS-ELASTICITY OF DEMAND

The existence of substitutes is another important factor affecting demand, and in fact own-price elasticity of demand may be looked on, to some extent, as an indication of the existence or otherwise of satisfactory substitutes for the commodity. If satisfactory substitutes exist, and price is raised, demand will be transferred to the substitutes. Commodities with close substitutes are, therefore, usually found to have a high own-price elasticity of demand. The substitutes with which many business decisions are concerned are the products of competitors. Thus, although the own-price elasticity of demand for cigarettes is low, that for any particular brand may be high. Cross-elasticity of demand is a measure of the relationship between the change in demand for one product and the change in price of another. It is defined as

$$\text{Cross-elasticity of demand} = \frac{\text{relative change in quantity of X}}{\text{relative change in price of Y}}$$

The formula is:

$$e_c = \frac{dQ_X/Q_X}{dP_Y/P_Y} = \frac{dQ_X}{dP_Y} \cdot \frac{P_Y}{Q_X}.$$

A similar concept is that of market share elasticity, which relates an individual firm's share of the total market sales of a commodity to the difference between its prices and general market prices. Sales, and the market share, of cigarette X, for example, are likely to fall if the price of cigarette Y in the same market falls. Other factors affecting demand, such as advertising, tastes, etc., will also have their relevant share elasticities.

Since the businessman is concerned not merely with total market demand for his product, but also with how much he can expect to sell, the relationships between the demand for his product and that for its substitutes is clearly of importance to him.

In general, the demand relationship between two commodities may be of two kinds: competing or complementary. If the demand for two commodities is competing, i.e., they are substitutes (e.g., herring and mackerel), then if one (herring) falls in price there will be a decrease (shift to the left) in the demand for the other (mackerel). In general, therefore, the demand for any commodity will move in the same direction as the price of its substitutes, and the cross-elasticity of demand will be positive; the higher the cross-elasticity, the greater the degree of substitutability. Complementary goods, such as cigarettes and matches, have a negative cross-elasticity. Thus, if the price of one of the complements changes, the demand for the other will change in the opposite direction i.e. an increase in the price of one will lead to a leftward shift in the demand curve for the other.

TASTES AND PREFERENCES

One of the fundamental determinants of demand for most non-necessary goods is the tastes or preferences of the consumer. There are some basic needs, such as a certain calorie intake of food, some warmth, some clothing, some shelter; but there are several ways of satisfying these needs, and given his income, the consumer's preferences or tastes frequently determine in what form he will buy the goods to meet these needs. These tastes are usually shaped by the kind of society in which we live, and in which part of that society; housing 'needs', for example, depend very much on professional and 'class' status; clothing needs usually far exceed the minimum necessary for warmth. One of the tasks of market research is to find out something about this society and the effects that it has on demand. Further, the businessman can influence the way in which his products are perceived as satisfying the desires of consumers or, possibly, can change the preferences themselves. We look more closely in the next chapter at the ways in which demand may be affected by the actions of the businessman.

SOME EMPIRICAL FINDINGS

To sum up the discussion so far, the main factors likely to influence the demand for a commodity are: the price of the commodity itself; the prices of its substitutes; the prices of complementary goods; the incomes of consumers; and the tastes and preferences of consumers. The quantity demanded will alter as one or any combination of these factors changes or is expected to change.[8]

There have been many attempts to quantify the basic relationships affecting demand, both for individual commodities in isolation and for many commodities taken together. The classic pioneering and comprehensive study for the UK was that of Stone,[9] which has been extended and up-dated by the work of Deaton.[10] When taking one product at a time, which is likely to be the prime interest of the businessman, one does not have to be concerned with a number of particular restrictions relating to the adding up, or aggregation, of all the individual demand functions to form total consumers' expenditure. Thus, for example, one does not have to take account of the fact that the sum of the expenditure on each good must be equal to the total expenditure. At this level, therefore, it is quite appropriate to take each demand equation on its own in an attempt to find that which bests fits the data for that commodity.

As noted in chapter 1, it is common in empirical work to use a logarithmic form for the demand function, which yields direct estimates of the elasticities and assumes that these are constant.[11] This means that we compare the logarithms of prices and quantities and other variables in a way that has the effect of relating percentage changes in the two directly. The results of applying this type of model for a number of commodities in the UK for the period 1954–70 are shown in table 4.2.

A number of features of the results in this table are noteworthy: all the own-price elasticities have the expected negative sign (except recreational goods, the coefficient of which is not statistically significant), but only gas and wines and spirits appear to have demand that falls in the elastic (> 1) range. A number of products appear to be inferior, with negative income elasticity – namely, sugar and sweets, gas, rail travel and newspapers. The rest have positive income elasticities, and those for wines and spirits, the running costs of motor vehicles and recreational goods are high. Most of the estimates fit in well with preconceptions about the nature of the goods, and the fact that the demand for potatoes and vegetables appears to have an income elasticity of roughly unity is probably explicable by the fact that this category includes frozen vegetables.

This last point raises an important issue. The level of aggregation of these commodities is rather high, and as such many close substitutes for individual products will appear in the same category. Thus, one might expect the price elasticities for the broad groups to be fairly low. Individual producers, moreover, are more likely to be concerned with the elasticities of demand for their particular products. Similar techniques can be applied to estimate, for example, the demand

Table 4.2 Own-price and income elasticities of demand for the UK, selected products*

	Income elasticity	Own-price elasticity
Bread and cereals	0.72	−0.12†
Meat and bacon	1.36	−0.27†
Sugar and sweets	−0.17†	−0.48
Dairy produce	0.86	−0.41
Potatoes and vegetables	0.99†	−0.20
Clothing	2.68	−0.99
Gas	−3.53	−1.65
Wines and spirits	3.55	−1.12
Running costs of motor vehicles	3.81	−0.63
Rail travel	−2.52	−0.73
Newspapers	−0.73	−0.43
Recreational goods	4.28	0.33†

* The results are derived from equations fitted to the period 1954–70. The elasticity figures quoted relate to 1963.
† Statistically, these results are not significantly different from zero.
Source: A. Deaton, Models and Projections of Demand in Post-War Britain (London, Chapman & Hall, 1975), table 5.3.

function for more specific commodity classifications, or even for particular brands of goods.[12] In a detailed study of individual brands across a number of European countries, Lambin[13] was able to find significant negative price effects for 37 out of 43 equations estimated for the demand for particular products. The average value of the own-price elasticity for these products was − 1.326 with a standard deviation of 0.92, and 23 of the elasticities had an absolute value greater than 1, indicating that in many cases the demand would be classed as own-price elastic. The frequency distribution of the estimated elasticities is shown in figure 4.2. Lambin's particular focus of interest was on the effects of advertising, and the products in his sample tended to be those with a high degree of advertising. Thus, it might be that these products are less price-sensitive than others that are not so heavily advertised. Nevertheless, for most of them price is important, and the results do confirm the belief that own-price elasticities will be greater the more specific is the commodity group analysed.

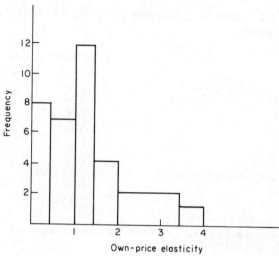

Figure 4.2   Distribution of own-price elasticities from a sample of branded products.

Source: J. J. Lambin, *Advertising, Competition and Market Conduct in Oligopoly over Time* (Amsterdam, North-Holland, 1976), p. 103.

DEMAND FUNCTIONS AND TOTAL EXPENDITURE

Much recent research on the estimation of demand functions has concentrated on seeking to examine the system of demand functions that comprise total expenditure. Here direct account has to be taken of the interactions and restrictions referred to earlier, and the statistical and analytical procedures required are well outside the scope of this book. The results of these techniques are, however, highly relevant for forecasting the overall pattern of demand, and it is appropriate to consider them. Table 4.3 reproduces the elasticities derived for broad commodity groups from a study by Deaton and Muellbauer.[14] It should be noted that the expenditure elasticity rather than the income elasticity is appropriate.[15] As might be expected, food and housing have low but positive expenditure elasticities, while the others all exceed unity. The commodity groupings are very broad,[16] but it appears that only for transport and communication does the demand appear to be own-price elastic. Food shows a positive own-price elasticity but, in fact, this coefficient is not statistically significant.

Table 4.3 Expenditure and own-price elasticities, UK, 1954–74, broad commodity groups

	Expenditure elasticity	Own-price elasticity
Food	0.21	0.07
Clothing	2.00	−0.92
Housing	0.30	−0.31
Fuel	1.67	−0.28
Drink and tobacco	1.22	−0.60
Transport and communication	1.23	−1.21
Other goods	1.21	−0.72
Other services	1.40	−0.93

Source: A. Deaton and J. Muellbauer, 'An almost ideal demand system', *American Economic Review*, 70 (1980), table 2.

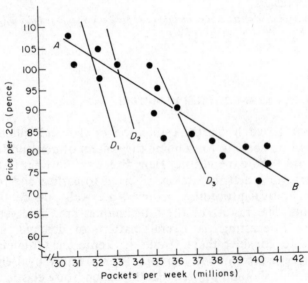

Figure 4.3   Prices and quantities consumed of cigarettes.

The careful estimation of demand functions is not easy and requires the use of sophisticated statistical techniques if meaningful results are to be obtained. The reader should be warned of a fairly common sort of error that can be made if care is not taken. One could collect data on the price of a particular product and the quantity sold for a number of years and plot the information in the form of a graph as in figure 4.3. It would be tempting to say then that the line of best fit (*AB* – fitted freehand) represented the demand curve for the commodity: it may possibly do so, but equally, the series of points on the graph, being observations for different years, may each be on different demand curves (for example, D_1, D_2, D_3, etc.), which represent the different conditions prevailing in each year and may reflect changes in incomes, tastes, prices of substitutes, etc., that have caused the curves to shift. This problem is what is known as the identification problem, i.e., of being able to isolate a demand curve from the many other factors that have led to a particular price and quantity being recorded at a specific time. If simple observations of price and quantity are to identify the demand curve correctly, a number of conditions must hold. Allan, in his study of the demand for herrings,[17] specified the six conditions that held in the particular market he was considering which were sufficient to provide reasonable certainty that the figures plotted did relate to the demand curve:

(1) a highly perishable product;
(2) a unified market;
(3) a homogeneous and divisible product;
(4) accurate statistical information;
(5) supply that varied in response to outside influences – the number of boats going out to fish for herring, for example, was heavily dependent on the day of the week, with no fishing on Sundays and little on Saturdays, since the fish could not be sold until Monday;
(6) demand that remains constant for long enough to enable a sufficient number of observations to be made.

While there are other circumstances in which a simple plot of price versus quantity would give a good approximation to the demand curve, the above list does provide an indication of the sort of conditions that are necessary to provide reliable estimates for any individual market. If these conditions are not met, then much more sophisticated estimation procedures are required.

MARKETS

In the introduction to this chapter, we provided a brief discussion of the nature of markets as a background to the treatment of demand in the following sections. It is now time to consider a number of additional features that need to be taken into account in examining actual markets.

The definition of actual markets in the real world is not itself easy. Of prime concern in the present context is the way in which any particular product is viewed by the consumer. We are not so much interested in either techniques of production or types of inputs used to produce the good or service, as in how the consumer appraises what is offered. Cross-elasticity of demand is a potentially useful tool for this purpose, since it provides a direct measure of the degree of substitutability between items. Thus, products with a high degree of cross-elasticity, being close substitutes, may be classified as part of the same market. In practice, data requirements and other problems discussed in previous sections make it rather difficult to conduct this sort of analysis on a wide scale.

The issues involved in examining any particular market arise, for example, in many of the reports of the Monopolies and Mergers Commission (MMC). Cases of mergers or dominant firms can be referred to the Commission for investigation under the Fair Trading Act 1973 if the firm concerned has over 25 per cent of the relevant UK market.[18] The first task of the Commission, therefore, is to ascertain whether this condition holds in any particular case. Consequently, they are required to discuss the nature and definition of the market. Two recent cases before the Commission aptly illustrate the issues involved.

In the report on cat and dog foods,[19] the reference to the Commission defined the products concerned as foods specially manufactured for consumption by cats and dogs or by both. It was noted that such foods currently comprise: canned foods, semi-moist foods, complete dry foods, biscuits and meal, and others, including quick frozen products and cooked foods not supplied in cans. The Commission also observed that other foods were consumed by cats and dogs, namely, fresh meat and fish, household scraps and milk, and that specially manufactured pet foods accounted for slightly under half of total consumption by cats and dogs. Prepared cat and dog foods are big business, and in 1975 total retail sales amounted to over £200 million. The market is dominated by Pedigree Petfoods (a subsidiary of Mars), with 50 per cent, and Spillers, with about 30 per cent. Particular sectors of the market show even larger shares for the main suppliers with, e.g., Pedigree Petfoods accounting for over 60 per cent of canned foods and Spillers over 70 per cent of biscuits and meal. The Commission noted, however, that owners have a considerable tendency to vary the diet of their pets, and that they appear responsive to price changes. In terms of the analysis of previous sections, therefore, it appears that the demand for particular types and brands is likely to be own-price elastic and that the cross-elasticity of demand between types and brands is quite high. The facts also indicate the dangers of taking a narrow view of any particular market, and suggest that attention must be paid to the existence of substitutes such as household scraps. The main companies themselves conducted extensive research into and analysis of the general market for their products as an essential part of their decisions.

In the report on the ready-mixed concrete market,[20] the Commission defined the good as 'concrete mixed to a fresh condition with the required properties for use, whether in a central mixer or truck mixer, and batched elsewhere than at the site where the concrete is required for use'.[21] It was also noted that a wide variety of types of concrete can be produced by varying the proportions of the basic ingredients or including different additives.

Ready-mixed concrete is heavy and bulky and tends to deteriorate markedly if not used within two hours of mixing. As a consequence, it can be transported only short distances (5–15 miles, depending on the roads), and there are a number of local markets that are small in area. The Commission estimated that over 70 per cent of concrete used on building sites was supplied in a ready-mixed state but that mixing on site remained an alternative available to consumers for a substantial portion of the demand. The Commission observed that producers of ready-mixed concrete needed to allow for this potential substitution in their pricing policy. The Commission also noted that all companies regularly examined local planning applications and other sources of information about forthcoming building work. The larger companies tended to conduct substantial market analysis, including, for example, a detailed analysis of the scale of business of competitors which may involve following the trucks from a competitor's depot.

The fact that it may not be a simple matter to isolate any particular market, especially when there are a large number of interconnecting elements, is illustrated by the recent failure of the Monopolies and Mergers Commission to come to a satisfactory conclusion in a reference on metal fasteners. Such fasteners covered nuts and bolts; cotters and cotter pins; nails, tacks and staples; rivets; and screws. In a press notice[22] it was announced that, among other things, definitional factors made it impossible for the Commission to collect precise information, and its deliberations, therefore, ceased without a report.

Each business needs to be aware of the nature and scope of the market or markets in which it is operating and, as noted above, the major companies do tend to take this task seriously. The firm also needs to be alert to new opportunities and challenges if it is to survive and prosper. The market is ever-changing, and failure to initiate or at least react to new developments can have serious consequences. A suitable lesson is provided by the experiences of the company manufacturing Gross cash registers, which was the largest UK manufacturer of mechanical cash registers. It unfortunately took a narrow view of the market and failed to recognize the implications of the new electronic technology. Continuing to manufacture only mechanical machines, its business declined substantially as electronic cash registers took over, and eventually the company was forced into liquidation.

The nature of the market for a product may depend crucially on the type of product concerned. At a minimum there is an important distinction between autonomous and derived demand. Autonomous demand is that for the product in its own right, for final consumption. Derived demand relates to demand for inputs that are required for further processing. Thus, the demand for an input is derived from the autonomous demand for the final product or service it will be used to produce. Cat and dog food discussed above illustrates autonomous demand,[23] whereas the bulk of the demand for ready-mixed concrete is derived from that for construction.

Just as in the case of a final product, the demand curve for an input will generally slope downwards from left to right showing that, the lower the price, the more will be bought. The downward slope occurs for two reasons: first, a reduction in price will change relative prices and tend to lead to the substitution of the relatively cheaper for the relatively more expensive input; second, the reduction in price will reduce marginal cost, which may encourage the firm to increase its output and consequently employ more inputs. Firms supplying inputs need to recognize that the demand for their products depends on the final demand for the good they are used to produce. For example, many firms in the West Midlands are heavily dependent on sales to British Leyland, and the ramifications of British Leyland going into liquidation would be far-reaching.

The own-price elasticity of demand is equally relevant for derived demand as for autonomous demand. The value it takes in the case of derived demand depends on four factors:

(a) the own-price elasticity of demand of the final output — the more elastic the demand for the final product, the higher the elasticity of derived demand;

(b) the proportion of total costs accounted for by the input – 'the importance of being unimportant'. If an input accounts for, say, 1 per cent of total costs, a doubling of its price would increase total costs by only one percentage point. Generally, although not always, the smaller the percentage of costs attributable to an input, the lower the own-price elasticity of derived demand;

(c) the ease with which the technology being used permits the substitution of inputs – the greater the substitutability, the higher the price elasticity;

(d) the elasticity of supply of other inputs: if increased quantities of other inputs can be bought with only a small increase in price, the own-price elasticity for any particular input will tend to be high.

A firm providing goods or services for use in other productive processes needs to be aware of these influences on the demand for its own output. It is often claimed that the demand for inputs is more rational than that for consumer goods, in the sense that the buyers are usually more expert and the motives for purchase purely economic, products being bought for profit prospects, not for themselves alone. Such a distinction is, however, a gross simplification of reality. It may be that the pricing and marketing strategies are different for the two types of good. For example, many inputs may be put out to tender, as is the case in ready-mixed concrete, or on long-term contract, rather than being bought 'off the shelf'. But, of course, tendering is not unknown in the household market – for example, house repairs and maintenance, installation of central heating, etc. The differences to some extent are simply those of scale: each household buys only a limited quantity of any particular good, whereas a company may be ordering substantial amounts.

These factors raise a further important issue. In the treatment of demand so far, nothing has been said about how the goods or services get from the producer to the consumer. Such a view neglects the important role of the channels of distribution. For consumption goods it is rare for the manufacturer to sell direct to the consumer; most consumers buy their goods from some type of retailer – shop, mail order catalogue, discount warehouse, etc. On the other hand, inputs are more commonly bought directly from the manufacturer. For consumer goods, therefore, it is necessary to pay particular attention to the relationship between the retailer/wholesaler and the manufacturer on the one hand and the consumer on the other.

The role of the distributor is likely to have an important influence on the pricing, marketing and other strategies adopted by any manufacturer. The retailer may exercise considerable bargaining power in relation to the manufacturer, as exemplified by the importance of Marks and Spencer to the UK textile industry. Further, following the virtual abolition of resale price maintenance,[24] the actual price charged to the final consumer is determined by the retailer and not the manufacturer directly. The emergence of low-price discount warehouses and catalogue showrooms (e.g., Comet and Argos) in the sale of consumer durables has been a notable trend of the 1970s and 1980s. Their role in relation to one particular market will be discussed in detail shortly. In any discussion of markets, the importance of the distributional channels should not be neglected.

There is a wide variety of distributional outlets, but as an aid to analysis they may be categorized into two broad groups:[25]

(1) convenience outlets: these are retail outlets where little or no sales assistance is provided and there tends to be a large number in any particular location;
(2) non-convenience outlets: these are outlets that provide sales assistance and they tend to be less densely located.

Correspondingly it is possible to distinguish two broad groups of products:

(1) convenience goods: i.e., goods with a relatively low unit price, purchased repeatedly, and for which the consumer desires an easily accessible outlet. Given the small outlay the consumer may not generally find it worthwhile to shop around in terms of both price and quality;
(2) shopping goods: for these goods the unit price may be quite high, the goods are purchased relatively infrequently (consumer durables, clothing, etc.), and it may pay the consumer to compare prices, quality and style in several shops.

It may be difficult to classify individual products into these two categories, but the characteristics of the retailer may provide a reliable indication of the type of good involved. Thus, if goods are predominantly sold with little sales assistance and in many shops in the same location (convenience outlets), consumer buying habits are likely to correspond with those associated with convenience goods. On the other hand, if considerable sales assistance is provided (non-convenience outlets), consumer buying habits are likely to follow those associated with shopping goods. The category into which the product falls can make a considerable difference to the manufacturer and his relationship to the retailer and consumer. For convenience goods, for example, the manufacturer may be concerned predominantly with developing a successful brand image which ensures that the retailer will stock the product and so reduces his bargaining power *vis à vis* the manufacturers. For goods sold through non-convenience outlets, the retailer is likely to wield considerably greater influence on the consumer's choice and, therefore, to exercise greater power over the manufacturer. At the same time, it has to be recognized that retailers have been creating their own branded products, which they normally have manufactured by an outside contractor, who may also be selling his own branded product, usually made to different specifications. For example, in the market for breakfast cereals, the brand leader in cornflakes is Kelloggs and the retailers' own brands (Sainsbury's, Tesco's, etc.) are largely produced by Viota. Weetabix, on the other hand, produces both its own brand and retailers' brands of its wheat biscuit cereal.

Consumers' buying habits and the various influences on the market will, therefore, differ to a considerable extent according to the type of good and the channel of distribution. Thus, the nature of the market for a product will depend to some extent on whether it is durable or perishable (or 'single-use'). Sales of durable goods are, as has been remarked, the subject of much more complex decisions by the buyer. The demand for most consumer durable goods is postponable, and much of it will be the replacement of already existing assets, e.g., new washing machine, car, etc. But from time to time, technological change produces sweeping consequences for the sales of durables. The recent introduction of reliable video recorders, small home computers and CB radios are clear indications of these trends. Indeed, all three illustrate the way in which changes in manufacturing technology rapidly lead to corresponding changes in related markets. The emergence of large numbers of outlets for the hire of video cassettes is a clear illustration. Similarly, the sale of small home computers illustrates the changing role of distributional channels. Thus, the Sinclair ZX80 and ZX81 were originally sold direct by the manufacturer to consumers via mail order. Having established a successful 'brand', access was then gained to large retail outlets such as W. H. Smith.

It is worth examining the demand for consumer durables in some detail.[26] The major characteristic affecting the market for durables is that there is a stock of the goods which is carried forward from one period to another. Further, since they constitute a relatively large expenditure for most households, the availability of credit is a significant factor. Taking hire purchase (HP) credit as an illustration, there are two crucial variables – the minimum percentage down payment required, and the maximum monthly repayment period. If either the down payment increases or the length falls, credit can be said to be tighter. The impact of changes in these variables during the 1970s was particularly marked. For instance, a change in the minimum deposit to $33\frac{1}{3}$ per cent from 10 per cent for domestic appliances and 20 per cent for cars led to a 12 per cent fall in expenditure during the same quarter. The overall finding of Cuthbertson's study[27] was that expenditure on durables was influenced not only by income and HP credit but also by monetary variables covering the liquid assets of consumers, bank loans and interest rates. The long-run income elasticity of demand was estimated to be 1.9.

A CASE STUDY: THE BICYCLE MARKET

The recent report of the Monopolies and Mergers Commission on the supply of bicycles[28] provides an excellent illustration of the factors we have been discussing in this chapter and the sort of analysis that is required to understand a market. In this section we shall discuss the main findings of the Commission on the nature of the UK bicycle market.

The case itself is important, since it is the first one under the Competition Act 1980 concerned with the power to investigate an anit-competitive practice. The practice related to the criteria used by Raleigh in determining whether to supply bicycles to particular retail outlets, and the main point at issue involves the refusal of the company to supply Raleigh bicycles to retailers such as Argos, Comet, Tesco and Woolworth. The case, therefore, provides an interesting practical application of the discussion on distributional channels in the previous section.

Sales of bicycles showed a markedly rising trend in the decade up to 1979 owing to a number of factors including an increase in the number of teenagers, the sharp rise in petrol prices and the change in fashion, which encouraged bicycles on both health and environmental grounds. The Commission noted, however, that the long-term prospects for bicycle demand remain uncertain – the number of children under 16 is likely to decline over the next few years, and whether the demand by adults increases depends on the real growth in consumer income, the relative price of petrol and public transport, and measures to improve road safety for cyclists. Demand is highly seasonal, with 50 per cent of sales taking place in the three months up to Christmas. Further, the main sales are to the under-16s. There is an active second-hand market which provides a real alternative to the purchase of a new bike.

Raleigh (part of Tube Investments) is clearly the leading UK manufacturer, with about 40 per cent of the market in 1980. No other British manufacturer had a share greater than 5 per cent. In the early 1970s Raleigh increased its market share largely at the expense of other UK manufacturers, but its market share has subsequently fallen from a peak of 67 per cent in 1972, largely because of imports. From being insignificant in 1970, imported bicycles accounted for over a third of the UK market by 1980 — a story not untypical of other manufacturing sectors of British industry.

As regards distribution, UK manufacturers normally distribute their bicycles directly to retailers, but there is some wholesale trade. Bicycles are sold to consumers through specialist bicycle dealers (about 2,500), the branches of Halfords (over 350), department and chain stores, Co-ops, catalogue and direct mail order, and more recently by discount stores, supermarkets and on garage forecourts — all of which serve to illustrate the variety of possible institutional arrangements making up a market. In table 4.4 the breakdown of total UK sales by outlets in 1976 is shown, as well as the particular pattern for Raleigh in 1980. Raleigh had refused to supply certain multiple retailers, as mentioned above, and they did not sell to direct

Table 4.4   *Distribution of bicycles in the UK*

	UK market 1976 (%)	Raleigh 1980 (%)
Bicycle dealers	55	43
Halfords	12	13
Department stores	8	8
Co-ops	3	5
Catalogue; direct mail order	15	19
Other (incl. discount stores)	7	5
Wholesalers	n.a.	7

Source: Monopolies and Mergers Commission, *Bicycles*, HC 67, (London, HMSO, 1980/81).

mail order organizations, although they have supplied major catalogue mail order houses. Raleigh operates a network of specialist dealers who buy exclusively from the company (120, accounting for 13 per cent of all Raleigh sales). Raleigh's response to increased competition, particularly from imports, has been to focus on brand image, and it regards a selective distribution policy as one way of enhancing this. It also produces bicycles to lower specifications and prices, which do not carry the Raleigh name but that of Sun and Triumph. The Commission was unable to estimate the own-price elasticity of demand for bicycles in general, but they did observe that consumers appear to shop around (non-convenience goods) and that there is considerable price competition, with discounts of 15 per cent or more from the manufacturer's suggested prices.

It is not relevant in the present context to examine the detailed arguments for and against the particular distribution policy adopted by Raleigh, but students should read the report for themselves. It would be misleading, however, not to record the findings of the Commission. They argued that refusal to supply was an anticompetitive practice which had adverse effects on the public interest: development of the type of retailing that relies mainly on keen price competition is being frustrated as far as Raleigh bikes are concerned; the general level of prices for Raleigh bikes is higher than it would otherwise be; and consumer choice is restricted in the sense that the purchaser of a Raleigh bike is not given the option of selecting a lower price at the expense of service. They therefore found the practice to operate against the public interest and recommended that Raleigh should not refuse to supply bicycles to retailers; but, recognizing the possible importance of the Raleigh brand image, they argued that the company could withhold the supply of bicycles under the Raleigh brand name provided it offered, under alternative names, bicycles that were of equivalent specifications and did not prevent the retailers from indicating that the bikes were supplied by Raleigh.

There are many other manufacturers who have refused to supply discount stores, and the Raleigh reference was to some extent a test case. These other goods include some manufacturers of audio and video goods, perfumes, watches, china and glassware. The report of the Commission on Raleigh suggests that there is no general presumption that refusal to supply is against the public interest, and each case will, therefore, have to be taken on its merits.

As a final observation, it should be noted that the distribution policy of a company may have important consequences for its market share and ability to compete. A question must be raised as to whether, at least to some extent, Raleigh's refusal to supply some major retailers had been one contributory factor in the increased penetration of imports into the UK market.[29]

THE CHARACTERISTICS APPROACH TO DEMAND

As a prelude to the discussion of marketing in the next chapter, it is important to consider an alternative approach to demand which relates not to the goods themselves, but to the characteristics they possess.[30] In this relatively new approach to demand, any individual product is regarded as being comprised of a bundle of characteristics, and the consumer is presumed to be interested not in the product itself, but in the characteristics it embodies. Thus, demand is fundamentally seen in terms of characteristics and not goods. A particular model of bicycle, for example, consists of a number of features such as style, size, colour, comfort, safety, ease of maintenance, etc.; and, subject to income and price, the consumer will choose that model which contains the most preferred set of characteristics. For some goods the characteristics are relatively straightforward, whereas for others they can be very complex. For example, brands of baked beans differ in relatively few dimensions, such as proportion and flavour of the tomato sauce, whereas the possible variations in stereo equipment, home computers and houses are substantial.

The characteristics approach offers a simple explanation for the fact that many manufacturers supply several different brands of the same basic good. We have seen earlier that Raleigh, for instance, supply a number of different models and brands of bicycles, all with somewhat different characteristics. Since consumer tastes differ, it is sensible for the manufacturer, depending on the effect on production, distribution and stock-holding costs, to offer consumers a number of varieties. Similarly, manufacturers will often seek to differentiate their products from those of other suppliers, and we saw that Raleigh viewed its brand name and associated quality image as a vital part of its strategy to compete with lower-priced imports.

The emphasis on characteristics means that the manufacturer has to be aware of the consumer's attitude to particular features, which places great importance on the role of market research, a topic we shall consider in the next chapter. Advertising also takes on a new significance. In the conventional treatment of demand, it is assumed that the consumer is aware of his or her own preferences and the availability of goods. In this context, advertising can be successful only if it changes the consumer's tastes, and on these grounds it has been the subject of much abuse. However, in reality the consumer is not fully informed as to the availability of goods and the characteristics of particular products. One function of advertising, therefore, is to inform the consumer of the existence and attributes of a 'brand'. This information enables the consumer to make better decisions. Again, we develop this point in the next chapter.

Further, given that different brands are not, in general, perfect substitutes, since their characteristics will differ at least to some extent, the consumer may operate with some 'brand loyalty'. This loyalty may mean that demand for a brand may not be particularly price-sensitive around the current price. When discussing Lambin's results on elasticity, it was noted that highly advertised brands might be expected to have lower elasticities, although, as we saw, there was some evidence from the particular sample that price was still an important determinant of sales.

The idea that characteristics are important and that the supplier has an active role to play in relation to the demand side of the market leads to a consideration of the marketing process, which is the subject of the following chapter.

NOTES

1 J. Nightingale, 'On the definition of "industry" and "market" ', *Journal of Industrial Economics*, 27 (1978).
2 C. M. Allan, 'The demand for herring: a single equation model', *Scottish Journal of Political Economy*, 20 (1972); S. F. Witt and C. L. Pass, 'The effects of health warnings and advertising on the demand for cigarettes', *Scottish Journal of Political Economy*, 28 (1981).
3 The reader should graph the demand curve for herrings as an exercise.
4 Such a good is known as a 'Giffen good'.
5 For a straight-line demand curve the elasticity would be different at every point.
6 Strictly, it is not permissible to speak of the demand for any product as elastic or inelastic in total: at very low prices the demand for most products, even for luxury goods, is inelastic: at very high prices the demand for most goods, including necessities, is elastic. Formally, elasticity of demand may be different at each part of the demand curve.

   The most that can usually be said of the demand for a commodity is that it is own-price elastic or inelastic at prices around those that have been general in the market; but since it is in this range of prices that most decisions will be made, and very large price variations are not common features of business policy, it is usually sufficiently accurate for practical purposes to talk of elasticity of demand without specifying the price range to which the statement refers. Nevertheless, there have been a number of cases of dramatic price changes in recent years. Among the most obvious are the introduction of the Skytrain to New York by Sir Freddie Laker; the rapid reduction in price of personal computers; and the 25 per cent reduction in fares by London Transport (until declared illegal in a celebrated case in the House of Lords in December 1981).

7 Witt and Pass, 'The effects of health warnings'.

8 Theoretical economists have developed neat ways of expressing the logic underlying demand theory, by the use of 'indifference curve' and 'revealed preference' analysis. This sort of analysis conveniently summarizes the fact that, with a limited income and known prices, a consumer's demand is restricted: a choice must therefore be made, and the consumer will have a system of preferences (these may be subconscious and not formalized in any way). One commodity may be substituted for another until, effectively, the satisfaction received from the expenditure is maximized. All of the factors influencing demand can be consistently analysed by the use of this sort of technique; but the analysis more of theoretical than practical interest and has been omitted from the present discussion. The interested reader will find convenient summaries in W. J. Baumol, *Economic Theory and Operations Analysis*, 4th edn (London, Prentice-Hall, 1977); and J. Hirshleifer, *Price Theory and Applications*, 2nd edn (London, Prentice-Hall, 1980).

9 R. Stone, *Measurement of Consumers' Expenditure and Behaviour in the United Kingdom, 1920–1938* (Cambridge University Press, 1954).

10 A. Deaton, *Models and Projections of Demand in Post-War Britain* (London, Chapman & Hall, 1975).

11 The equation actually used by Deaton was:

$$\log Q = \alpha + (\beta^0 + \beta'\theta) \log \frac{\mu}{\pi} + (\gamma^0 + \gamma'\theta) \log \frac{P}{\pi}$$

where π is a price index of all prices and μ is total consumers' expenditure. The term θ is a time trend based on 1963 and allows the elasticity of both own-price and income to change over time.

12 In this context it may be preferable to work in terms of market shares rather than quantity sold, as was mentioned above.

13 J. J. Lambin, *Advertising, Competition and Market Conduct in Oligopoly over Time* (Amsterdam, North-Holland, 1976).

14 A. Deaton and J. Muellbauer, 'An almost ideal demand system', *American Economic Review*, 70 (1980).

15 The expenditure elasticity measures the responsiveness of the quantity demanded to a change in total expenditure rather than disposable income.

16 The requirements of the system are such that it can be estimated only at a highly aggregated level.

17   Allan, 'Demand for herrings'.
18   For a discussion of the Fair Trading Act see, for example, D. Swann, *Competition and Consumer Protection* (Harmondsworth, Penguin, 1979).
19   Monopolies and Mergers Commission, *Cat and Dog Food*, HC 447 (London, HMSO, 1976/77).
20   Monopolies and Mergers Commission, *Ready Mixed Concrete*, Cmnd 8354 (London, HMSO, 1981).
21   Ibid., para. 2.2.
22   Issued by the Department of Prices and Consumer Protection, 17 November 1978.
23   The distinction is not always clear-cut; for example, what about the demand for dog food by kennels?
24   Resale price maintenance occurs when manufacturers are able to specify the prices at which their products will be re-sold by dealers. For a discussion of the UK law that effectively prohibits the practice, see e.g. Swann, *Competition and Consumer Protection*.
25   See M. E. Porter, *Interbrand Choice, Market Strategy, and Bilateral Market Power* (London, Harvard University Press, 1976).
26   For a recent empirical study of the demand for consumer durables in the UK on which this section is based see K. Cuthbertson, 'The determination of expenditure on consumer durables'. *National Institute Economic Review*, 94 (1980).
27   Ibid., p. 67.
28   Monopolies and Mergers Commission, *Bicycles*, HC 67 (London, HMSO, 1980/81). See also Office of Fair Trading, *Report on TI Raleigh Industries Ltd and TI Raleigh Ltd*, 27 February 1981.
29   See, for instance, D. Harris, 'TI Raleigh: why Mr Borrie will be disappointed', *The Times*, 17 December 1981.
30   The name most associated with the characteristics approach is that of Kelvin Lancaster: see, e.g., K. J. Lancaster, 'A new approach to consumer theory', *Journal of Political Economy*, 74 (1966); and *Variety, Equity and Efficiency* (New York, Columbia University Press, 1979). The analytical methods employed in this literature are very similar to linear programming discussed in chapter 2.

5

Marketing

Marketing is that part of business activity that is concerned with the assessment, manipulation and fulfilment of demand. The borderline between production and marketing is indistinct, and in the final analysis both are concerned with meeting demand; it is frequently convenient, however, to separate them for purposes of analysis.

Marketing orientation is the feature that identifies the mature business enterprise. The majority of businesses in the past have started with a distinct product orientation, typified by a concentration on the manufacturing of the product; at a later stage management consciously identifies consumer wants and does something about meeting them; the next phase may come with a realization that the facilities of the firm are capable of producing new products, or with the recognition of the fact that the market may suggest profitable opportunities; eventually, marketing becomes the basic motivating force of the business and is integrated with top management decision-making. The ultimate stage of development is that in which the enterprise is viewed as an integrated business-cum-technological system, the whole of which is aimed at the profitable satisfaction of the needs of the consumer.

In most firms, therefore, the aim of marketing management is to develop an integrated marketing programme through the co-ordination of its resources in the attempt to achieve the objectives of the enterprise.

It is sometimes argued that marketing is unproductive and wasteful, because it adds nothing tangible to the product. It is true that much marketing activity may be inefficient, that distribution may be carried out wastefully, and that much of the effort and resources put into the manipulation of demand may possibly be put to better use, but the same is true of much manufacturing activity. A certain amount of marketing activity is necessary to get the goods to the consumer at all, and the creation of a market for goods and the provision of information about them is just as necessary as their production. Marketing adds value (or utility) to goods in the sense that it puts the goods where they are wanted when they are wanted; it is analogous to the addition of value in production. Efficient marketing adds no more to the cost of goods than is necessary for the fulfilment of these functions.

An indication of the size of the contribution of the distribution function can be obtained by examining the gross margins (or value added) in both retailing and wholesaling in the UK.[1] Gross margins among all retailers in the UK amounted to just over 27 per cent of total receipts in 1978, and in wholesaling the corresponding figure was 13 per cent. The margins differ from trade to trade and by size and type of firm; for example, among grocers and general food retailers the average margin was less than 17 per cent, whereas in clothing, footwear and textiles and household goods it averaged nearly 40 per cent.

The largest gross margins are in the service trades, in which purchases are a relatively small proportion of total costs, while wages and salaries are a high proportion; wholesale margins are lower on average than retail margins, largely because purchases are a high proportion of total costs and value added by processing and services is small.

MARKETING PRACTICES AND POLICIES

Marketing is an essential part of the competitive process, given the lack of information about products and their attributes noted in the previous chapter. The various marketing practices and policies are judged by their effectiveness as weapons of overall marketing policy. The marketing mix is the combination of resources required in a marketing programme in order to fulfil the company's marketing objectives. Each element in the mix is interdependent, and a coherent policy requires programmes for marketing research, promotion, product development, distribution and pricing.

MARKETING RESEARCH

Marketing decisions depend on the acquisition and interpretation of information. Back in 1962, the British Institute of Management[2] defined marketing research as: 'the objective gathering, recording and analysing of all facts about problems relating to the transfer and sales of goods and services from producer to consumer'. As can be seen from this definition, the concept of marketing research is wide-ranging and covers: identifying and quantifying the market and market conditions (often given the more narrow name of 'market research'); the development of new products; and the methods of promotion, distribution and after-sales service facilities.

Four major divisions of marketing research can be identified:[3]

(1) product research – the design, development and testing of new products as well as improvements to existing products;
(2) sales research – a full-scale examination of the selling activities of the company, including sales trends, market share and effectiveness of the sales force;
(3) customer research – investigations of buyer behaviour, whether by consumers, distributors or industrial purchasers;
(4) promotion research – an evaluation of the effectiveness of the promotion strategies employed by the company.

Thus, the major uses of marketing research are: to inform management of the position of the firm in the industry and its share of the market; to provide information about present and possible future trends in the market; to help in the introduction of new products and the improvement of old ones; and to provide for the appraisal and improvement of the effectiveness of sales management.

Marketing research is a tool of management, but it cannot by itself solve marketing or other problems; it can only narrow the range of uncertainty and help to make decisions more intelligent and less of a guess. The ultimate value of marketing research depends on how the results are used. It is a method not of formulating decisions, but of providing guidance, and in the last analysis the evaluation of results and the formulation of policy are the job of the manager.

There is a tendency to think of marketing research simply in terms of surveys of a cross-section of the population by interview and questionnaire, but as has been argued, the issues involved are much more comprehensive. Table 5.1 shows the results of a survey conducted by the Industrial Marketing Research Association which lists the main functions of marketing research among companies selling industrial products (i.e., inputs to other processes).[4] It is noted that this pattern is very similar to that found for marketing research in general in the USA. Thus, sales forecasting and analyses of the market are clearly seen as the main functions in the majority of companies conducting such research, and much of the requisite information is obtained from published sources (desk research), the company's own records and expert sources.

Table 5.1 Main functions of industrial marketing research

Functions	Percentage regularly carrying out
Sales forecasting	76
Analysis of market size	70
Trends in market size	61
Estimating demand for new products	51
Competitive position of comparing products	48
Determining characteristics of markets	43
Determining present use of existing products	41
Studying economic factors affecting sales volume	38
General business forecasting	30
Evaluating proposed new products and services	30

Source: Industrial Marketing Research Association; quoted in P. M. Chisnall, *Effective Industrial Marketing* (London, Longman, 1977).

Having decided to embark on marketing research, management still has to determine how the research should be conducted, and there are several possibilities. Some firms employ outside agencies, some do their own, but most do a bit of both. To be effective, marketing research is generally seen as consisting of five key steps: [5] the definition of the problem and preparation of the research brief; the design of the research proposal; data collection and fieldwork; analysis and evaluation of the data; and the preparation and presentation of the report. If the research is to be successful all of these stages need to be carried out, whether the firm conducts the work itself or contracts it out. Central to the process is the collection and analysis of the data relevant to the research objectives. Depending on the nature of the problem, such data can be either primary or secondary, or an appropriate combination of the two. Primary data relate to those items collected specifically, and for the first time, for the particular project. The main sources of such data are questionnaires and other survey techniques, observation or experimentation. Secondary data can be derived either from the existing data flows within the firm itself or from outside sources. The specific uses of some of these sources are discussed below.

The decision of a firm to perform a particular piece of marketing research itself is a straightforward one, similar in nature to the firm's decision to manufacture instead of sub-contract; it depends very much on the scale of operation of the company. The costs of marketing research must be weighed against the returns expected from it; almost all marketing research expenditure is overhead cost, and whether or not to use a particular method depends on whether the firm can work on a large enough scale to justify the expenditure involved. Small firms can rarely afford the specialized staff for field research; indeed, most big firms prefer to have such work done outside by specialized agencies. The cost of field research, surveys, etc., is rather high, and this sort of work involves a great deal of specialized knowledge and planning which is rarely possible even in very large firms. Firms that have their own research departments frequently buy regular, specialized services, such as the products of retail audits, in addition to their own work. But most firms can do a great deal of intelligent marketing research on their own at relatively little expense.

However the research is done, few firms can afford to do without some marketing research, carried out independently of the sales department. For example, in one firm manufacturing electrical components, the production and sales side of the firm had worked for several years on the assumption that their trade was seasonal (largely because everyone said so). A statistician was engaged by the company, and, in order to determine the magnitude of the seasonal fluctuations, he examined the sales of the firm over a period of years; there was no seasonal pattern whatsoever! In the same firm, the production department had relied for several years on the sales forecasts provided by the sales department, with some adjustment in the light of past experience. These forecasts were becoming increasingly unreliable. Since the scale of operation of the company was increasing, more accurate forecasts were required, and the statistician prepared a demand forecast. His predictions turned out to be much more accurate, and have since superseded those of the sales department. All of this work was done internally by one man, at very little cost to the company.

As has been noted, one of the main objectives of marketing research is to establish a market profile for the products of the organization. Such a profile is simply a detailed practical analysis of the factors considered in the previous chapter. Table 5.2 outlines these main factors and provides a convenient check list.

Possibilities in the field of marketing research can be enumerated briefly. Even the vaguest hunches can be improved by a quick look at some of the mass of published information now available. From government sources, for example, one can consult the *Monthly*

Table 5.2   The elements of a market profile

THE CONSUMER
  Total number of consumers
  Regional distribution
  Total income
  The effect of income and wealth; measures of elasticity
  Income per household
  Distribution of income
  Consumers' tastes
  Behaviour characteristics — where do consumers buy, when do they buy, etc.?
  The effect of design

THE BUSINESS ITSELF
  Current level of sales
  Current stocks
  Trends in sales and stocks
  Share of the market
  Seasonal fluctuations
  Trends in research and development
  Company strengths and weaknesses
  New product possibilities

THE MARKET
  The effect of price, measures of own-price elasticity, etc.
  Characteristics of products
  Identification of competitive products
  Numbers and nature of competitors
  Institutional arrangements, channels of distribution, etc.
  Forms of competition (price, advertising, brand policy, etc.)
  Expected technological changes
  General price levels
  Prices of similar commodities

GENERAL CONSIDERATIONS
  The economic climate, level of activity, employment, etc.
  Government policy
  Taxation

Digest of Statistics, Economic Trends, Social Trends, Overseas Trade Statistics, Family Expenditure Survey, Business Monitors and the *National Income Blue Book* as well as a host of specialized statistics on energy, finance, construction and so on. There also exist a wide range of non-official sources of data published by trade associations, banks, academic institutions, the trade press and commercial research organizations.[6] Increasingly, access to data banks is being made available through telephone links using computers (Viewdata) in services such as those provided by Prestel and other specialized sources. Even in its raw form, such information is useful, but its utility can be increased enormously by intelligent statistical analysis.

Similarly, the analysis of the firm's own sales patterns can give useful clues to markets. It is frequently possible, for example, to find out, with little trouble, the patterns of distribution (does the firm sell, for instance, mainly to small corner shops or large chain stores?), and from this to devise an intelligent sales policy. Masses of such information comes into most firms daily and is frequently ignored, or treated unsystematically.

Even so, there are usually important gaps in the information required for policy-making, and there are many forms of marketing research that the typical firm cannot conduct for itself and for which it needs to employ a specialized agency. External marketing research is often carried out on the basis of sample surveys, either by interviewers, through the mail, on the telephone (particularly common in the USA, where practically everyone has a telephone), by consumer panels and so on. Such surveys cover a wide field and there is a range of alternatives: they may concentrate on past sales, or on the buying intentions of consumers, or they may approach the problem from a psychological standpoint.

Surveys of past sales are useful, partly because they give an indication of the firm's share of the market, and partly because the proper statistical analysis of past trends is necessary for forecasting.[7] In terms of such analysis, outside agencies may possibly provide the necessary sophisticated statistical expertise and techniques required to make more accurate forecasts. The degree of sophistication applied to demand analysis and forecasting has increased substantially in recent years, and only the large firm or specialized agency may be able to afford the required skills.

Ascertaining a firm's market share is also an indispensable function of marketing research. Again, such a function can often best be carried out by an external agency, which can, as part of its normal activities and at small extra cost, collect a great deal of the available information about the market, much of which is inaccessible to the firm without considerable expense. One such method is the retail audit, effectively developed by the A. C. Neilson Co., which consists of regular periodic visits to a selected sample of retail shops, during which checks are made of stocks and purchases of the commodities under review, enabling sales of brands to be computed. Another method is the consumer panel, members of which keep diaries of products purchased. For example, the Attwood Consumer Panel consists of a random sample of over 5,000 households in Great Britain where information is recorded in a pre-coded diary for a wide range of products detailing such factors as day of purchase, brand name, price, where bought, etc. The information that can be obtained from consumer panels is, therefore, extensive and includes the extent of the market, market structure (geographical distribution, household composition, etc.) and prices. From these data it is possible to study consumer buying habits such as the frequency of purchase, quantities bought, brand loyalty, seasonal pattern, pattern of distribution and types of retail outlet. The information may also help in the assessment of advertising and other promotional strategies.

Useful information about market shares can also be obtained without the use of an external agency. In many industries a trade association or similar body acts as a source of information concerning the market and its members' shares. The regular publication of information by the Society of Motor Manufacturers and Traders is a clear example. The Bicycle Association of Great Britain also provided much of the information used in the recent Monopolies Commission report on the industry which was discussed in the previous chapter. The role played by many trade associations in this way means that much marketing research is possible within the firm at relatively small cost.

Surveys of consumer buying intentions are useful, within broad limits, as guides to market expansion, and they may help to narrow the range of error of forecasts. In Britain such surveys are usually available only from specialized agencies. A danger of relying on such surveys is that people do not always act in accordance with their expressed intentions, however honest they may try to be; there is a similar difficulty with public opinion polls, which are now published regularly in many newspapers on a variety of subjects. However, experience does allow intentions to be checked against realizations and some correction of estimates is possible.

Motivation research and its related concepts has been a major development in the field of marketing research since the 1950s, which has led to a growing interest in finding methods of measuring the attitudes and behaviour of consumers. The intention is to find out why consumers reach particular decisions, and its rationale is that if one knows why people buy things, one can not only predict how they will behave in given conditions, but can also decide on ways in which they can be influenced and the appropriate choice of promotional and brand strategies. Increasingly, techniques borrowed from the behavioural sciences (such as psychology) have come to be used in marketing research as a means of measuring attitudes and behaviour involving various methods of scaling.[8] Further, over recent years there has been a movement towards the use of group discussion as a guide to the development and marketing of new products in particular.

Marketing research is now a complex activity involving advanced statistical and behavioural methods. It has also been recognized as being as valuable in the marketing of industrial products as it is for consumer goods.[9] Further, for many British companies account has to be taken of the fact that many of the markets that they serve are international in nature, both through competition from imports and in the supply of exports. Whatever the type of marketing research used, if it is competently carried out it can provide valuable information for decision-making. The more and the better the information a firm has about the market and the demand for its products, the better it is able to formulate marketing, production and financial policy.

AN EXAMPLE OF MARKETING RESEARCH IN PRACTICE:
EMBASSY CIGARS

In order to illustrate the application of some of the techniques discussed in the previous section, it is useful to examine one particular piece of research in some detail. In chapter 4 the cigarette market was considered, and we shall be looking at various aspects of the Imperial Group in later chapters. It is appropriate, therefore, to take as our example the research leading up to the launch of Embassy Slim Panatella cigars in 1968.[10]

This research was conducted by an outside agency whose brief was to conduct a planned programme of consumer research designed to assist in the development of a new medium-sized cigar. The company itself had already ascertained that there was an existing strong brand leader in this market and that the first task of the research should be to examine consumer attitudes to the successful brand and determine the factors leading to its success.

This qualitative study was conducted by means of group discussions and depth interviews with 50 smokers of medium-sized cigars, half of whom had smoked the existing leading brand. Tests were conducted under 'blind' conditions, and it was observed that the product had an important advantage over other brands particularly in that it was mild and regarded as slow-burning, which gave the impression of value for money.

At the same time the company was considering a name for its new product, and 'Embassy' was suggested, since the cigarette of the same brand was already highly successful. Group discussions suggested that the name 'Embassy' carried suitable associations for the brand name in terms of such factors as quality and reliability. During the same test, the agency also evaluated a number of alternative packs for the new cigar.

On the basis of this early work, it was decided to proceed with a full-scale product test. Four alternative blends of cigar were tested in blind conditions against the existing brand leader among a sample of over 1,000 cigar smokers using various test procedures. This aspect of the research suggested that one blend was far more acceptable than the main competitor and that it had its greatest potential among the younger end of the market and among those who had never asked for the competitor by name. A new test blend was tried against the previous 'winner' and the competitor using a similar but smaller sample. This time the previous successful blend performed very badly against the competitor, but it was discovered that a wrong batch of tobacco had been used to produce the blend! On a second test, the original preferred blend was again successful and, in fact, became the blend that was eventually launched.

The earlier research had found that the main competitor's advertising had been highly successful and the project turned to an evaluation of three alternative commercials for the new cigar. Tests were carried out in London and Manchester, whereby samples of consumers were shown alternative programmes consisting of general short films and advertisements for both Embassy and the competitor. At various stages, the consumers were asked which brand of cigar they would like to win in a raffle. On the basis of the test, one particular Embassy advertisement appeared superior to the alternatives and those of the main competitor and was, therefore, selected to launch the product.

To quote the researcher:

every aspect of the Embassy cigar had been tested on consumers before the launch: the name, the pack, the product, and finally the advertising. The success of the brand to date itself justifies the meticulous attention through the vehicle of market research that each of these aspects received.[11]

ADVERTISING[12]

Advertising is only one of a number of alternative promotion expenditures that can be incurred by the firm as part of its marketing strategy. Other items include special promotions (e.g., 'money-off' offers), samplers in stores, display material, special discounts to retailers, etc. Generally, the different items of expenditure are complementary to each other. For example, it is rather pointless to undertake a major advertising campaign unless the product is adequately stocked and displayed by retailers. The precise mix of promotional expenditures depends on many factors, including the nature, age and market share of the product. The factors involved in each item are, however, in general similar, and we shall concentrate on advertising since it is usually the major item of promotional expenditure.

Advertising is a major feature of all market economies and is a vital part of the market process. In the UK in 1979 total advertising expenditure amounted to £2,129 million, or 1.34 per cent of gross national product. In the USA advertising expenditure is even more significant, amounting to some 2.1 per cent of GNP, while in some other advanced countries it is rather less important – 0.93 per cent in Japan and 0.52 per cent in West Germany. It is necessary, therefore, to examine the significance of advertising for the firm and the role that it can play in the marketing of products.

As was noted in chapter 4, in the traditional textbook view of markets, where consumers are fully informed as to the number and variety of goods, their attributes, prices and locations, advertising can only have a very limited role. More realistically, however, advertising is an essential part of the market process, in that it attempts to create awareness in the consumer of the existence, location and attributes of a particular product or service. In so doing it also clearly seeks to persuade the consumer to purchase the particular product advertised; this may require the use of a catchy jingle, colourful presentation, clever story-line or other device to attract the interest of the potential customer. This feature should not detract from the fact that at least some information is being provided – namely, the existence of the product. It may be questioned as to whether the right sort of information is being provided by advertising, but it is rather meaningless to attempt to distinguish the so-called informative from the persuasive aspects of advertising. Thus, advertising may help to overcome the existence of imperfect information in the real world and hence make markets work better. It also plays an essential role in the process of innovation and the introduction of new products. On the other hand, it is closely associated with product differentiation and possible harmful effects of monopoly and the associated market power. While these issues are of relevance to the welfare of society in general, it is of greater concern in the present context to examine the advertising decision of the individual firm, bearing in mind these general issues.

The main role of advertising to the individual firm can be seen as changing the demand curve facing the firm, principally in the sense that it is designed to shift it to the right, so that the firm can obtain a higher price for any given output or, what amounts to the same thing, sell more at a particular price. If advertising has this effect, how much should the firm spend on it? If the firm wishes to maximize profits, the rule is quite simple and follows that for most other decisions: i.e., the firm should advertise up to the point where the marginal revenue from an additional amount of advertising is equal to the marginal cost of that advertising. In chapter 4 various measures of elasticity were discussed, and there is a further one that is relevant to the present discussion – the advertising elasticity of demand. Advertising elasticity is defined as the proportionate change in quantity demanded, divided by the proportionate change in advertising. If we consider a firm that has only two marketing decisions to make – the price to charge and the amount of advertising to undertake – there is an important relationship between the advertising and own-price elasticities of demand. It can be shown that the profit-maximizing firm should have a ratio of advertising to sales that is equal to the ratio of the advertising elasticity of demand to the own-price elasticity of demand.[13] Thus, if both elasticities remain constant, the rule would suggest that the firm should adopt a constant advertising–sales ratio.

Having looked at the theory, what is the practice? Surveys of the way in which advertising decisions are reached tend to show that many firms adopt some fairly simple rule of thumb, but recent work suggests that companies have become rather more flexible in their approach to the determination of the advertising budget.[14] Four alternative rules of thumb are usually suggested in the marketing literature.

1 The all-you-can-afford approach

Using this method, the firm would set its advertising budget at the limit of its cash resources. But the rule is rather empty of content, since it is by no means clear what is meant by the limits of the firm's cash resources, which would presumable be decided on some basis by discussion between the finance and marketing directors.

2 *The competitive-parity approach*

Here the firm would set its budget at the same level in terms of percentage of sales or some other criterion as its main rivals. It is a simple rule, but since firms are likely to differ in their product range, size, age, etc., it is not likely to lead to an appropriate level of advertising for the individual firm. The evidence seems to suggest that companies do collect information on the advertising expenditure of their competitors, but it does not appear that they use it in the simple way implied by this rule.

3 *The objective and task method*

The firm would set its advertising budget by determining the objectives of the advertising, assessing the tasks needed to achieve the objectives and adding up the costs of executing the tasks to obtain the budget. However, one should really assess the relevance of the chosen objectives in terms of the overall performance of the firm and ask whether the costs involved justify the objectives and tasks. Once objectives and costs are being compared, the analysis approaches that of a more complicated cost–benefit analysis.

4 *The percentage-of-sales method*

In this case, the advertising budget would be set at some predetermined proportion of either past or predicted sales. This method appears to be the most popular among those used by companies, for not only is it simple, but it incorporates some of the desirable features of the other methods. Thus, for instance, an advertising budget based on sales revenue will tend to vary with what the company can afford, and it may produce a result similar to that adopted by competitors. Further, as has just been shown, it may have a strong theoretical rationale in some circumstances.

The interested reader is referred to the study by Rees (see note 14), which contains a number of interesting examples of the practical determination of advertising budgets. To take one of these for illustrative purposes, one company (a multinational food manufacturer) uses several guidelines, including in particular (1) the task method, (2) historical data and (3) competitors' actions. A target is set, usually in terms of sales volume, and the company believes that to obtain a certain level of sales a proportion of the population must see its advertisements a certain number of times each week. This task implies a level of expenditure, and the historical data show the results of certain actions in the past. Finally, analysis of the actions of competitors reveals its share of the market and the relative share of its promotion expenditure. The company makes use of a complex mathematical model which enables it to assess the likely consequences of certain actions. It also spends a considerable amount on pre-testing research of its advertising.

A considerable amount of empirical evidence has been collected on the relationship between advertising and demand. Table 5.3 reproduces some results for the UK derived by Cowling for a number of products. There are several relevant features of the table. The estimated advertising elasticities are all positive but less than 1; this suggests that firms operate in the range where there are diminishing marginal returns to advertising. The own-price elasticities all have an absolute value greater than 1, which indicates an elastic demand. The advertising–sales ratios are shown in column (4). We have just observed that a profit-maximizing firm should advertise to the point where the advertising–sales ratio is equal to the ratio of the advertising to own-price elasticity. Column (3) shows this ratio and column (5) shows the results of dividing the 'optimal' advertising–sales ratio by the actual one. This column, therefore, gives an indication of the extent to which actual advertising expenditure was optimal. Cowling concludes that for non-durable goods there is relatively little divergence between actual and optimal, but for durable goods the difference is pronounced. However, there may be special factors at work

Table 5.3 Estimated price and advertising elasticities and advertising to sales ratios for selected products, UK

	(1) Advertising elasticity	(2) Price elasticity	(3) Ratio (1) ÷ (2)	(4) Advertising sales ratios	(5) Ratio (3) ÷ (4)
Cars	0.19	−1.95	0.096	0.007	13.7
Tractors	0.49	−3.29	0.148	0.0136	10.88
Margarine	0.59	−4.3	0.138	0.098	1.41
Coffee	0.14	−0.2	0.678	0.162	4.15
Toothpaste	0.24	−1.98	0.12	0.153	0.78

Source: K. Cowling, 'Optimality in firm's advertising policies: an empirical analysis', in K. Cowling (ed.), *Market Structure and Corporate Behaviour* (London, Gray-Mills, 1972).

in these markets, notably associated with the introduction of major new models and the fact that advertising may have its most pronounced effect on the timing of durable purchases rather than on the amount.

Advertising is generally regarded as having some long-term effects in that it creates 'goodwill'. In the case of Embassy cigars discussed earlier it will be remembered that one key factor in the choice of name was the goodwill already attached to the brand name. The effectiveness of advertising will, therefore, depend to some extent on how long the message is retained by relevant consumers. Two separate issues are really involved: the extent to which consumers in the market from period to period are different individuals, and the degree to which individuals forget the message. Clearly, in this case it is not just the amount of expenditure on advertising that is relevant, but the way in which it is spent. These issues cover the quality of the advertising copy itself (in terms of sales, not aesthetically); the usage of specific media (newspapers, TV, posters, etc.); and the timing or placement of the advertisement within the particular media chosen. The appropriate choice involves a number of complex issues and increasingly sophisticated techniques are being applied to help determine the solution.[15] But vital to all these is the assessment of the effect of advertising on demand.

The effects of advertising can in principle be assessed in two main directions: the communications effect, and the direct effect on sales and profits. The former seeks to ascertain the success of any particular advertisement or campaign in communicating its message to the consumer. Such research is usually the main focus of that conducted within companies and specialized agencies. It also generally falls into two categories: pre-testing and post-testing. The former is designed to reject poor advertising copy and campaigns that are likely to be unsuccessful in meeting their objectives. The Embassy cigars case study provides an illustration of the sort of techniques that can be used. Thus, pre-testing acts as a screen to weed out advertising that appears likely to be unsuccessful: but there is, of course, no guarantee that an advertisement that passes the screen will be successful. Tests of the communications effects of advertising are usually conducted in terms of the ability of random samples of individuals to recall various aspects of the message in different circumstances and, as in the Embassy case, to try and assess the effect of the message on consumer attitudes. But whatever the success of the advertisement in communicating its message, ultimately the only relevant criterion is its impact on sales and profits. There is no necessary relationship between the communications success and the sales success of an advertisement. Thus, it is important for the firm also to conduct direct tests of the impact of advertising.

Direct testing of the effects of advertising uses statistical techniques such as linear regression to quantify the relationship between advertising and sales allowing for the effect of the other variables that also influence demand. Many of the studies make use of data that have been collected over time — time-series analysis — but their use requires the exercise of considerable care. There are a number of problems of which one needs to be aware; for example as noted earlier, advertising expenditure incurred in one period is likely to affect sales in a later period through its effects on goodwill, and allowance has to be made for these time-lags. Not only is advertising likely to affect sales, but there may also be a relationship between advertising and sales; i.e., the higher the level of sales, the greater the advertising budget, particularly if the budget is determined as a percentage of sales; consequently, sophisticated analysis is necessary to determine the direction of causality and to measure the variables, particularly in adjusting for inflation.

As an illustration of a recent study, table 5.4 reproduces the results of an investigation into the demand for cigarettes which has been used earlier in chapter 4.[16] The effects of advertising on the

Table 5.4 Advertising and the demand for cigarettes, UK, 1955-75

Dependent variable: $\ln Q/P$	
Explanatory variable	Coefficient
$\ln C$	−0.32
	(−4.59)
$\ln Y/P$	0.13
	(2.88)
$\ln A/P$	0.068
	(2.68)
Health scares	(−0.34 to −0.071)
Constant	(7.268)
R^2	0.957

Source: S. F. Witt and C. L. Pass, 'The effects of health warnings and advertising on the demand for cigarettes', *Scottish Journal of Political Economy*, 28 (1981), p. 8.

demand for cigarettes is an area of great contention, and is linked to pressure for the banning of all advertising in addition to the current ban on television advertising in Britain. It is not our intention to enter into that debate here but merely to illustrate some of the relatively simple techniques that can be used.

The data used in the study are annual and relate to the period 1955–75. During this period major health scares occurred as a result of the publication of three influential reports by the Royal College of Physicians (1962 and 1971) and the US Surgeon-General's Advisory Committee (1964). It is suggested that the health scares have an effect on demand of limited duration, and from the results it appears that the reports caused a decline in demand in the year in which they appeared and in the subsequent year. The actual model fitted was of the following form:

$$\ln \frac{Q_t}{P_t} = \alpha_0 + \alpha_1 \ln C_t + \alpha_2 \ln \frac{Y_t}{P_t} + \alpha_3 \ln \frac{A_t}{P_t}$$

$$+ \text{ health scare variables} + U_t$$

where Q_t = number of (manufactured) cigarettes consumed in year t

P_t = UK population over 15 years of age in year t

C_t = real price of cigarettes in year t

Y_t = UK real personal disposable income in year t

A_t = real (press and television) advertising expenditure in year t[17]

U_t = random error.

Since the equation is in logarithms, the coefficients on income, price and advertising are direct estimates of the respective elasticities. Table 5.4 shows that demand for cigarettes is highly price- and income-inelastic (as observed in chapter 4). Advertising also has a small effect on total cigarette consumption, with an elasticity of about 0.07. The health scare effects were all negative and indicated, for example, that the 1962 report of the Royal College of Physicians led to a fall in cigarette consumption of just over 4 per cent in 1962 and 1963.

It should be noted that the advertising effect measured is that of advertising by all producers on the total demand for cigarettes. This does not imply that advertising on particular brands does not induce brand-switching. The empirical evidence does tend to suggest that the effect of advertising becomes more pronounced the lower the level of aggregation; that is to say that, taking due account of the problem of causality discussed earlier, total consumption appears to be little affected by the level of advertising expenditure, whereas at the brand level it can have a marked impact. Such a fact leads naturally to a discussion of product differentiation as a marketing strategy.

PRODUCT DIFFERENTIATION

In one of the classic works to incorporate the concept of product differentiation, Chamberlin[18] stated that:

A general class of product is differentiated if any significant basis arises for distinguishing the goods (or services) of one seller from those of another. Such a basis may be real or fancied, so long as it is of any importance whatever to buyers, and leads to a preference for one variety of the product over another.

Such differentiation is a pervasive feature of many markets particularly, but not exclusively,[19] for consumer products. Products may be differentiated in a variety of ways — by exclusive patent features and trade marks, brand policy, packaging, design or advertising — and it is possible to extend the notion to include such factors as reputation (of manufacturer or distributor), location of distribution (e.g., in a 'high-class' district) and a whole host of intangible and personal factors that may bind a consumer to a seller.

Product differentiation fits readily into the analysis discussed in chapter 4, where commodities are seen as bundles of characteristics. Differentiated products, therefore, are those that combine the same characteristics in different proportions. It is open to the firm to change the mix of characteristics in its products and to move to a new location in terms of the characteristics of its product in relation to its rivals. In addition, a new differentiated product can be introduced if there is an identifiable gap in the market. Take, for example, the position illustrated in figure 5.1. Here it is assumed (for simplicity) that only two characteristics are relevant (beans and tomato sauce, for instance) and there are currently two products on the market (A and B) which combine the characteristics in the proportion shown by the lines OB and OA. Consumers are presumed to have preferences in terms of the characteristics, and it might be that marketing research identifies a gap in the market since a significant number of consumers prefer a combination somewhere between the two existing products,

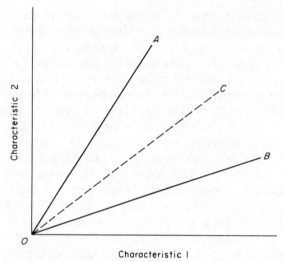

Figure 5.1   Characteristics approach to demand.

such as that shown by the line *OC*. Depending on costs and the consequent selling price, it might pay a firm to introduce a new variety
with that particular combination of characteristics. Clearly, the
greater the number of available varieties, the less scope there is for
finding such a gap. The Monopolies and Mergers Commission in its
study of household detergents[20] argued that, among other things, the
large number of brands produced by the two main suppliers (Unilever
and Proctor and Gamble) did deter the emergence of new competitors and weaken competitive pressure on prices and profits.

The analysis of differentiation on these lines also reveals two
possible effects of advertising and other promotion expenditure. The
first is to inform consumers as to the particular mix of characteristics
offered by the firm's product(s); the second is to seek to establish
brand loyalty by reinforcing consumer preferences for the particular
bundle of characteristics.

For many goods, the range of characteristics involved is wide: in a
study of the UK car market,[21] the characteristics measured included
horsepower, passenger area, fuel consumption, length, inclusion of
power-assisted brakes, inclusion of four forward gears and the quality
of trim. Using these characteristics, it is possible to adjust the price
of the product for differences in quality. Such quality-adjusted prices
were found to be significant determinants of market shares, and the
own-price elasticity of demand taking account of these quality differ-

ences was much higher than the simple own-price elasticity. This type of work points to the importance of distinguishing between different quality products when analysing many real-world markets.

Product differentiation really arises because consumers have different tastes, and to provide full satisfaction of these requires variety in the goods and services available. One advantage of product differentiation, therefore, is to widen the range of choices available to the consumer. Indeed, if there were no economies of scale at either the production or distribution stage, it would in principle be possible for every good to be custom-made to suit each individual. But as discussed in chapter 2, and illustrated by specialization and the division of labour, some economies of scale are inevitable. Thus, there will always be a trade-off between productive efficiency and product variety. Recent literature has discussed what factors determine the 'best' amount of product differentiation,[22] but it is clear that, given differences in tastes, and recognizing the importance of characteristics, product differentiation is not necessarily wasteful; and indeed, it can be socially beneficial to increase product variety at the expense of productive efficiency.

To the producer, as noted in chapter 4, product differentiation and the associated brand image creates an important link between the manufacturer and consumer, which reduces the power of the retail and wholesale stages of distribution. There is thus a further incentive for the producer to establish, through promotion strategies, the precise characteristics of the product. For goods where the quality can be easily assessed by the consumer (convenience goods), it is important that the producer provides reliable information to consumers. Even in the case of more complex goods, such as consumer durables, which are bought infrequently, repeat purchases may still be important; also, most manufacturers offer a range of different products (hi-fi units, portable radios, televisions, etc.), and will presumably wish the consumer to purchase other items from that range. Thus, there is a strong incentive for the producer to provide reliable information rather than attempt to mislead consumers.

THE MARKETING PROCESS AND SELECTION OF CHANNELS OF DISTRIBUTION

The importance of the distribution stage has been discussed briefly in both this chapter and the preceding one. It is appropriate, therefore, to consider the marketing implications in rather more detail.

Many firms have no consciously formulated policy about channels of distribution. Standardized procedures save time and trouble and make the control, prediction and evaluation of success much easier; co-ordination within the firm is simpler; and the firm's channels of distribution themselves find advantages in standardized policies. A possible danger is that competitors, too, will find prediction easier, but reasonable flexibility reduces the risk of this. Channels should be subject to frequent review and re-appraisal.

The simplest channel of distribution is from producer direct to consumer, but this is rare for manufactured goods, although some firms, such as Sinclair (suppliers of the ZX81 microcomputer), have been notably successful in using direct mail order at least in the initial stage of the product's life. In general, goods pass through some form of middleman (wholesaler, retailer, agent), and the commonest arrangement for consumer goods is a chain of producer–wholesaler–consumer. But the growing importance of large retailers with their own central distribution depots (e.g., Sainsburys), who take direct delivery from manufacturers, is reducing, to some extent, the importance of the wholesale trade. Further, as the case of the bicycle market showed in chapter 4, there are other circumstances in which manufacturers will sell direct to retail outlets. The growth of cash-and-carry warehouses is also leading to a decline in the traditional wholesale role. However, wholesalers may be necessary because the costs to the manufacturer of providing specialized storage facilities at widely dispersed points may be excessive (much depends on the scale of operation of the firm), and the wholesaler provides useful services to the retailer by maintaining large, and usually varied, stocks from which choice is possible.

The choice of channels of distribution depends partly on the nature of the product, partly on the nature of the market, and partly on the sort of consumer at whom the product is aimed; it may also depend on the existing structure of distribution, although it is frequently possible to change this. The final selection of the channel will depend on the sales expected from the use of the channel balanced against the costs of using it. Frequently, the most costly methods are those that involve selling direct to final buyers, but there are cases where this may be cheaper.

Co-operation with the distributor is part of marketing policy. It may be necessary to supply display material, to guarantee rapid delivery, to provide financial aid in the form of extended credit, to be prepared to offer after-sales service and so on. The co-operation may be mutual, and the distributor may be prepared to offer long-term contracts and special facilities. Much depends on the customs of the trade, particularly in the case of credit and discounts.

The sole agency is one such form of co-operation, which has mutual benefits. These accrue to the retailer in the form of a degree of local monopoly, advertising by the producer, elimination of duplicate brands and lower stock costs. The producer gains by having a semi-guaranteed and regular outlet; he can concentrate his promotional effort, and he benefits from the fact that the distributor can carry complete stocks of his range of goods and provide after-sales service and repairs. For some goods, particularly those bought on impulse, sole agencies offer fewer advantages.

Another aspect of the marketing process is the decision about the number of outlets. Complete coverage may be desirable, as in the case of detergents and many foodstuffs; but selective distribution through a limited number of outlets is often preferable, as in the case of products sold largely to a few income groups or to specialized sectors of the economy, where large-scale distribution would be wasteful. In general, expensive durable goods such as refrigerators and motor cars, which usually have to be maintained in fairly large stocks at the outlet, with relatively infrequent turnover, are best distributed selectively; goods such as foodstuffs, groceries, cosmetics, detergents, etc., which are manufactured on a large scale, are best distributed through as many outlets as possible. With selective distribution care is necessary in choosing outlets; with large-scale distribution such care is neither possible nor in most cases necessary. Many goods are sold by grocers, chemists, confectioners and multiple stores, and have to be distributed through the appropriate wholesale channels for each type of shop. It also has to be borne in mind that, as the Raleigh case (see chapter 4) illustrates, the terms of the Competition Act may apply in relation to refusal to supply as an anti-competitive practice.

As was noted earlier, the growth of supermarkets, large chain stores and discount retailers has tended to take the marketing initiative away from the producer towards the distributor. There have been big changes in both the scale and technology of distribution in recent years. In the UK, Marks and Spencer are renowned for the fact that they employ their power over manufacturers in the interests of securing goods of consistent quality for the consumer. The economic principles underlying such situations are quite clear; the balance of power depends on the relative share (of output or market respectively) of the manufacturer and the distributor. The power of Marks and Spencer depends largely on the fact that they buy from many dispersed and independent producers. On the other hand, the power of companies such as IBM and British Oxygen rests with their domination of the sources of supply. The large distributor is tending to gain ground, which has led many small retailers to band together to achieve some of the economies of scale and bargaining power of the large concerns.

Manufacturers are, therefore, having to think much more deeply about distribution policy than they have in the past because the choice of distribution channels is narrower and distributors have more power. Effective marketing now involves much closer co-operation with distributors. At the same time, there has been the growth of retailers' own-brand products which compete on the shelves with manufacturers' branded products. Indeed, as noted earlier, many leading manufacturers also supply products to retailers' own specifications. It is in fact, generally worthwhile for a manufacturer to supply own-brands to retailers as long as such sales exceed the marginal costs of production.[23]

As an illustration of the factors involved in a choice of distribution policy, it is useful to examine in some detail the arguments put forward by Raleigh for its choice of distribution policy in bicycle marketing.[24] Raleigh argued that specialist products were often sold more effectively under a selective distribution policy. A manufacturer's choice of outlets was one of the most effective means of competing in, for example, providing technical service, achieving the right balance of coverage and selling effort and promoting brand image. The company also argued that there were broadly two alternative methods of bicycle marketing: (1) to produce to a low specification, competing primarily on price and selling through supermarkets, discount stores, etc., often under the retailer's own brand; or (2) to produce to a high specification, selling primarily through specialist cycle dealers and emphasizing quality, service and the promotion of brand image and loyalty. Raleigh traded, and had traditionally traded, at the upper end of the bicycle market — predominantly through specialist dealers and up-market department stores. In the mid-1960s, faced with difficult trading conditions, they had also started selling to catalogue mail order houses under brand names other than Raleigh. Raleigh also operates a network of '5 Star' dealers buying exclusively from it, the numbers of whom were increasing.

Raleigh placed great emphasis on quality and the associated effect on brand image. In particular, they regarded it as important that a Raleigh bicycle should be seen as a safe and reliable vehicle. They argued that this image was reinforced if the bicycle was sold through a specialist outlet which provided technical services. In effect, they saw themselves as offering a package – a bicycle together with service for road safety.

In defending their refusal to supply discount retailers they argued that selling at low prices would detract from the quality image and that discount stores generally had no technical expertise or facilities for pre-sale checking and provided no guidance to the customer. Also, they argued that discount stores in some cases would stock bicycles only at certain times of the year and be interested only in leading brands, and hence would restrict the consumer's exposure to the full Raleigh range. The buying of bicycles on a seasonal basis, and the lack of long-term commitment to cycles by the discount stores, would impair the utilization of productive capacity throughout the year. If they supplied discount stores Raleigh believed this would have important implications for the market, namely, that many dealers would abandon service to compete on price, and that dealers would be forced out of business, reducing the number of outlets available to provide service.

Although, as was shown in chapter 4, the Monopolies and Mergers Commission regarded the refusal to supply as anti-competitive and against the public interest, the case does reveal the thoughts of a leading British manufacturer on the factors determining its distribution policy.

SALES MANAGEMENT AND PERSONAL SELLING

The term 'sales management' means different things in different firms. In some firms the sales manager or director is responsible for all aspects of marketing; in others (s)he is merely responsible for the management of the sales force; in still others (s)he may be the person responsible for personal selling, or for price policy, or for any other aspects of marketing. It is defensible, if not completely logical, to think of sales management as the function of organizing the sales force and personal selling, and that is the sense in which the term is used in this chapter.

Supervision of sales personnel is largely an administrative task: the manager will want to know how well the sales staff are doing their work, what their problems are and what assistance is required; and this means that the necessary information must be available. Much of the data comes from records within the sales department itself; some comes from other departments, occasionally in the form of rebukes. Volume of sales is not necessarily the best measure of performance, since this will depend on the size and complexity of the sales area, the number of calls and the number of other tasks required to be performed by the sales staff; against these, the personal selling ability of the individual may have little chance. The 'super' salesperson, though frequently successful in the short run, often antagonizes customers and works against the long-term interests of the firm. Experience and research can usually help management to set and maintain reasonable performance standards.

Personal selling by the sales force of manufacturers and distributors is the oldest marketing method, and is the most effective in many circumstances. The term embraces over-the-counter selling, house-to-house selling, the calls of sales staff on wholesalers and retailers, and the calls of specialist sales staff and executives on important customers. More often than not, personal selling is the method used to close the sale. Effective personal selling, though it is frequently left to less skilled personnel, depends on a knowledge of the market and the products, on locating the buyers, on concluding the sale and on the maintenance of goodwill. A whole industry has developed based on the training of sales staff, and training courses of this sort usually ring the changes on a few basic ways of being good at selling; these include finding out the customer's needs, presenting the product as effectively as possible, meeting objections, and ways of closing the sale. But effective personal selling depends much more on the representative just being there than on tactics or gimmicks. Contact, above everything else, is the essence of salesmanship.

Personal selling usually has a high cost per contact, but it is also, as a rule, more effective than other methods. How large a sales staff to use and where to concentrate them is an integral part of the whole marketing decision and has to be seen as part of the promotional mix, but personal selling remains a key part of the marketing process.

CONCLUSIONS

It is possible to sum up the main elements of the marketing decision. There are three essential managerial aspects of demand:

(1) analysis and forecasting – the main function of marketing research;
(2) organizational effect – the effect that demand may have on the organization and activities of the firm. The problems involved are related partly to production and partly to administration. The main concerns are product development and design, organization

or the marketing department, adaptation of the production process to meet the conditions of the market, and policy with regard to stocks;

(3) the positive approach to demand or marketing. The issues include the choice of channels of distribution, problems of transport and storage, problems of finance, the provision of services before and after sales, co-operation with distributors and pricing policy.

Policy decisions are necessary about all three aspects, and they have to be made in the light of the firm's assessment of the factors affecting markets — factors within the firm itself, general considerations affecting the market, and specific considerations relating to consumers and distributors.

Within the firm itself, marketing largely determines overall policy, which is affected by production capacity, its flexibility and projected changes, the production time-lag (which determines the length of forecast necessary), research, development and design, the storability of the product, the number of suppliers and the flexibility of supplies.

In the market in general, the main points to consider are: the size and structure of the market, transport facilities, distance from the main parts of the market and main centres of demand, credit possibilities, and seasonality of demand, the number of competitors, their share of the market and the forms of competition, the number and type of substitutes, prices, prospects for various types of sales promotion, and the relative powers of producers and distributors.

Coming to the consumers, the main factors affecting policy are: the number of consumers and the number of economic units (such as households), their incomes, tastes and preferences, their demand patterns, their consumption capacity over a period of time, the storage capacity of the household or other unit, and the time-lag of consumption (the increasing number of freezers, for example, tends to impose new time patterns on consumption, since people can buy larger amounts of perishable foods less often).

The main considerations relating to distributors are: the structure of distribution and the variety of channels, the number of distributors and their power, the ability of distributors to handle products, the attitudes of distributors, warehousing facilities, the customs and traditions of the trade, trade association policies, discount and credit opportunities, possibilities of mutual co-operation and the costs of distribution.

The reconciliation of all these factors and individual decisions forms the marketing policy of the firm, which must be consistent with its overall objectives.

NOTES

1 The *Business Monitor*'s, SDA25 and SDA26, from which these figures are derived are a valuable source of information on the retail and wholesale trades respectively.

2 British Institute of Management, 'Survey of marketing research in Great Britain', Information Summary 97 (London, BIM, 1962).

3 This classification follows that of P. M. Chisnall, *Marketing Research: Analysis and Measurement*, 2nd edn (London, McGraw-Hill, 1981).

4 Quoted in P. M. Chisnall, *Effective Industrial Marketing* (London, Longman, 1977), p. 120.

5 See, for example, P. Kotler, *Marketing Management: Analysis, Planning and Control*, 3rd edn (London, Prentice-Hall, 1976).

6 To give some idea of the availability of information, the book *Where to Find Business Information* (Chichester, John Wiley, 1979) lists over 5,000 major sources.

7 See chapter 10.

8 See, for example, M. Christopher, 'Non-metric scaling: the principles and marketing possibilities', *European Research*, 1 (1973).

9 For an excellent discussion of this field see Chisnall, *Effective Industrial Marketing*.

10 P. Hoult, 'Embassy slim panatellas', in M. K. Adler, *Leading Cases in Market Research* (London, Business Books, 1971).

11 Ibid.

12 This section is based on B. Chiplin and B. Sturgess, *The Economics of Advertising* (London, Holt, Rinehart & Winston, 1981).

13 This result is known as the Dorfman–Steiner condition (see R. Dorfman and P. O. Steiner, 'Optimal advertising and optimal quality', *American Economic Review*, 44 (1954). There are many complications and refinements that have been made to allow for differing circumstances, but its essence remains as stated in the text.

14 R. D. Rees, *Advertising Budgeting and Appraisal in Practice,* Research Studies in Advertising 11 (London, Advertising Association, 1980).

15 See, for example, S. H. Kennedy and D. R. Corkindale, *Managing the Advertising Process* (Farnborough, Hants, Saxon House, 1976).

16 S. F. Witt and C. L. Pass, 'The effects of health warnings and advertising on the demand for cigarettes', *Scottish Journal of Political Economy*, 28 (1981).

17 It should be noted, however, that poster advertising is of considerable importance in the cigarette market.

18 E. Chamberlin, *The Theory of Monopolistic Competition* (Cambridge, Mass., Harvard University Press, 1935).

19 Think, for example, of the variety of products available in office equipment, typewriters, small computers, etc.

20 Monopolies and Mergers Commission, *Household Detergents*, HC 105 (London, HMSO, 1966).

21 K. Cowling and J. Cubbin, 'Price, quality and advertising competition', *Economica*, 38 (1971).
22 See, for instance, K. Lancaster, *Variety, Equity and Efficiency* (New York, Columbia University Press, 1979) and A. M. Spence, 'Product differentiation and welfare', *American Economic Review Papers and Proceedings*, 66 (1976).
23 See, for instance, S. Nickell and D. Metcalf, 'Monopolistic industries and monopoly profits, or Are Kellogg's cornflakes overpriced?', *Economic Journal*, 88 (1978).
24 See Monopolies and Mergers Commission, *Bicycles*, HC 67 (London, HMSO, 1981). The bicycle market was discussed extensively in chapter 4.

6
Pricing

The pricing decision is an integral part of marketing policy. Not all firms are able to set prices for their products; they are *price-takers* rather than *price-makers*, and under the pressure of competition must accept what they can get for their products. Sellers of many basic commodities such as rubber, cotton and tea are in this category, and their prices are determined by supply and demand; sellers of many other commodities have to accept prices fixed by government or international agencies. Sometimes the opportunity to charge a higher price than that ruling in the market may be made by producing a superior grade of product or one that is specially adapted for its market; but in many industries short-run market conditions approximate to what the economist refers to as *perfect competition*. The characteristics of such markets are the presence of large numbers of buyers and sellers dealing in a homogeneous product with full knowledge of the market; the fact that firms are free to enter or leave the industry; and the fact that all factors of production are fully employed. In these conditions price is market-determined and firms are price-takers.

In sharp contrast to conditions of perfect competition are conditions of *monopoly*, where one seller dominates the market for a clearly differentiated product with no close substitutes. A monopolist is not at the mercy of competitors, but what the firm can sell at any price depends on what the consumer is prepared and able to buy at that price (effective demand); the monopolist cannot fix both prices and sales.

Manufacturing industry does not generally operate in conditions of either perfect competition or monopoly. Many firms, in agriculture, distribution, and services as well as in manufacturing industry, sell in a market in competition with a small number of other firms. Economists refer to this state of affairs as *oligopoly*; its essence is that the actions of any firm greatly affect the others in the market. Another economists' term, *monopolistic competition*, describes a market generally involving more producers than oligopoly, all of whom are affected to some degree by the actions of others. Nevertheless, they may have some scope for independent action without experiencing serious retaliation from their competitors. In monopolistic competition firms are able to differentiate their products from those of their competitors by advertising, design, trade-marks, selection of location, etc.; price, however, remains a vital element in the strategy and tactics of the firm. When there is only a small number of buyers the market condition is referred to as *oligopsony*, and where there is a single buyer the term *monopsony* is used. Oligopolists may sell to oligopsonists or monopsonists or to a multitude of buyers, and buyers and sellers may be matched in a variety of other ways.

Important though pricing is, it must not be looked at in isolation from the other activities of the business. Since price is a determinant of sales, it must be related to output and production costs and in turn to decisions to invest. The ability to sell at particular prices is quite likely to determine what can be spent in making the product and in ensuring its quality; production may have to be tailored to a price as often as a price has to be fixed to cover production costs.

The need to relate these elements of business decisions applies to all firms, whatever the precise ends they set themselves. But the way they fix prices, when they have the discretion to do so, is likely to reflect the objectives they are pursuing and which were discussed in chapter 1: we might, for example, expect those firms concentrating on expanding their turnover to set lower prices than those concerned with maximizing profits in the short run.

Opinions differ as to what is characteristic in these respects. It has to be recognized that in modern industry there is a substantial divorce between ownership and control for almost all but the smaller companies. Thus, the owner − the shareholder − is generally able to exercise little direct control over the running of the company, which is the responsibility of professional managers who have their own particular objectives to pursue. Such an idea is the basis of theories of the firm that stress the importance of managerial discretion.[1] Bearing this fact in mind, some, including Professor J. K. Galbraith,[2] argue that modern industry is constantly changing; periods of gestation tend to be long and effective planning of industrial operations for years ahead is unavoidable. Planners attempt to reduce the uncertainties inherent in long time-horizons and try to plan for the comparative stability of certain elements over which they can exercise control. One of these elements is price, which can fluctuate more than the costs of production if price determination is left to the market. Such fluctuations can be reduced either by achieving close relationships with suppliers and distributors, or by extending control to earlier or later production processes by *vertical integration*. Price is thus reduced to a secondary role in planning decisions. This assumes, however, that the ultimate prices charged to consumers can be controlled so as to maintain the profitability of companies and to provide them with the resources necessary to expand their businesses.

The Galbraithian thesis on the power of the corporation is exaggerated, but oligopoly is becoming increasingly common in industry. Oligopolists are unlikely to indulge in price-cutting or raising prices ahead of their competitors; they fully recognize that they have a common interest in maintaining prices, as retaliation is bound to follow a price cut; they also know that if they attempt to raise prices individually their competitors may not follow suit, preferring to gain a larger share of the market. However, in conditions of widespread inflation, as has been experienced in Britain in recent years, it becomes more likely that competitors will tend to follow a price rise. In such circumstances, where the reactions of rivals is crucial, it is fairly common for price-leaders to emerge (which may or may not be the dominant firms in each market), and their decisions about price levels are tacitly followed by competitors.

If it can be assumed that all firms effectively operate in collusion and attempt to maximize their pooled profits, the theoretical analysis is fairly simple.[3] It is in fact the case of monopoly, and output may be determined in conditions of complete knowledge in such a way as to maximize profits. The basic postulate is that of the downward-sloping demand curve (as discussed in chapter 4), which expresses the fact that demand will be greater at a lower than a higher price. Every increase in sales, holding the other factors that influence demand constant, necessitates a reduction in price, and this means that the additional (marginal) revenue from increasing sales by one unit is less than the price at which the unit is sold because all units are sold at the same, lower, price. The position is illustrated in figure 6.1. The average revenue curve (or demand curve) shows the price at which various levels of output can be sold; the marginal revenue curve (which is always less than this)[4] represents the increase in revenue that results from selling an additional unit after allowing for the fact that the price of all units, and not just the marginal unit, has to be reduced. The curves relating to costs show both marginal (additional) costs incurred in producing an extra unit and the average cost of producing the various levels of output.[5]

If the intention is to maximize profits, that output for which

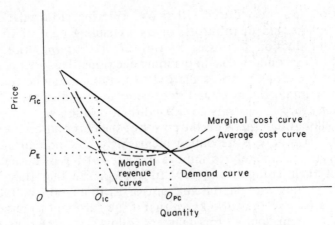

Figure 6.1   Price and output under monopoly.

marginal cost equals marginal revenue should be produced. The logic behind this rule is quite simple. If marginal cost exceeds marginal revenue, an expansion of output means that each successive unit produced adds more to cost than to revenue, with the result that incremental profit is negative and total profits fall; it would be point-less to expand output in these conditions — in fact, it would pay to contract. If marginal revenue exceeds marginal cost, an expansion of output results in the addition of more to revenue than to costs, and further expansion is, therefore, justified. It follows that the equilibrium condition, in which it pays neither to expand nor to reduce output, is where marginal cost equals marginal revenue. It should be noted, however, that in formal terms the analysis assumes profit-maximizing behaviour, and the conditions do not apply if the firm is pursuing some alternative objective.

It is possible for a firm that possesses market power not to maxi-mize profits, and in this case it will produce either a smaller or greater output than that of the profit-maximizing firm. It may do this with the intention of achieving other objectives, such as increasing sales revenue, generating growth, preserving goodwill or charging a 'fair' price. One consequence of concentrating on other objectives may be that the pressure on the firm to produce at lowest possible cost will be reduced. Thus, the cost curves shown in figure 6.1 may be higher than those that are attainable in principle. Such a difference in costs is a measure of inefficiency which is known as 'X-inefficiency'.[6]

The description of the behaviour of firms in terms of the selection of a price–output combination is sound enough so far as it goes, but it is not always easy to fit it to actual conditions, and it is certainly an over-simplified model of what happens, whether or not competition is experienced. Fitting the product to the price is as important as selecting the price for a given product. Also, in many consumer markets it would be unwise to act on the assumption either that the prices set by apparent price-leaders should be followed invariably, or that consumers are so loyal (or so ignorant) that their purchases will not be affected by the price set or by that charged by competitors. Interesting work on buyer response to price and the role of price as an indicator of quality has suggested that in some cases there may be a range of prices for any particular brand within which the consumer may be unresponsive to price changes. Thus, the consumer is seen as having an upper price limit beyond which the good would be considered too expensive, and a lower limit below which the quality would be suspect.[7]

Pricing policy is likely to differ in a number of complex ways depending on the particular circumstances facing the firm. Alfred, a practising businessman, has conveniently categorized a number of these alternative circumstances that are likely to be relevant:[8]

(a) type of product:
 consumer
 industrial
(b) geographical market:
 home
 export
(c) type of competition:
 competitive
 oligopolistic
 monopolistic (including many products or services in the public sector)
(d) age of product:
 existing product
 new or development product
(e) nature of production:
 joint products
 multi- (interchangeable) products
 vertically integrated products
(f) variations in capacity:
 utilizing existing capacity (short-term)
 anticipating new capacity (long-term growth).

These categories are not, of course, unique, and in addition to the possibility of the addition of further items, combinations of the various sub-divisions are possible, all of which may have different implications for price. The categories are, however, reasonably self-evident, and do provide a guide to the relevant issues. Space does not permit a detailed examination of all the possible circumstances, but we shall seek to highlight a few of the major alternatives and provide a discussion of some of the general principles involved in pricing decisions.

The pricing decision for a new product is likely to involve somewhat different factors to those involved in the pricing of an existing and mature product. The development of new products is essential for the success of a company, but the failure rate is high.[9] It is common to suggest that there are two alternative pricing strategies for new products: the setting of either a 'skimming' or a 'penetration' price.[10] For the former, the company would set a price that greatly exceeds the average and marginal costs of production, with the intention of skimming the cream of the market. Such a high price allows for substantial promotional expenditure, which may be necessary to launch the brand, and it also aids the early recoupment of the development costs associated with the product. At the same time, it may enhance the 'quality' image of the product. It also follows that subsequent price adjustments are likely to be downwards, with beneficial effects on demand, and it opens the possibility of introducing lower-price varieties at a later stage once the product is secure – a policy of market segmentation.

The alternative of setting a penetration price is designed to obtain large sales of the product at an early stage in its life, which may be important if demand is highly responsive to price (own-price elastic) and can act as a deterrent to the introduction of rival products by potential competitors. It can be argued[11] that a penetration price is most suitable if the product is functionally similar to already existing products. It is also suggested that the appropriate process for a new brand is to choose the price first and then work backwards to determine the appropriate limit for the cost of production – a policy of pricing backwards from the market. On the other hand, if the product is genuinely innovative, it may be preferable to set a creaming price.

One difference between consumer and industrial goods is frequently assumed to be that industrial buyers are better informed, particularly about quality and costs of production, than are consumers. However, such a view may over-state the case in practice. Many industrial buyers may be in a similar position to the average consumer, with a reasonable idea of the prices in the market, the quality of different brands and the reliability of suppliers. The industrial buyer, like the consumer, may also be presumed to be willing to pay a higher price for a higher-quality item, and may not be particularly price-sensitive (see, e.g., the laws of derived demand discussed in chapter 4). Also, factors such as delivery dates, reliability, technical advice available, etc., are likely to be important for some industrial products, which might tend to reduce the importance of price.

As has been mentioned earlier, for some industrial products competitive tendering may be the main market process, particularly in fields like construction, but also for many other products, and the award of long-term contracts for the supply of inputs can be determined on the basis of a tender bid. To the firm bidding for the tender, much depends on the degree of information available – i.e., what is known about the behaviour of the buyer and other potential contractors. Such information is likely to be influenced by the extent to which the particular project is one-off or part of a regular series. As was noted in the case of ready-mixed concrete (see note 3), such tenders may not be as competitive as they appear. For major contracts, however, complex factors are involved, and there are available a number of mathematical models, based on probability, which can be used to attempt to assess the likely success of any particular bid.[12] To give a simple example of the principles involved, if records exist of bids submitted on previous occasions for similar classes of work, it may be possible to estimate the probability that rivals' bids will fall above or below the estimated costs by various percentages, and to work out the chances of success of a particular bid. Thus, a bid that would give a rate of return of 5 per cent and have a 20 per cent chance of acceptance would not, on average, yield as much as one with only a 15 per cent chance of acceptance at a 10 per cent rate of return. Strategies of this kind are likely to work only so long as a reasonable number of contracts is coming forward; there is a danger that, if few but large contracts are placed and the bidder is unsuccessful in most tenders, it will be difficult to meet overhead costs. Further, if competitors adjust their tactics in reaction to the company's bid behaviour, the whole basis of the analysis will need to be changed. Inflation in costs is also a particular problem where long-term contracts are concerned, and the supplier needs to be particularly careful that the terms of the contract adequately reflect this possibility.

Tender prices, and pricing in other circumstances, may well not be independent of the current usage of capacity of the firm. If capacity is under-utilized, it may pay the firm to undertake extra work as long as the revenue exceeds the variable costs incurred. In the construction industry at present, with the cut-back in local authority expenditure, some builders are prepared to tender at very low prices just to remain in existence. Similarly, many manufacturers are prepared to supply retailers' own brands at somewhere near the marginal costs of production to make full use of their productive capacity.

Companies that work on a jobbing basis, e.g., many engineering firms, carrying out a large number of specific but small jobs, may face particular difficulties in selecting an appropriate pricing strategy. Here there may be no clear guidance as to the 'going' market price for the work. Many such firms may set prices on the basis of a simple cost-related rule, but they may be forgoing important opportunities for profit and market development if no account is taken of demand.[13]

For industrial products it is also important to recognize that many sales may be to other parts of the same company, both within the same country, and across national frontiers in multinational companies. A British Institute of Management survey of 293 companies in the UK showed, for example, that in more than a third of the companies involved inter-company sales accounted for between 10 and 25 per cent of total sales.[14] The question here is the determination of the transfer price, which may be particularly important to the individual managers concerned if the company operates its divisions as profit centres with target rates of return. If the same goods and services are available on the market, it is generally argued that it is sensible policy to transfer them within the company at current market prices. However, it may be possible to gain in terms of tax liability, especially for multinational companies, if taxable profits are shifted through appropriate transfer prices, such that total tax payments are reduced.

Export pricing is little different, in principle, from pricing for the domestic market, but due account has to be taken of differences between conditions in the home and export markets. It is generally assumed that the export market is rather more competitive than the home market for the large manufacturer. Additional costs in the form of transport, special packaging and insurance as well as the existence of import controls, both tariff and non-tariff barriers (e.g., safety regulations, administrative requirements, etc.), need to be considered. There may also be extra difficulties involved with changes in exchange rates.

As an illustration of the determination of price in an export market, it is informative to look at the Price Commission's study in early 1979 of the market for video tape recorders in the UK.[15] All video recorders were imported, mainly from Japan, but also from Austria and Germany. There were 12 importers in the UK, and although there are differences between systems, the Commission considered that the number of importers and the basic similarity of the systems meant that prices would not get much out of line with each other. It was clear that the UK consumer had to pay somewhat more than the Japanese consumer and considerably more than the American consumer for recorders, but additional manufacturing costs to meet, e.g., different electrical standards, freight charges, import duty, sales taxes, and in the case of the American market its larger size and more prevalent discounting, largely accounted for the differences.

The above treatment of some of the issues involved has done little more than provide a brief introduction to the important questions and specific features that apply to particular market environments. Another difficulty needs to be analysed: it is not always clear what precisely is meant by the term 'price'. The price actually paid by the consumer for an item is frequently different from the list (published or catalogue) price because of discounts, special offers, the amount bought, transport charges and the method and timing of payment (cash, credit card, hire purchase, etc.). On the last point, there has recently been considerable dispute about surcharges applied to credit card users by certain retailers, most notably garages. Garages that honour credit cards have to pay between 2 and 3 per cent of the cost of the petrol to the credit card companies. Following a Monopolies and Mergers Commission report (September 1980) that approved the practice, many garages imposed surcharges for a time of between 15 and 25 pence per transaction for petrol bought using credit cards.[16] When other aspects of credit purchase are taken into account, it is clear that both the price paid and the price received by the supplier are not simple matters. For instance, a Monopolies and Mergers Commission report on trading checks made in 1981 showed that the cost of credit varied enormously even within a particular category.[17] In the case of hire purchase, for example, the annual percentage rate of interest at 1 October 1980 ranged from 19.7 to 56.2 per cent.

As well as the role of credit, there is a further factor influencing the effective price to the consumer for durable goods, namely the trade-in allowance on existing assets. Trade-ins are of considerable importance in electrical goods as well as in the car market. For example, a retailer of electrical goods was offering a vacuum cleaner at a price of £47 but with a flat-rate £5 allowance against any old cleaner. In the January sales the price had been reduced to £39 but the £5 trade-in allowance had been discontinued – not such an improved bargain to those with old vacuum cleaners!

It also has to be remembered that the quality of products can differ enormously. Take, for instance, the car market, where the 'price' may include all sorts of extras, such as radio, heated rear window, etc., or where these may be optional extras. Again, the determination of price for comparative purposes is no simple matter when quality varies. Variation of quality and other attributes of the product is one way in which a producer can adjust to rising costs without necessarily increasing price. In the confectionery market, for example, it has been a common occurrence for suppliers to change the size of their chocolate bars, not only in response to tax changes but also as a consequence of variations, among other things, in the price of cocoa. We discussed the possible importance of obtaining quality-adjusted prices in chapter 5.

The prices for many industrial transactions are determined by negotiation, tender or secret reductions from published list prices. Thus, for both consumer and industrial goods, not only may there be many dimensions to price, but also care has to be taken in any empirical work to ensure that the prices obtained are those actually paid (transaction prices), and not simply list prices.[18]

RETAILERS AND PRICES

In chapter 5 we mentioned the significance of retailers in determining the prices of many goods, and in the present context it is important to examine their role in greater detail. Until 1964, resale price maintenance (RPM) was a common practice (at least in branded goods) whereby manufacturers compelled retailers to sell their product at a minimum prescribed price. Goods typically passed from manufacturer to wholesaler to retailer, and the manufacturer set prices that gave each stage a gross margin to cover costs and provide profit. The typical wholesale margin was between 10 and 15 per cent, and the corresponding retail margin between 15 and 33 per cent. The Resale Prices Act 1964 abolished this practice, with certain exceptions, largely on the grounds that resale price maintenance kept prices higher than necessary and reduced competition. In those sectors where RPM had been significant it was generally replaced by a system of manufacturers' recommended retail prices.

Changes in the pattern of distribution, including the growth of discount stores, resulted in actual retail prices in some sectors being substantially below the recommended price and differing considerably between sectors. In its report in 1977,[19] the Price Commission found three distinct types of price distribution between retailers across 87 different products. These distributions are illustrated in figures 6.2–6.4.

Figure 6.2 shows a distribution where prices are clustered around the recommended retail price, with about 50 per cent or more of the observations at the recommended price. It was prevalent in the prices of cinema admission, living-room furniture, cosmetics and clothing and footwear. Figure 6.3 is distinguished by two peaks in the price distribution, with about 15–30 per cent of observations being at the current recommended price and a second concentration of observations some 20–30 per cent lower. Such a pattern was found to be prevalent in products such as beds, kitchen furniture and toothpaste. Most of the lower prices occurred in discount houses and department stores, whereas the higher prices were more likely to be observed among the independents and multiple chains. The third distribution is shown in figure 6.4, which is a more bell-shaped (or normal) distribution and includes products without a recommended retail price (those where the price is limited only by market forces) as well as products with recommended prices. In the last category, a much smaller proportion of observations occurred at the recommended price in comparison with the other two distributions. It should be noted that in all cases there is a very small proportion of observations above the recommended price, many of which occurred through mistakes, or rounding up of prices involving 0.5p prices.

Table 6.1 provides evidence on the average percentage discount from the recommended price both by type of product and by outlet. It will be observed that there is considerable variation, and on average prices are lowest in discount stores. These figures illustrate the wide range of retail prices actually found in practice, but they should not be interpreted as implying that the manufacturer has no control over the price charged by the distributor. Many of the high discount prices may occur because of special terms granted by the manufacturer to large retailers, although the retailer may still have considerable discretion over the actual price charged. Raleigh, for example, were most concerned to prevent their bicycles being priced as 'loss-leaders' by discount retailers.

In his major study of the distribution process in the UK, Ward[20] argued that the abolition of RPM and, therefore, the control by

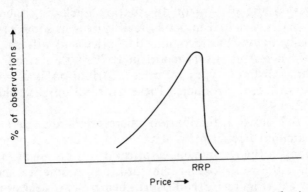

Figure 6.2   Price distribution type A. RRP, recommended retail price.
Source: Price Commission, *Recommended Retail Prices*, Report 25 (London, HMSO, 1977).

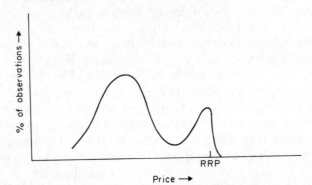

Figure 6.3   Price distribution type B. RRP, recommended retail price.
Source: Price Commission, *Recommended Retail Prices*.

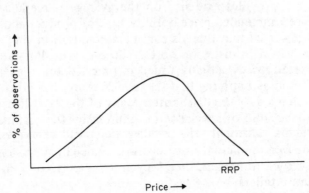

Figure 6.4   Price distribution type C. RRP, recommended retail price.
Source: Price Commission, *Recommended Retail Prices*.

Table 6.1 Average percentage discounts from current recommended retail prices*

	Co-op	Discount house	Dept store	Multiple specialist	Indepen- dent	All outlets†
Photographic goods	5	14	9	8	8	8
Consumer electronics	22	28	23	23	19	22
Carpets	20	23	25	18	21	21
Beds	11	25	15	15	18	16
Kitchen furniture	12	17	10	9	12	12
Living room furniture	5	16	7	3	9	7
Fabrics	7	–	6	8	14	10
Clothing	5	–	1	2	1	1
Footwear	1	4	2	2	2	1
Hardware	21	31	16	20	13	18
Groceries	12	18	10	12	10	12
Spirits	14	–	8	11	10	11
Toiletries	16	26	16	12	13	15
All sectors	12	20	12	11	12	

* Weighted within sectors by number of observations.
† Unweighted column average – illustrative only.
Source: Price Commission, *Recommended Retail Prices*, Report 25 (London, HMSO, 1977).

manufacturers of retail selling prices would have the following consequences:

(a) a decrease in the services offered by the distribution sector as a whole, including a reduction in the number of retail outlets and wholesale warehouses;

(b) a switch in sales towards the more efficient traders and hence an overall increase in the productivity of the distributive trades;

(c) a reduction in the average price paid for particular commodities, as traders exercise their option of substituting lower selling prices for part of the service provided;

(d) a fall in the average gross margin earned by distributors;

(e) the development of new methods of selling based on lower prices, and in particular the growth of self-service at both retail and wholesale levels;

(f) price competition at the distributive stage would tend to lead to increased pressure on manufacturers for additional discounts, and the diversion of trade towards larger distributors would tend to increase their bargaining power still further.

It has been noted in chapter 5 that many of these developments have, in fact, occurred in recent years in the distributive sector. The arguments also serve to emphasize the complexity of price as noted above; for the purchase of a commodity involves both the product itself and the service associated with its purchase. Price, to some extent, will reflect differences in the quality of this service.

The determination of prices at the retail stage will be the outcome of a complex set of factors:[21] marginal costs, the range of stock carried, the service given and the strength of competition are all likely to be important. Prices and standards of service are closely interrelated; there are many forms of retailing, each with a characteristic mix of overhead and variable costs, and standard of service. Correspondingly, the prices charged can vary considerably. The attraction of a store does not depend solely on the prices charged and location; variety of stock, standard of display and advertising, as well as service, can be important. But recent trends would suggest that price is increasingly the dominant influence. Retailers generally offer a combination of goods, and complementarity between sales of different items means that demand for a particular product, and the price charged for it, must be seen in relation to the effect on other goods sold in the same store. A product priced as a 'loss-leader' is easily understood in this connection, since the loss on the product is presumed to be more than compensated by the additional demand generated. This is related to the choice between two alternative general pricing strategies: a series of deep price cuts in relation to competitors' prices on a limited number of products, or smaller cuts on a wide range of products. In general, it seems that stores that cut prices across the board make greater headway. In addition, the store has to consider its own-brand policy and the corresponding prices.

As these discussions have illustrated, the retail stage has become an important influence on the prices charged to consumers for branded goods since the widespread abolition of resale price maintenance. The manufacturer, therefore, needs to take account of these developments in the determination of his pricing strategy.

PRICING BY MANUFACTURERS

Most analyses of price recognize the importance of costs and some stress their role − independent of the level of demand, where price is determined by a mark-up on some measure of costs. In the economists' textbook model discussed earlier in this chapter, both costs and demand come into play, and price and output are set such that marginal cost equals marginal revenue for the profit-maximizing firm. Assuming that average costs are constant, the profit-maximizing relationship can be converted to a simple formula in terms of the price–cost margin:[22]

$$\frac{P - AC}{P} = \frac{1}{e}$$

where the left-hand side is the price–cost margin in terms of average cost and the right-hand side is the reciprocal of the absolute value of the own-price elasticity of demand. Thus profit-maximizing behaviour does, as might be expected, carry direct implications for the profit margin. The crucial questions, therefore, are whether actual pricing behaviour conforms to this rule, and whether the margin responds to changes in demand in the way predicted by the analysis.

There are essentially three wholly different views as to how prices actually respond to short-run changes in demand at given levels of costs.[23]

(1) Competitive forces are important, and prices fall relative to costs in recessions and rise relative to costs in periods of expansion.

(2) Prices rise relative to costs in a recession and fall relative to costs in expansionary periods; the rise occurs as firms seek to attain a target profit rate when average cost falls as output expands.

(3) Prices are determined by standard (or normal) costs and do not react to temporary changes in either demand or costs. The firm is seen as calculating the level of costs at a normal level of output and sets prices as a mark-up on normal costs independent of any temporary variations in demand.

This last category reflects the original work of Hall and Hitch, who suggested, on the basis of interviews with a number of businessmen, that costs were the predominant influence on prices and that many firms adopted simple cost-plus rules.[24] These rules can take two broad forms. The first – full-cost pricing – takes account of the full average costs of production of a product including an allocation for overheads and adds a 'conventional' profit margin to determine the selling price. The second takes only the more easily measurable cost components, such as labour, raw materials, fuel and transport per unit, as a basis and allows for overheads together with profits by the addition of some conventional margin. The costs used, whether including overheads or not, can be based on current actual unit costs, average costs over some period, expected unit costs, or 'standard' or 'normal' costs as suggested in category (3) above. In essence, therefore, the firm is seen as following average cost pricing rules.

Although the alternatives seem simple, it needs to be remembered that allocation of costs, both variable and overhead, can be difficult in the case of multi-product firms.

Cost-plus pricing is sometimes interpreted as indicating that only supply-side factors are important in determining prices. However, as was shown above, profit maximizing behaviour, which would take full account of demand-side influences, can also be interpreted in terms of a margin on top of average costs. The crucial question is whether the margin remains unaltered, independent of the state of demand. It may be that margins do not vary in response to temporary changes in conditions, as suggested by category (3) above, but it is quite another matter to suggest that they are immutably fixed. It makes no sense for a company to seek to hold its margins constant, at some historical or conventional level, irrespective of demand. We have, for example, already seen the impact of reduced margins operated by the new discount stores on the retail trade. On the other hand, it would not be sensible, in terms of both long-run profitability and other objectives, to vary prices constantly with minor changes in conditions.

PRICES AND THE LAW[25]

Many aspects of the law are of direct relevance to pricing and marketing policy, e.g., the Trade Descriptions Act 1968 and Consumer Credit Act 1974, as well as contract law in general. However, in the present context it is proposed to concentrate on the main aspects of competition policy in the UK and the operation of price controls.

We have already referred on several occasions to various provisions of competition policy in the UK, notably the Resale Prices Act 1964 and the Restrictive Trade Practices Act 1956. In most cases these acts effectively prevent the enforcement of resale prices and formal collusion between suppliers of both goods and services. The other major part of competition policy comprises the Fair Trading Act 1973 and the Competition Act 1980.

Under the Fair Trading Act, the Office of Fair Trading, or the relevant secretary of state, may refer a firm that has more than 25 per cent of a relevant market (including a local market) to the

Monopolies and Mergers Commission for investigation. That body is then required to report whether the firm is operating, or might be expected to operate, against the public interest. Further, on reference from ministers only, mergers involving either a market share of 25 per cent or more or assets of over £15 million may be examined. Under the public interest guidelines of the Act (section 84), the Commission is required to consider a number of issues and in particular the desirability 'of promoting the interests of consumers, purchasers and other users of goods and services in the United Kingdom in respect of the prices charged for them and in respect of their quality and the variety of goods and services supplied'.

The Commission in practice does pay great attention to the pricing policies and the level of profits of the companies it investigates, and as such must be regarded as forming some constraint on the activities of firms that have the requisite market share. Further, the Competition Act 1980 gives the Director-General of Fair Trading the power to investigate anti-competitive practices and if necessary refer them to the Monopolies and Mergers Commission for examination. We saw in chapter 4 the results of the first such investigation by the Commission under the Act. But some practices are stopped without full investigation by the Commission; for instance, the fact that free newspapers can now carry a listing of television programmes is as a result of the action taken by the Director-General of Fair Trading.

Competition policy is, therefore, well developed in the UK, although its direct impact on prices and pricing policy should not be exaggerated. Of more significance perhaps has been the imposition of various forms of price control since the mid-1960s. Statutory price controls were introduced in 1966 by the Labour Government, under which applications for price increases were examined by the National Board for Prices and Incomes. A period of voluntary control ensued. A virtual standstill on prices at the end of 1972 was followed by the creation of a Price Commission in 1973. The larger firms (over £5 million) were required to give prior notice to the Commission of price increases and to submit quarterly returns of their net profit margins. Smaller firms had to keep appropriate records so that the Commission could assess whether they had kept to the price codes. The original Price Code set a reference profit margin (the average of the best two trading years out of five prior to April 1973), and manufacturers could raise prices only if allowable costs per unit of output had increased and their net profit had not risen above the reference level. This Code was relaxed as time went on and as recession began to take hold.

Any form of price control carries the danger that it distorts the operation of market forces and prevents needed adjustment in relative prices. To one of the economists concerned with the policy,[26] it appeared that many pricing decisions became based almost entirely on what was permissible under the Price Code, and the pricing decision came to be taken largely by accountants and not entrepreneurs. In its later life the Price Commission came to be more concerned with the operation of market forces and competition under the Price Commission Act 1977, and it performed something of a regulatory role in the pricing and performance of British industry. However, its effective powers ceased in May 1979 and it was finally disbanded in 1980.

This brief review of policy has been designed to indicate that firms are not entirely free to determine their own prices even in those cases where they have some market power. The price control legislation was, of course, concerned predominantly with the control of inflation, and not with the specific price-setting practices of individual firms.

PRICING METHODS IN PRACTICE

All firms need a pricing policy, but given the wide variety of different market circumstances discussed in this chapter it should not be too surprising if we find no simple pattern.

The most commonly adopted policy according to researchers, who seek to obtain evidence from direct observation of firm behaviour, is that of cost-plus or full-cost pricing.[27] But, as might be expected from our previous discussion, there is a variety of different cost measures used as the baseline. Further the arbitrary nature of the allocation of certain costs, especially overhead costs, can lead to marked differences between firms. The margin also tends to differ and may be related to a target rate of return on capital or to some concept of a 'conventional' margin. To re-emphasize a point we made above, it does not follow that, just because the firm used a mark-up on costs, it is not taking account of demand circumstances: it depends whether the margin itself varies according to market conditions.

In their study of industrial pricing in the UK, Coutts, Godley and Nordhaus tested the normal cost variant of cost-plus pricing, i.e., that prices are set as a mark-up on normal unit costs and are independent of demand conditions. They used econometric testing rather than asking company executives what they did. Such an approach avoids the problems associated with questionnaires and interviews, but in its turn raises measurement and specification issues. The basic procedure of these researchers was to compare quarterly predictions of prices based on the assumption that they were set as a fixed gross margin on past normal unit costs with the actual quarterly movement of prices. The period tested covers 1957–73 for some industries and 1963–73 for others. Their general conclusion was that demand did not affect prices relative to normal unit costs. They also looked at the impact of price controls and concluded that the Labour Government's policy between 1965 and 1970 (largely voluntary) had little effect on the mark-up of prices over costs, but that the statutory policy of the Conservative Government introduced in 1972 did reduce, at least temporarily, the level of prices relative to costs.

There are many complications involved in using econometric methods to assess pricing policies, and it is perhaps dangerous to argue that prices and margins are totally independent of demand conditions. The experience of falling margins in the early 1980s in both manufacturing and retailing is indicative of this point.

The main advantage of cost-plus pricing is that it is simple to operate, particularly when little is known about demand conditions. With this system prices respond to changes in production costs and not to demand. Although such a response may be acceptable to customers, who understand the logic of a price increase based on cost increases, its failure to emphasize the importance of demand and competitive conditions is a major weakness. The effectiveness of the measure also depends on having the right definitions and accurate measurement of costs; ideally, the measure should reflect opportunity costs and be concentrated on marginal or incremental rather than average costs.

Flexible mark-up pricing is a slightly more sophisticated variant, which permits the firm to adapt its mark-up to market changes to some extent; administratively, it may be expensive if frequent demand estimates are required, and many firms may restrict the use of flexible mark-ups to products sold to customers they know well. The emphasis in this approach is on what the market will bear.

In appropriate demand and cost conditions a variety of other methods may be used, including price lining (the adoption of a limited number of prices at which goods are to be sold); loss-leader pricing on selected products; and simply following the prices of other firms (following a price-leader). The economics textbooks also discuss the possibility of limit pricing, which involves setting a price such that any potential new entrant to the market is unable to make a suitable profit and is, therefore, deterred from entering that market. It may well be, however, that there are superior strategies available, such as building excess capacity, which can be put into operation if necessary to push down the market price if entry is threatened.

Further, it is open under certain circumstances to the producer to supply essentially the same product to different consumers at different prices, or even to charge an individual consumer a different price for different quantities. The wide number of different prices available for an inter-city journey on British Rail at the current time or concessions for old-age pensioners on public transport are examples of the former, and the latter is well illustrated by the pricing of public utilities such as gas and electricity, which involve a standing charge and alternative rates per unit for actual consumption. A standing charge is not necessarily discriminatory if there are some costs independent of the number of units supplied. To be effective, price discrimination requires the existence of separate markets with different elasticities and little possibility of resale from those buying at the lower price to those who have to pay more.

The firm that wishes to maximize profits should fix prices and sales at the level that equates marginal cost and marginal revenue, taking account of the expected reactions of rivals; this is difficult, but incremental or marginal-cost pricing frequently approaches this ideal in practice. The advantage of the marginalist approach is that it gets away from prices based on average cost plus some fixed mark-up and makes an attempt to take account of demand conditions.

A CASE STUDY OF PRICES AND MARKETS:
IMPERIAL TOBACCO LTD[28]

In order to try and draw together our discussion of prices and markets, it is appropriate to consider in some detail the response of one particular company to changed market circumstances. The company we have chosen is Imperial Tobacco, part of the Imperial Group, to which we refer in many parts of the book.

Cigarette smoking, in terms of weight of tobacco consumed, has fallen since the early 1960s from a peak of 243.1 million pounds to just under 200 million pounds by 1977. The number of cigarettes smoked has shown a less marked decline and peaked much later (in 1973).

Tobacco prices have a weight of nearly 5 per cent in the retail price index. The main change in the tobacco market affecting Imperial has been the alteration in the system of taxation, which occurred as a result of EEC membership as Britain moved towards the common EEC taxation policy for tobacco products. The previous British system had levied a tax based on the weight of leaf used in the cigarette, but under EEC rules this was changed to an *ad valorem* duty based on the retail price plus a specific element (so much per cigarette). This new system came fully into force in January 1978. The implications for the prices of various sizes of cigarettes were marked. In particular, the difference between small-size filter cigarettes and king-size cigarettes narrowed, so that, for example, a differential of 15p in 1975 was reduced to 6p by January 1978. This implied, and led to, a marked expansion of the king-size sector, so that the share of king-size cigarettes increased from 11 per cent in 1975 to 50 per cent in 1978.

In the 1950s Imperial had accounted for 80 per cent of the total market; competition from Gallahers had reduced this to about 55 per cent by the mid-1960s, but it subsequently rose again to 66 per cent in the mid-1970s.

The changes in taxation had particularly serious implications for Imperial, since it had a very much smaller proportion of its sales in the king-size category (about 2 per cent in 1976) compared with its main competitors, especially Carreras Rothmans, for whom the proportion was over 40 per cent.

The Price Commission noted in 1978 that competition in the industry had traditionally taken the form of promoting a brand image and that price was relatively insignificant in determining brand shares. It was also apparent that Imperial acted as an effective price-leader. With the ending of resale price maintenance on cigarettes in 1968 retailers began to develop price competition; but the price reductions were not generally significant, and during this period the manufacturers used coupons which could be exchanged for goods as a means of retaining brand loyalty.

Recognizing the need to improve its position in the king-size market, Imperial launched John Player King Size at a price that was the same as that of standard filter brands (penetration price strategy for the new brand). A tax increase followed almost immediately which caused Imperial to raise its price, but the competitors held their king-size prices constant, thus beginning a phase of intense price competition. Changes in the tax rules, which required the value of coupons to be included in the price for tax purposes, effectively ended the success of coupon brands at the same time.

In order to compete on price, the producers initially used 'flash packs' (i.e., packs marked at, say, '2p off'), but these were replaced by matched deals originated by Imperial's competitors. These matched deals occur when the manufacturer offers a discount off each pack of cigarettes on condition that the distributor will match the cut. Thus a discount of 2p by the manufacturer means a cut of 4p to the consumer. The Price Commission pointed out that at that time manufacturers' recommended retail prices were realistic in that most cigarettes were sold at such prices. Over 25 per cent of sales are through independent confectioner/tobacconist/newsagent outlets, and over 50 per cent of retail sales are made at the recommended retail price. Thus the Commission argued that Imperial set its price to yield a satisfactory margin for distributors at the same time as giving itself a reasonable margin. The Commission also pointed out that over the period 1973–77 the net profit margin earned by Imperial fell by over a third as a consequence of the increased promotional expenditure and reduced prices. The effect of the 'matched' deals on its market share forced Imperial to introduce a similar scheme.

Further important developments took place in the market in 1978. Rothmans reduced the price of Dunhill King Size, and Imperial introduced Players No. 6 King Size and Regal King Size and backed the launch with trial offers. British and American Tobacco (BAT) entered the market with its 555 brand at a price of 48p for 20 as compared

Table 6.2   *Manufacturers' shares of UK king-size filter market*

	Imperial (%)	Gallaher (%)	Carreras Rothmans (%)	Philip Morris (%)	BAT (%)	KS filter as % of total UK cig. market (%)
End 1975	9	54	34	3	–	11
End 1976	33	38	27	2	–	18
End 1977	37	38	23	2	–	29
1978						
February	50	28	20	2	–	40
March	46	31	21	2	–	43
April	45	32	21	2	–	44
May	43	33	20	2	2	46
June	40	31	18	2	9	49
July	39	31	18	2	10	49
August	39	32	18	2	9	50

Source: Retail Audits Ltd; quoted in Price Commission, *Imperial Tobacco Ltd – Cigarettes and Cigarillos*, HC 28 (London, HMSO, 1978/79).

with 53–55p for the competing brands and including tokens worth 2p off next purchase in each pack. The effect of this launch was marked with the results for market shares shown in table 6.2. This table demonstrates that market shares can change substantially in a short period of time.

Imperial's marketing strategy had been to spend heavily on advertising and sponsorship in 1976 and 1977 in order to seek to establish its king-size brands. But matched dealing, increased price competition and the use of trial offers during 1977 and 1978 increased the importance of price reductions, and advertising expenditure fell substantially.

Thus, the cigarette market in recent years illustrates the profound changes that can be brought about by external events, and how a once stable pattern can soon be eroded by new entry and changed marketing and pricing strategies.

NOTES

1 See, e.g., O. E. Williamson, *Economics of Discretionary Behaviour: Managerial Objectives in a Theory of the Firm* (Chicago, Markham, 1967).
2 See, e.g., J. K. Galbraith, *The New Industrial State* (London, Hamish Hamilton, 1967).
3 Under the Restrictive Practices Act 1956 (consolidated into the Restrictive Trade Practices Act 1976), restrictive agreements have to be registered and are presumed, in general, to be against the public interest. Although, on the surface, the legislation was successful in leading to the abandonment of many restrictive practices, collusion often continued in one form or another. For example, investigations by the Office of Fair Trading in 1977 revealed the existence of over 200 unregistered local agreements in the ready-mixed concrete market (this market was discussed briefly in chapter 4). These arrangements were mostly in the form of 'unwritten understandings' between suppliers who met regularly and allocated contracts and/or fixed prices for the supply of ready-mixed concrete. In most cases the main restriction related to the selection of a 'preferred tenderer' who would quote the lowest price, with the other parties agreeing to quote higher prices. (See Monopolies and Mergers Commission, *Ready Mixed Concrete*, Cmnd 8354 (London, HMSO, 1981).
4 In fact, at any price the marginal revenue curve is always halfway between the price axis and the demand curve.
5 See chapters 2 and 3.
6 See H. Leibenstein, 'Allocative efficiency vs X-efficiency', *American Economic Review*, 56 (1966).

7   A. Gabor and C. W. J. Granger, 'Price as an indicator of quality: report on an enquiry', *Economica*, 33 (1966).

8   A. M. Alfred, 'Company pricing policy', *Journal of Industrial Economics*, 21 (1972).

9   Gabor suggests that more than 50 per cent of new products brought to the market result in losses. See A. Gabor, *Pricing: Principles and Practices* (London, Heinemann, 1977).

10 Joel Dean, 'Pricing pioneering products', *Journal of Industrial Economics*, 17 (1969).

11 See Gabor, *Pricing: Principles and Practices*.

12 Ibid.

13 Product analysis pricing, developed at Glacier Metals, is one such technique. See, e.g., F. Livesey, *Pricing* (London, Macmillan, 1976).

14 British Institute of Management, *Transfer Pricing* (London, BIM, 1971).

15 Price Commission, *Prices, Costs and Margins in the Distribution of Video Tape Recorders and their Accessories* (London, HMSO, 1979).

16 See, e.g., *Financial Times*, 11 December 1981.

17 Monopolies and Mergers Commission, *Trading Check Franchise and Financial Services* (London, HMSO, 1981).

18 See, for example, K. Coutts, W. Godley and W. Nordhaus, *Industrial Pricing in the United Kingdom* (Cambridge University Press, 1978).

19 Price Commission, *Recommended Retail Prices*, Report 25 (London, HMSO, 1977).

20 T. S. Ward, *The Distribution of Consumer Goods: Structure and Performance* (Cambridge University Press, 1973).

21 For a discussion of the various alternatives see, e.g., Gabor, *Pricing: Principles and Practices*, ch. 9, and Livesey, *Pricing*, ch. 12.

22 For a formal proof of this relationship see, e.g., D. Needham, *The Economics of Industrial Structure, Conduct and Performance* (London, Holt, Rinehart & Winston, 1978), p. 58.

23 Coutts, Godley and Nordhaus, *Industrial Pricing in the United Kingdom*.

24 R. L. Hall and C. J. Hitch, 'Price theory and business behaviour', *Oxford Economic Papers*, 2 (1939).

25 For a clear and comprehensive summary and discussion see D. Swann, *Competition and Consumer Protection* (Harmondsworth, Penguin, 1979).

26 J. D. Gribbin, 'The United Kingdom 1977 Price Commission Act and competition policy', *Antitrust Bulletin*, 23 (1978).

27 Most of the major studies are reviewed in, e.g., D. A. Hay and D. J. Morris, *Industrial Economics: Theory and Evidence* (Oxford University Press, 1979).

28 The details in this section are based on: Price Commission, *Imperial Tobacco Ltd – Cigarettes and Cigarillos*, HC 28 (London, HMSO, 1978/79).

7

Finance

Finance is required so that a firm may carry on its day-to-day operations and undertake investment projects. This chapter examines the sources of finance available to satisfy these needs. In general, the most appropriate form of finance depends upon the amount required, the time when it is required, the purpose for which it is required and the type of firm requiring it. Broadly, there are three sources of finance: internal funds, external long-term funds and external short-term funds. Each will be considered in its turn below.

The main types of institution providing these funds are shown in figure 7.1. *Short-term finance*, which may be regarded as funds required for up to three years ahead, relates to temporary working capital (i.e., funds needed for day-to-day activities), capital to meet seasonal fluctuations in activity, and funds for short-lived assets. In the medium term, up to ten years, funds are required for most plant and machinery and for overdraft financing. Over ten years, in the long term, funds are needed for buildings and financing acquisitions.

Equity finance, which also tends to be long-term, relates to an arrangement whereby providers of funds take an ownership stake in the business in return for taking a variable rate of return on their funds. *Long-term loans*, on the other hand, tend to be provided for a fixed rate of interest. The balance between loan and equity financing is of crucial importance for the firm and we shall return to it below.

Clearly, the sources of funds shown in the figure are many and varied, and care is needed in choosing which combination of them best meets the loan and equity needs of each particular firm. In general, the clearing banks and hire purchase companies and factoring companies, which buy debts, are better for short- and medium-term finance. The stock exchange and insurance and pension institutions tend to specialize in channelling long-term finance to companies, in the form of both equity participation and loans. In addition, a number of organizations provide funds for medium-

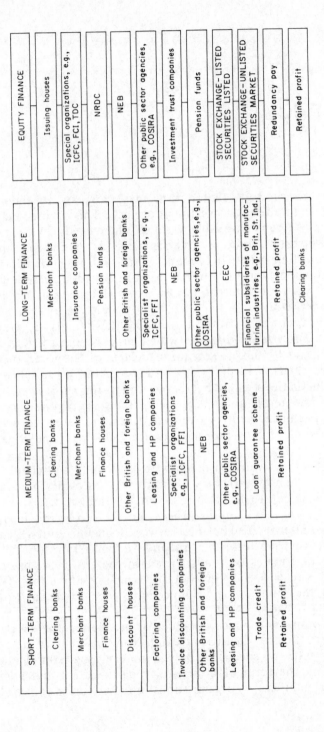

Figure 7.1 Sources of finance.

term, long-term and equity needs of firms, for example, the National Enterprise Board (NEB) and the Industrial and Commercial Finance Corporation (ICFC). The ICFC is a particularly important provider of finance for smaller firms and we shall return to it below.

The size of the firm is very important for the type of finance used. Some sources specialize in providing finance only for larger firms and these can be prohibitively expensive for the small firm. The consequence is that small firms have faced severe problems in obtaining external finance for growth purposes. As the success of smaller firms is crucial to the long-run success of the economy, we shall examine the long-run external financial sources available to smaller firms separately, after considering the general sources of such funds. This will be followed by a discussion of short-term financial sources. However, we begin with an examination of internal funds, which provide about three-quarters of the finance of both large and small firms.

INTERNAL FUNDS

Profits are the principal source of internal funds. Profit is defined as the surplus of revenue from a trading operation left over after the expenses incurred in employing factors of production have been met. It is important to understand from the outset that profits do not equal cash.

Calculations of profits are made at regular intervals. This arises from the need to provide regular financial reports in order to satisfy the requirements of the Companies Acts. In so doing the accountant matches the revenues of the period, usually one year, with the expenses of the period. It is unlikely that cash payments for factors of production or cash receipts for sales will fit neatly into the period, since in most industries there are standard credit periods; also, for example, the electricity bill for the last quarter may be received after the end of the financial year, so that cash has not been paid out at the year end. Even so, the revenues and expenses must be recognized, or accrued, to provide an accurate calculation of the profit for the year. Having said that, however, there are many different definitions of profit. The most appropriate one to use depends upon circumstances. These differences may be illustrated by examining the income statement of Imperial Group (table 7.1). The normal accounting definitions distinguish between gross and net profit. *Gross profit* is the excess of sales over the part of the cost of goods

Table 7.1   Imperial Group Ltd, income statement, 1980

		£m	£m
(1)	Sales		3,929.1
(2)	*less:* Wages and salaries	(509.0)	
(3)	Expense on materials, services, etc.	(3,212.7)	
(4)	Hire of plant and machinery	(11.7)	
(5)	Depreciation	(54.6)	
(6)	Audit fees	(1.3)	
(7)	Directors remuneration	(1.0)	
(8)			(3,790.3)
(9)	Group operating profit		138.8
(10)	*add:* Surplus on disposal of premises		2.5
(11)	Share of profits of associated companies		5.0
(12)	Investment income		33.5
(13)	Interest charges		(52.9)
(14)	Group net profit before taxation		126.9
(15)	Taxation		(46.1)
(16)	Group net profit after taxation		80.8
(17)	Minority interests		(0.3)
			80.5
(18)	Extraordinary items		11.6
(19)	Group profit attributable to the parent company, available for distribution		92.1
(20)	Ordinary dividends		(51.8)
(21)	Retained profit		40.3
(22)	Earnings per share after taxation		11.3p
(23)	Dividends per share		7.25p

Source: Imperial Group Ltd Annual Report and Accounts 1980, p. 22.

sold that is directly attributable to putting the goods in a saleable condition. The cost of goods sold is specified as the value of stock at the beginning of the period plus the cost of purchases (less returns), less the value of stock at the end of the period. While gross profit will be calculated for internal purposes, the Companies Acts do not require its publication. Hence, in the example it is not shown. *Net profit* is the surplus remaining after charging against gross profit all the expenses, including depreciation, properly attributable to the normal activities of the business. *Depreciation* is the allocation of the cost of an asset over its whole life; it measures the benefit from the asset used up each year. This benefit is deducted from profit as an expense. Depreciation does not involve the movement of funds. The funds have already moved when cash was paid to acquire the asset. Imperial Group's net profit before taxation is shown at line 14. From this figure taxation is deducted, and after adjusting for various other items the profit available for distribution to the owners is derived (line 19). Again, it must be borne in mind that the *retained profit* (line 21) does not take the form of pound notes lying around somewhere. Rather, it is a recognition of the owners' remaining claim on the business; and it will already have been used to acquire further assets or to increase working capital. The accumulated retained profits are shown in the balance sheet as *reserves* (line 14 in table 7.3). We discuss the balance sheet below after we have examined the various sources of finance.

The surplus gained on the firm's trading activities gives an indication of how well the firm is using its productive assets (line 9). However, for the economist the important figure is that for net output, or value added, which is the difference between sales and direct costs. His view of gross profit is thus closer to the accountant's net profit, as defined above. The economist's net profit is struck after deducting as expenses management salary payments, interest on borrowed funds (which excludes share capital) and any imputed rent on the buildings owned by the firm. In this way the economist endeavours to obtain a better view of the residue available to the owners of the company.

The answer to the question of what constitutes management salary depends on whether one takes the accountant's or the economist's standpoint. In many firms the directors receive no salary but are rewarded entirely in the form of directors' remuneration. The accountant is required by the Companies Act to regard this as profit. However, for the economist an accurate assessment of profit, which is the return for entrepreneurial activity, requires allowance for a managerial wage. This is a particular problem when comparing large and small concerns. The latter, for tax purposes, tend to class some of what would be considered as profit in a large firm as managerial salaries.[1]

Strictly speaking, the residue available to the providers of capital should be calculated after providing for replacement of fixed assets and stocks at current prices, which assumes that the firm is a going concern. Detailed discussion of this point is left to the section on inflation accounting in the next chapter. However, simply it may be taken that this means that historical cost depreciation provisions are inadequate in a time of inflation. Hence, if full allowance for inflation is made the profit available for distribution will be reduced.

The amount of funds distributed as dividends to shareholders will obviously affect the level of internally generated resources available for investment. Whether firms have or have not distributed sufficient dividends to owners in recent years has been the subject of some discussion. On the one hand, it has been argued that ordinary share prices have not kept up with inflation owing to insufficient dividends since 1969.[2] However, it has been forcibly suggested by Lawson and Stark that, on the contrary, too much profit has been distributed; this has led to an increase in long-term borrowing to pay for it. Such substitution of debt for equity capital is estimated to have accounted for about 38 per cent of the real decline in equity values between 1961 and 1978.[3] That the payment of excessive funds to shareholders and an increase in interest payments, occasioned by higher borrowing to finance dividends, leaves less for investment is clear. In the absence of any tax changes which remove the current bias against payments of dividends, and any change in practice to bar dividend payments on profits not adjusted for inflation, such a trend is likely to persist.

It is sometimes argued that one of the major advantages of the use of internal funds is that they are free from borrowing costs, since the firm does not have to pay interest on its own money. The argument is illusory: the opportunity cost of internal funds is the alternative earnings from the money if it were put to other uses, such as the purchase of securities or the buying of another firm. In some firms the rate of return on internally financed assets is so low that the firm would have done better to purchase stock exchange securities or other paper assets. Failure to recognize this point may result in bad investment decisions which do not reflect the true cost of capital. This point is discussed further in chapter 9.

LONG-TERM EXTERNAL SOURCES

For any firm seeking to raise long-term finance externally, the distinction between share and loan capital is important.[4] *Share capital*, as the name implies, is in the form of a share in the ownership or a prior right to a share of the profits of the firm. *Loan capital* is in the form of a prior right, both to interest and usually also over the assets of the firm, in the form of a mortgage or debenture. Share capital is never repayable except by permission of the High Court, though in quoted public companies it is marketable and is bought and sold on the stock exchange. Long-term loan capital is repayable, the period varying from about 10 to 50 years. Lenders cannot demand repayment before the 'term' of the loan, but are entitled to a fixed rate of interest, whether the firm is profitable or not. The security is usually marketable, but if the general level of interest rates increases the holder will receive less than the nominal value, owing to its fixed return. If the firm is unable to pay the interest, loan creditors have the right to put it into liquidation in order to recover their principal and interest from the proceeds of the sale of its assets.

Share capital may be of two kinds. *Ordinary share capital* carries a vote proportionate to the number of shares held and receives a dividend in the form of part of the residual income of the firm. *Preference shares* rarely carry a vote, but have as compensation a prior right to dividend and the residue of assets, should the company cease to trade, over the ordinary shares. Preference shares usually carry a fixed return, while ordinary shares receive a dividend only if there are adequate profits. To compensate for the risk of receiving nothing, the returns to ordinary shares are higher than to preference shares when profits are good.[5]

The relative proportion of each type of funding is of crucial importance for the rate of return on equity and the cost of raising additional capital. In the extreme, the very survival of the firm depends upon it. If a company is unable to meet interest commitments when profits are low, creditors may foreclose.

The *capital gearing ratio* of a company indicates the relative proportions of a company's variable interest and fixed-interest capital. The greater the proportion of fixed-interest capital, the more highly geared is the company. The simple gearing ratio for Imperial Group is shown in table 7.2 and may be considered to be low. Notice that reserves are included in the denominator, since they represent further investment in the business by the ordinary shareholders. However, such a ratio based on the book value of share and loan capital may give a misleading assessment of the extent to which management have been successful in maximizing the value of the shareholders' investment and thus minimizing the cost of raising extra capital.

A more appropriate definition of the gearing ratio is based on the market values of loan and share capital and includes total short-term borrowings ('market' gearing ratio in table 7.2). The reasoning behind this is as follows. According to economic theory, the profit-maximizing firm will continue to raise funds by means of fixed-interest securities until the rate of return from the marginal investment project, for which the funds are to be used, equals the rate of interest payable on the fixed-interest securities. However, in practice, since the rates of return on projects are uncertain, the firm will seek a margin of safety to prevent losses occurring, after interest is paid, if returns are low. Management will also try to increase the return to equity (lever it up) by using a proportion of lower-cost fixed-interest debt such that more profit is left after interest for each

Table 7.2 Imperial Group Ltd, capital structure and gearing ratio, 1980

$$\text{Simple 'book' gearing ratio} = \frac{\text{Debentures} + \text{preference shares}}{\text{Equity share capital} + \text{reserves}}$$

$$= \frac{£263.0\text{m} + 0}{£178.7\text{m} + £911.6\text{m}}$$

$$= 0.24$$

$$\begin{array}{l}\text{'Market' gearing ratio} = \\ \text{(at 31.10.80)}\end{array} \frac{\text{Total market value of debentures} + \text{total market value of preference shares} + \text{total short-term borrowings}}{\text{Total market value of equity shares}}$$

$$= \frac{£201.4\text{m} + 0 + £309.5\text{m}}{£539.8\text{m}^*}$$

$$= 0.95$$

$$\text{Interest cover} = \frac{\text{Net trading profit before interest and taxation}}{\text{Interest}}$$

$$= \frac{£179.8\text{m}}{£52.9\text{m}}$$

$$= 3.4 \text{ times covered}$$

*= 714,932 shares at 75.5p each.
Sources: Imperial Group Ltd Annual Report and Accounts 1980; *Financial Times; Stock Exchange Daily Official List.*

remaining shareholder than if a greater proportion of share capital were used. But, if the process of gearing-up is carried too far, and profits fluctuate, equity earnings will become too volatile, hence depressing share prices and reducing market capitalization. At the same time, the cost of debentures increases as the market demands a higher return to compensate for the increased risk of profits being inadequate to cover interest commitments. Thus, an assessment of gearing based on market value gives an accurate reflection of how well the management have performed in maximizing the shareholders' return.

The degree of riskiness in receiving debenture interest may be measured by the *interest coverage ratio*. The greater the excess of profits over debenture interest, the more secure debenture holders feel. In the case of Imperial Group the interest coverage ratio of 3.4 (see table 7.2) is quite comfortable. Clearly, the effects of different capital structures and different profit levels can be analysed by substituting different figures into this ratio.[6]

Short-term borrowings are included in the market gearing ratio as they too represent fixed-interest commitments of the firm which will affect the shareholders' return.

Besides considerations of gearing, the form that new finance will take is influenced by ruling market conditions, the existing structure of interest rates and taxation considerations. A time of historically very high interest rates is rarely the best time from the point of view of the firm since, once committed to raising loan or preference share finance, interest or dividends on these have to be paid regardless of future profitability or interest rates. But high nominal interest rates may not be a problem if real rates of interest are negative, as they have been in the recent past and are expected to continue. The raising of ordinary share capital is usually easier at times of good trade and high stock exchange values, and it is in times like that that the issue of shares tends to be over-subscribed. There may be other reasons for over-subscription, however, and we return to these below. Tax considerations are important in so far as they make it more or less costly to the firm to issue equity or loan capital. Current company taxation is biased against the payment of equity dividends, since it aims to encourage profit retention for investment.

A firm wishing to raise ordinary share capital generally does so through the New Issue Market of the stock exchange. This organization consists of a small group of issuing houses and merchant banks specializing in the issue of new share capital whose prime function is to act as an intermediary between those who wish to issue share capital and those who are willing to invest in share capital. They will usually advise on the best form of capital, work out a financial plan, make sure that the stock exchange regulations are complied with, arrange any underwriting that may be necessary[7] and lend the weight of the house's name and reputation to an issue.

There are seven main possibilities for the large firm wishing to make a new issue of shares:[8] issue by prospectus; offer for sale; private placing; stock exchange introduction; issue by tender; rights issue; and capitalization issue. With an *issue by prospectus* the issuing house undertakes to find subscriptions for the new issue of shares; with an *offer for sale*, an issuing house buys the shares from the company and offers them direct to the public. *Private placing* is a method by which an issuing house will sell shares through brokers or jobbers on the stock exchange and thence to private investors. The *stock exchange introduction* is a method by which the issuing house makes an application, on behalf of the shareholders, for the shares of the firm to be quoted on the stock exchange. This method does not result in any extra capital being raised. *Issue by tender* constitutes an invitation to the public to bid for shares above a minimum price which is based on the anticipated market price. In this way, the company should benefit by minimizing the difference between the ultimate market price and the issue price. The *rights issue* gives existing shareholders the opportunity to buy a new issue of shares at less than the anticipated market price. *Capitalization issues* (or bonus or scrip issues) do not raise any new funds but merely result from a rearrangement of the existing capital structure.

In terms of costs, offers and prospectus issues are the most expensive, followed by rights issues and private placings in order of decreasing cost. In 1978 it was estimated that to raise £2 million through ordinary shares would cost £152,900 (7.6 per cent of proceeds) by means of an offer or prospectus, £80,700 (4 per cent) by rights issue, or £52,700 (2.6 per cent) by means of a placing.[9] Hence, because of the high fixed-cost element (advertising costs, legal fees, etc.), offers or prospectus issues are not worthwhile for smaller sums. For many companies whose shares are widely held and quoted on the stock exchange, the rights issue is the favourite form of raising new finance since it is relatively inexpensive and reduces the likelihood of a change in the balance of control. Rights issues may also be a most attractive method of raising finance when a company is facing liquidity problems and is deterred from other sources of funds, such as debentures and bank loans, by their high cost.

Whether shareholders will take up a rights issue is another matter. Their decision should not be influenced by the relation of the issue price to the current market. To see why, consider two companies X and Y whose share prices currently stand at 50p each. Company X decides to raise a sum of money equivalent to one-eighth of its current market value. It offers shareholders one new share at 25p for every four already held. When the market has adjusted to the issue, the number of shares will have increased by 25 per cent and their price, the 'ex-rights' price, will have fallen to 45p ($(4 \times 50) + 25 \div 5$). A shareholder who held four shares now has five and the value of his total holding has risen to 225p. However, company Y decides to raise the same amount by offering one new share at $12\frac{1}{2}$p for every two held. The number of shares rises by 50 per cent and their 'ex-rights' price will fall to $37\frac{1}{2}$p ($100 + 12\frac{1}{2} \div 3$). A shareholder originally owning four now has six and the value of his total stake rises to 225p, as for company X. Hence, in theory at least, it does not matter what the issue price is, since the market will adjust the price of shares to reflect the rights issue. However, in practice, if the market considered that the future prospects for company X were poor and for company Y were good, the actual price for company X might be lower than the theoretical 'ex-rights' price while for company Y it might be higher.

The current economic recession has seen a big increase in the number of rights issues. What is interesting about this is that the companies raising finance in this way are not facing cash flow problems. It appears that these well-placed companies intend to invest overseas, owing to prevailing favourable interest rates and little sign of economic recovery in this country. For example, in September 1980 Rio Tinto Zinc raised £126 million primarily for overseas mining development. The reason that such companies have been able to raise finance relatively easily is that the institutions with regular funds to invest have a limited number of options open to them at the moment.

In talking about raising finance it has been implicitly assumed that the company obtains a price for its shares that accurately reflects its performance and prospects. In other words, it has been taken for granted that the market works efficiently. However, this may not be the case. If prices of the shares are revised upwards after issue, this implies a loss to the company when issue receipts are compared with the free market value of the share. It may be argued that such a market discount reflects an allowance for risk and uncertainty required to encourage investors to take up a large stock of shares in a relatively unknown company. But there is evidence to suggest that the levels of market discount, particularly in the case of placings, are much higher than appears necessary. In a study of 275 firms coming to the London New Issue Market between April 1965 and March 1971, it was found that the average discounts were as follows:[10]

Offers for sale	(172 firms)	8.88 per cent
Placings	(60 firms)	19.08 per cent
Tenders	(41 firms)	6.95 per cent
Others	(2 firms)	4.75 per cent

However, the degree of disparity is dependent on the volatility of the stock market at the time the issue was made, being most marked in rising and uncertain (bull) markets. In conditions of falling and uncertain (bear) markets no systematic relationship between method of issue and revealed market discount occurs.

It may be thought that on these figures the speculator can make a great deal of money by bidding for new issues. Unfortunately, this is unlikely to be the case, because anyone trying to buy issues that are 'cheap' will find that only a few shares will be available, since other investors will be doing the same thing.

When the above points are coupled with the finding that small firms are discriminated against by the financing institutions in terms of discount in certain market conditions, the efficiency of financial institutions is called into question. Further evidence for these shortcomings has been provided in another study,[11] which used the same data source as above, updated to 1975. By using the ratio of subscriptions for a given share (x^1) to the number of shares available (x) as an estimate of excess demand for the share, it was possible to assess the accuracy of pricing new shares by issuing houses.

The following equation was tested using regression techniques:

$$\log \frac{x^1}{x} = a + bD_r$$

where $\log \dfrac{x^1}{x}$ = logarithm to base 10 of the subscription rate;

D_r = revealed discount (calculated as in note 10);
a = constant
b = slope coefficient.

Under all market conditions together, the equation derived from the data was:

$$\log \frac{x^1}{x} = -2.666 + 0.032 D_r \quad \text{(no. of observations} = 297)$$

The same equation and other non-linear forms were used to examine the relationship in stable bull and bear markets. Bearing in mind the difficulties in classifying all market conditions as unambiguously stable, bull or bear, the analysis demonstrated that, no matter what the market conditions, there was a highly significant relationship between market discount and the subscription rate. Moreover, it was also found that favourable press comment increased the likelihood of a price rise after issue.

While private sector companies have a choice in their sources of long-term external funds, this is not the case for nationalized industries. These enterprises normally derive all their long-term external finance from the government. It may be argued that this means of funding produces an adverse effect on the performance of some nationalized industries as they become caught in a vicious circle of raising extra finance to cover high interest payments, and hence incur greater deficits. One method of relieving this problem has been to use public dividend capital (PDC), but as this too is provided by the government it may be regarded as a soft option, since if little profits are made then PDC does not need to be paid. Three nationalized industries have had PDC for at least a decade (British Steel, British Airways and Giro), and their dividend record has been anything but satisfactory. Recent attempts have been made to change the capital structure of some nationalized industries by injecting a substantial share of private ordinary share capital. The first industry to benefit in this way was British Aerospace, which in April 1981 became partly privately financed in a share issue that was heavily over-subscribed. In those, possibly less successful, nationalized industries where private share capital may not be appropriate, it has been suggested that the capital structure could be changed with the introduction of government preference shares and private variable interest debt.[12] These methods would relate the dividends payable to the performance of the industry and would remove some of the Treasury control over the nationalized industries, replacing it by private capital market discipline. This suggestion raises issues that are outside the scope of this chapter. Suffice it to say that it would require government commitment to the running of the industries as profitable commercial enterprises rather than as instruments of macroeconomic policy. Otherwise, there would likely be a return to the writing-off of debt payments to compensate industries for losses incurred as a result of being obliged to follow non-commercial practices. However, changes in the financing arrangements for nationalized industries appear to be needed to circumvent the undesirable effects of the government's external financing limits, which arise mainly from macroeconomic considerations.

THE BALANCE SHEET

Now that the various long-term sources of finance have been discussed, it is useful to examine the balance sheet of our example company, Imperial Group (table 7.3). The Companies Acts require businesses to publish a summary of their financial position at the end of each financial year, in order that owners and other interested parties can ascertain the use to which sources of funds have been put. Unlike the Sources and Applications of Funds Statement, which we shall examine in the next chapter, and which relates just to this year, the balance sheet represents the accumulated sources and uses of funds since the firm began to trade. In the balance sheet, sources are referred to as liabilities, that is, money owed by the business to the providers of funds. Uses of funds are assets. As the name 'balance sheet' suggests, liabilities must equal assets. This is because, from the dual aspect of accounting, when a firm receives funds it must automatically do something with them, such as putting them into the bank. Hence the funds received are both a liability and an asset. Contemporary practice shows the balance sheet in vertical form, as is shown here for Imperial Group. This contrasts with the traditional approach of showing liabilities on the left-hand side and assets on the right. It has the merits that funds for day-to-day activities, net working capital (line 8 = line 5 − line 6 − line 7), are grouped together, and that funds used to finance fixed assets and working capital are clearly shown.

Long-term external finance takes the form of ordinary shares (line 13) and loan capital (line 17). Notice that here there are no preference shares. Under the heading of reserves (line 14) there are five types. *Share premium reserve* represents the excess over nominal value received when new shares were issued. This amount may not be distributed to shareholders. *Revenue reserves* mainly represent accumulated undistributed profits. The retained profit for 1980 of

Table 7.3 *Imperial Group Ltd, balance sheet, 1980*

		£m	£m
	Assets		
(1)	Fixed assets		805.4
	Current assets		
(2)	Stock	483.3	
(3)	Debtors	378.5	
(4)	Cash and bank balances	20.9	
(5)		882.7	
	Current liabilities		
(6)	Creditors	(604.3)	
(7)	Proposed dividends	(32.2)	
(8)	Net working capital (line (5) — lines (6 + 7))		246.2
(9)	Goodwill arising on consolidation		353.2
(10)	Interest in associated companies		18.8
(11)	Investments		265.0
(12)	Total		1,688.6
	Financed as follows:		
(13)	Issued ordinary shares		178.7
(14)	Reserves		911.6
(15)	Shareholders' funds		1,090.3
(16)	Minority interest in subsidiaries		2.7
(17)	Loan capital		263.0
(18)	Short-term borrowings		309.4
(19)	Future taxation		23.2
(20)	Total		1,688.6

Source: Imperial Group Ltd Annual Report and Accounts 1980, p. 23.

£40.3 million (line 21 in table 7.1) is part of this figure. Imperial Group has also taken the unusual step of creating an *investment revaluation reserve*. Many firms do not revalue investments since, if they are in the form of marketable securities, the value may be quite volatile and it would therefore be misleading so to do. But it is common practice, particularly in times of high inflation, to revalue physical assets. This recognizes the increase in the owner's equity, but it *does not* contribute any funds to the firm. The revaluation surplus would be shown in a *fixed asset revaluation reserve*. Finally, in the case of a company such as Imperial Group, which has an ownership stake in other enterprises, a figure for the *share of associated companies' reserves* is included. It is worth reiterating that the reserves are a recognition of the owners' equity, and do not represent cash in a bank account. The funds they represent will have been incorporated into the assets and working capital of the business.

Short-term borrowings relate to bank loans and overdrafts outstanding for one year or less. Future taxation represents a source of finance since although the liability must be recognized it has not yet been paid out.

The use to which long-term funds have been put is demonstrated by fixed assets (line 1), which comprise buildings, plant and machinery; investments in marketable securities (line 11); interests in other companies (line 10); and goodwill (line 9), which represents the excess of the purchase price of subsidiaries over their value in the accounts.[13]

We now turn to examine the special financing problems faced by smaller firms. In the context of the economy as a whole, their needs are important, since future growth prospects may depend a great deal on this sector of industry.

LONG-TERM EXTERNAL SOURCES OF FINANCE FOR SMALLER FIRMS

The main problem in respect of finance for smaller firms is not really acquiring start-up capital but rather the inability to obtain sufficient funds to promote growth. This difficulty is not a recent phenomenon; it was highlighted as long ago as 1931 by the MacMillan Committee and has been subsequently discussed in the Radcliffe Report (1959), the Bolton Report (1971) and the Wilson Report (1980). As Martin Binks has summarized it, the problem is that: 'the smaller the firm, the larger the proportionate increase in capital base required to respond to an increase in demand, but the lower its ability to command loan and equity finance'.[14] This is because increases in demand for the firm's product tend to occur in discrete steps. If the firm is newly established, it lacks a track record of success to encourage individuals and institutions to provide funds. Similarly, such firms have been, until recently, just too small to take advantage of the equity finance-raising opportunities afforded by the stock exchange. In addition, particularly if they are trying to obtain loans from the clearing banks, smaller firms are likely to experience difficulties because they are in possession of little collateral or financial expertise.

Economists have shown concern for the problems of finance for small firms, because the restriction of growth so produced can have serious implications for employment, innovation, the ability to compete with foreign firms, the ability to counteract the undesirable effects of increasing industrial concentration and so on. The capital cost per job created tends to be lower in smaller firms than in larger ones. Smaller firms may provide 'seed-beds' for innovation and growth, as they are more flexible since they often possess less specific capital and labour. But this argument can be turned on its head, because, rather than being more flexible, when its existing markets decline the small firm may simply go out of business, as it is unable to offset losses in one area by gains elsewhere. This introduces arguments about birth and death rates, which are returned to below. Increasing concentration often produces undesirable side-effects, as many reports of the Monopolies Commission demonstrate: economies of scale may not be realized, consumers may have to pay higher prices, choice may be restricted, etc.; so that many mergers that produce increased concentration may be regarded as disappointing marriages.[15] Hence, there has been a movement towards the small-is-beautiful theme.[16]

However, it should be remembered that by no means all small firms are innovators or fast growers. They are in fact a very heterogeneous sector of the economy. It is even difficult to agree on what is a small firm and how big is the small firm sector. The Bolton Report was concerned with manufacturing firms employing fewer than 200 people. But within this size range the financial problems faced by firms are likely to vary substantially. At the top end of the range many firms may be subsidiaries of larger holding companies. Their financial problems may centre on competition with other subsidiaries for funds. At the bottom end of the range independent firms may struggle to obtain funds from the local bank manager.

The size of the small firm sector will be affected by birth and death rates. But the availability of such data is limited, and its interpretation difficult. Deaths may arise because firms leave the size classification owing to growth or merger, in addition to liquidation. So the sector may *appear* to be shrinking as a result of faster growth. Birth rates may be affected by differing company forms becoming more or less attractive. The age make-up of the sector is also important, since at any time there will be small, young, fast-growing firms requiring capital but lacking a track record and small, old, slow-growers requiring capital to replace worn-out machinery but lacking potential. Both face problems in raising finance, but of a different nature.[17]

It should be clear that such heterogeneity demands different forms of finance to satisfy the differing requirements of small firms. This means different and new institutions providing equity and loan capital, adjustments in the tax system and other forms of organization of the firm.

One of the most important financial institutions specializing in finance for smaller firms is the Industrial and Commercial Finance Corporation (ICFC). Set up in 1945 and reconstructed in 1973, it is 85 per cent owned by the London and Scottish clearing banks, the rest being owned by the Bank of England. About one-third of new funds advanced by ICFC are to new businesses, the remaining funds are to aid the expansion of existing firms. In 1980/81 ICFC helped finance 261 start-ups and advanced over £100 million of new long-term loans to 1,000 companies. At the end of that year 3,500 companies in total had outstanding loans from ICFC amounting to some £400 million. Funds are provided on both an equity and a loan basis, often to the same firm. As we have seen, it is necessary to strike a balance between equity and loan finance. There is well-known resistance to the holding of outside equity in small firms, while too much loan capital can be risky in terms of capital gearing ratios which are too high. As such, the ability to take both types of finance from the same source can be an advantage. ICFC has been particularly active in providing this type of combination of finance in cases of managers wishing to purchase the company for which they work (management buy-outs), where it is the dominant source of finance.

In addition to ICFC, a plethora of equity and loan institutions have been set up over the last 30 years. But relative to the needs of small firms the amount of funds actually provided has been fairly small.[18] The reasons are not hard to find. Some have minimum cut-off points (for example the NEB, before the setting up of its Oakwood Loan Finance subsidiary). Many institutions appear to be very slow at providing funds, while there also has been some hesitancy among small firms to approach the institutions. For those that do not deal exclusively with small firms, the disproportionately high cost of processing applications and the higher risk involved would lead them to prefer investment in larger projects. Any new institution would have to overcome these problems to be successful.

In respect of the tax system, a number of recent changes have sought to encourage investment in small firms. For example, the Budget of 1981 increased the VAT threshold and lowered the rate of corporation tax for small firms. But the small size of these changes was unlikely to produce significantly higher profit retentions, particularly when it is remembered that the amount of mainstream corporation tax actually paid is very small. If the tax system is to be of any significant use in helping small firms, it is likely to be through the encouragement of investment in small firms. For example, the 1981 Budget introduced a three-year trial of income tax relief on amounts up to £10,000 p.a. for investors in small companies; though this is still small-scale, and to date there have been problems in its practical use.

In respect of the third area, different forms of organization refer mainly to worker co-operatives. Co-operatives, of course, are not a new idea, but they have recently come to the fore as a means of providing job security and growth while being run in the interests of employees rather than of the providers of capital. Aside from a number of well publicized failures in the mid-1970s, over 300 small co-operatives have been formed in the last five years.

Co-operatives, in addition to being able to approach the government institutions already noted for funds, can obtain funds from the Co-operative Bank and Industrial Common Ownership Finance (ICOF). However, they are prevented under the Industrial Common Ownership Movement (ICOM) model rules from issuing voting shares, since this would be contrary to the whole ethic of producer co-operatives. Also, the principal of working in the interest of employees is likely to discourage the more conventional providers of finance, particularly if there exist other suitable outlets for their funds. The setting up and growth of banks specifically designed to help co-operatives, along the lines of those found in Spain and France, and the use of initially hybrid capitalist/co-operative structures with full common ownership achieved later, are two suggestions for the promotion of this form of organization.[19] The strengthening of the role of the Co-operative Development Agency, which is precluded from providing funds, in respect of its ability to persuade institutions of the benefits of financing this sector is also a possible solution. A second newer form of organization is the management buy-out, already referred to above.

Two recent developments in the provision of external funds for smaller firms have been the introduction of the Loan Guarantee Scheme and the Unlisted Securities Market. These are now discussed in detail.

Loan Guarantee Scheme
The Wilson Report recommended the establishment of a Loan Guarantee Scheme, which would remove the constraints imposed by security requirements which restrict bank lending to small firms. Under such a scheme, the government would underwrite loans provided by the financial institutions. The problems here relate to how to select suitable firms for investment, the accountability of public funds and the gaining of the co-operation of the financial institutions. The main issue is the amount of risk the clearing banks should have to bear. The most persuasive argument here appears to be to follow US practice and exempt the banks from bearing any of the risk. If it is the firms with the highest potential growth rates that stand to benefit most, then the scheme could be cost-effective in terms of the use of government funds. The evidence from the USA indicates that the banks there use the guarantee facility responsibly.[20]

An experimental Loan Guarantee Scheme was introduced in the 1981 Budget. It provided for a total funds availability of £50 million annually for three years, with government guaranteeing 80 per cent. The loans are to be for up to seven years, at the full commercial rate of interest plus a 3 per cent premium. The scheme as formulated appears to have a number of shortcomings: the amount of money available is small; the loan period is only medium-term; and, rather than being subsidized, the interest rate is punitive. However, in the first six months after its introduction the whole of the first year's allowance was committed to some 1,350 loans. The annual sum available was increased to £100 million. It is worth noting that only 58 per cent of these loans were for new firms, the rest went to expanding existing firms. The average loan size was £35,000.

Unlisted Securities Market (USM)
The introduction of the USM, towards the end of 1980, was made partially in response to the recommendations of the Wilson Committee and partially in response to the general lack of venture capital that is provided for existing firms to expand. By reducing the percentage of equity required to be in public hands, from 25 per cent for a full listing to 10 per cent on the USM, and by reducing the cost of entry, it is hoped that smaller and medium-sized firms will be able to raise external finance more easily than hitherto.[21]

The three ways of obtaining entry to the USM are, in order of increasing cost:

(1) by introduction (cost under £10,000);
(2) by placing (cost £40,000 plus);
(3) by offer for sale (cost about £65,000).

The most appropriate method depends upon the particular company. An introduction is possible when the company already has 10 per cent of its equity publicly owned, and it is the cheapest method since no marketing is required. In most circumstances, placing the shares with a sponsoring merchant bank, who will then sell the shares to its clients, will be the preferred route. Extra costs are incurred because of this and the need to provide an accountant's report on the company. If the company wishes to raise more than £3 million or expects the total market capitalization of the company to be above £15 million, then it should make an offer for sale of shares at a fixed price to the general public. Underwriting and advertising expenses are responsible for the higher cost of this method. Even so, advertising costs will still be substantially less than for a full listing, and a full listing may be obtained later by application for an introduction to listing once 25 per cent of its equity capital is publicly owned. This means of obtaining full listing is considerably less expensive than the usual method.

The emphasis of the USM on the regional stock exchanges means that locally well-known companies can take fullest advantage of their equity being marketable, their additional options in raising further finance, their ability to issue shares to acquire other companies, and the general enhancement to their reputations that appearing on the USM conveys. However, in order to be considered for the USM it is necessary that detailed financial statements and unqualified auditors' reports are available for the previous three years. Even so, investing in USM companies is probably a riskier venture than investing in the listed securities market, since newer smaller companies seeking growth are likely to be more volatile in their operations and less likely to have a well-established, coherent management control structure.

After its first year of existence, 76 companies were included in the USM. However, many of these companies were not raising new finance by entering it: prior to its opening, dealings had taken place elsewhere and were simply transferred to it. Most of the Market's membership reflects the relatively buoyant sectors of the economy at present, such as firms servicing North Sea oil installations, microelectronic technology, computer services and finance.

In addition to these two schemes, a number of larger firms, for example British Steel, have begun to provide funds to encourage small firms to locate in parts of large factories that have closed down.

Although at the time of writing it is a little too early to assess fully the success of these new schemes to help small firms, they have contributed to bringing Britain more into line with her competitors. Until the introduction of the Loan Guarantee Scheme, Britain lagged markedly behind Canada, France, West Germany, Japan, Netherlands and the USA, all of which made use of credit guarantee and subsidized loan and equity finance schemes for smaller firms.[22] In two of these countries – the USA and West Germany – over £1,000 million of funds were provided under these schemes in 1979. The Netherlands and Canada each made over £200 million available, while France and Japan contributed about £100 million and £35 million, respectively. In Japan the schemes were unusual in that 85 per cent of funds were for working capital, that is, short-term funds. Clearly, great emphasis is placed on this aspect of firms' financial needs in Japan. The next section examines short-term financing in detail. The French credit guarantee scheme is interesting as it provides for an interim period of a few years before interest payments begin, something in which the UK scheme is lacking.

SHORT-TERM EXTERNAL CREDIT

The importance of this aspect of company finance cannot be over-estimated. If the company has problems here it may not survive into the long term, even though it may appear to be profitable. This section examines the main sources of short-term external finance and then presents a short study of the experiences of a small company. The four main sources of short term finance are: trade credit, factoring, bank credit, and hire purchase and leasing.

Trade credit
Trade credit works in two directions: the firm gives credit to its customers (debtors), and it itself receives credit from suppliers (creditors). The length of these trade credit periods and the changes in them found in a particular firm may be explained by an examination of two distinct motives for extending trade credit: the 'transactions' motive and the 'financing' motive. The transactions motive produces a certain level of trade credit which exists merely as a consequence of doing business. The financing motive relates to that

proportion of trade credit that responds to economic stimuli, especially monetary policy (i.e., the relative difficulty in borrowing money and the level of the rate of interest).

For any particular company, the level of trade credit held for the transactions motive will be a function of the type of business environment the firm finds itself in. The three main determinants, apart from the actual level of sales, will be: seasonal effects in sales, long lead-times in the production process, and the extent to which cash discounts are used to encourage payment. Successful management of trade credit requires the company to minimize the adverse effects of these factors.

Seasonal effects in sales means that at certain times of the year sales will be substantially higher than at other periods. As a result, the total amount of credit given to customers will rise. Also, because more materials are required to meet the increased sales, ahead of the greater demand, the firm will have to take more credit from its suppliers. This will affect the balance sheet interpretation of debtor and creditor figures if firms in the industry have different financial year-ends but are otherwise the same. Many retail trades experience seasonalities in sales.

When the production period is long – over one year – as in ship-building, civil engineering and aero-engineering, then, in order to prevent profit and trade credit figures becoming irregular, a procedure is adopted of adding to the cost of work in progress on each contract an allowance for profit deemed to have been earned to date. As each stage of the work is certified as completed, the customer becomes liable for progress payments, usually 90 per cent of the contract value of the work completed, so smoothing out trade credit levels. The other 10 per cent is termed 'retention money', payable after the contract is completed.

Table 7.4   Rolls Royce (Aero-engines); an illustration of the effects of long lead-times

Financial year	Orders (£m)	(% change)	Inventories (£m)	(% change)	Progress payments (£m)	(% change)	Turnover (£m)	(% change)	Cash (£m)	(% change)
1976	915	18.1	368.1	15.6	95.4	16.6	620.2	3.0	0.6	−53.8
1977	935	2.2	372.9	1.3	89.6	−6.1	703.9	13.5	16.8	280.0
1978	1,378	47.4	441.0	18.3	129.6	44.6	763.0	8.4	59.8	356.0
1979	1,949	41.4	631.9	43.3	173.4	33.8	847.9	11.1	15.1	−74.7
1980	2,160	10.8	871.0	37.8	228.2	31.6	1,258.4	48.4	5.6	−62.9

Source: Rolls Royce (Aero-engines) Annual Reports and Accounts, 1975–80.

The effects of long-term contracts may be illustrated by the example of Rolls Royce (Aero-engines), as shown in table 7.4. In 1978 the company experienced almost a 50 per cent increase in orders. From this date progress payments increase rapidly, and in the following year inventories begin to reflect the effects of the increased amount of work undertaken However, it is not until two years after the increase in orders that turnover rises significantly. The changing cash position illustrates the effect of having to finance increased purchases of materials before cash is received from customers. Though not represented in the table, the annual report of the company shows corresponding increases in creditors and debtors over the period, with progress payments clearly ironing out violent fluctuations in these variables.

The extent to which cash discounts for prompt payment are granted is often based on the traditional trading arrangements of an industry, although there may be wide variations within the industry. For example, in the textile industry, among those firms giving a discount, reductions of between 1 and 5 per cent for payment within seven days are offered. Otherwise, settlement of the invoice within 35 days is expected, when no discount will be given. In the electronics industry, discounts range from 2 per cent for payment within seven days to 5 per cent for payment within 30 days. In any case, settlement is required within 45 days.[23] But textiles companies are more disposed to offering discounts than are electronics firms (95 per cent of the former as against 35 per cent of the latter).

However, in deciding whether or not to take a discount it is necessary to examine the effective return from the discount relative to the return from the alternative uses to which cash may be put. The effective returns from discounts may be calculated and compared by expressing their value in terms of annual interest rates. To take the example of trading terms of a 3.75 per cent discount for payment within seven days or settlement within 45 days, and assuming full discount is allowable for payment within ten days, as is normal practice, the maximum annual effective return would be:

$$\frac{3.75}{(100-3.75)} \times \frac{365}{45-10} = 40.6 \text{ per cent.}$$

If we assume that payment may be made in 75 days, one month after the due date, without affecting supplies, the return from taking the discount becomes:

$$\frac{3.75}{(100 - 3.75)} \times \frac{365}{75 - 10} = 21.9 \text{ per cent.}$$

If it is assumed that the customer has to draw on an overdraft facility or forgo a return from another investment in order to take the discount, at a cost of 22 per cent, then figure 7.2 enables decisions to be made about whether or not to take the discount.

In the example, it is always worthwhile taking the discount if payment would normally be made in up to 75 days. It is left to the reader to work out the best decision for other terms of payment.

Clearly, the effective return to the customer and cost to the supplier of taking and giving cash discounts is an important aspect of trade credit management. Problems arise in adapting cash discount terms to changing circumstances, such as customers' resistance to changing traditional methods, the cost of continually reprinting invoices and the reaction of competitors.

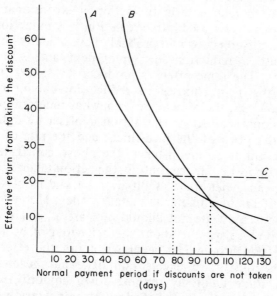

Figure 7.2   The decision to take a cash discount. Curve A, terms 3¾%, 10 days; curve B, terms 2½%, 38 days; curve C, alternative cost or return, 22%.

Source: adapted from S. Goddard and S. Jay, 'Medium-sized companies and the cash discount trap', *Accountancy* 91 (1980).

The extent to which a company has been successful in controlling its trade credit will be examined in the next chapter. One of the biggest problems to look for is evidence of over-trading, or expansion to the point that short-term commitments exceed liquid assets or the ability to meet these payments. Budgeting is one way of avoiding these problems and will be considered in chapter 10. But, over-trading may go undetected by the reader of accounts because of the phenomenon known as 'window dressing', whereby companies manipulate current assets and liabilities to present a better picture of liquidity than actually exists.

The second aspect of trade credit, the financing motive, has attracted attention because of the argument that it 'supplements capital market credit in a manner that presumably reduces the efficiency of any given amount of aggregate monetary control'.[24] In other words, in conditions of tight monetary policy, trade credit provides a means by which money is transferred from economic entities that have idle liquid balances to entities that need them. However, this is not necessarily the case, as can be seen by an examination of how a net trade credit-giver finances it.[25] If the method used to make up the excess of trade credit given over trade credit taken is to reduce cash, the action is expansionary, since an amount of money is released into circulation.[26] A reduction in stocks to finance the difference would probably have a depressing effect on prices or cause a reduction in employment and would thus be contractionary. The same effect is produced by selling fixed assets. However, if the firm chooses to reduce investment holdings or increase borrowings, the effects are somewhat indeterminate, as the direct expansionary effect of this action is offset by indirect reper-cussions on the price of the investment and the rate of interest. If the firm is a net trade credit-taker, the above conclusions will be precisely the opposite. Hence, only if the action taken is to pass idle cash balance can a net trade credit-giver be said to offset the con-tractionary effects of a tighter monetary policy. Moreover, since all takers of trade credit are not illiquid, nor are all givers very liquid, it is necessary to be specific about the behaviour of both givers and takers before conclusions can be drawn about the effects of trade credit. Givers must have excess liquidity and must finance the extension of trade credit by running down liquidity, while takers use the funds to increase inventories, for monetary policy to be frustrated.

A number of studies both in the USA and the UK have examined the effects of inter-firm movements of net trade credit in reducing the effects of a tight monetary policy. Space permits only the examination of UK studies. Brechling and Lipsey[27] concluded that such movements did frustrate monetary policy. However, their study used aggregate data, which were biased towards the few large companies at that time publishing turnover figures. Whittington[28] examined whether more liquid companies gave relatively more net trade credit in monetary 'squeeze' years than would be expected in monetary 'ease' years, and found little evidence to support his hypothesis. David and Yeomans,[29] in their study of whether large firms used their market power to lean on small firms or vice versa, similarly attempted to distinguish behaviour in 'ease' or 'squeeze' years. They conclude that there is a tendency for smaller firms to be more adversely affected by tight monetary policy than are larger companies, since the former display an increase in net trade credit given between 'ease' and 'squeeze' years while the latter do the opposite. However, both the Whittington and Davis and Yeoman findings depend crucially on the classification of years into 'ease' and 'squeeze'. Since whether a particular year is classified as one or the other depends upon the method chosen, the findings of these studies must be treated with caution. The effect of trade credit in frustrating monetary policy must, therefore, still be regarded as unclear.

Factoring and bank credit
One of the ways in which a company can reduce its trade debtors is by resorting to factoring. The principle is simple: the firm sells its trade debts to a factor; the factor then takes over the responsibility for the collection of the debt. By instantly providing up to 80 per cent of invoice value, the firm has the advantage of liberating the cash tied up in debtors. Liquidity is thus increased, and the dependence on outside resources is reduced. However, many firms are dissuaded from resorting to factors because they regard interest at rates in excess of bank overdraft rates, in addition to servicing fees, as too expensive. In addition, many companies fear, wrongly it seems, the loss of customers if this method of debt collection is used. Factoring services have recently succeeded in altering their image from the 'heavies' in debt collection to the providers of credit control facilities, particularly to smaller companies with limited skills and resources. By providing computer facilities, guidance on sales ledger procedures and payment collection methods and information on credit ratings of customers, they are able to prevent firms from getting into difficulties in the first place.

The use of factoring has also increased in the current economic climate of recession, with clearing banks becoming more involved. This has had a beneficial side-effect on companies with bank loans, who under the terms of the loans had previously been precluded from factoring debts.

The bank's role here reflects its traditional one as a provider of short-term funds. The main disadvantage of the traditional bank overdraft is its relatively short duration, although once a facility is granted it is seldom withdrawn. But the bank usually wants to know what the money is for; the bankers are not happy about lending for long-term projects. The fear of withdrawal of an overdraft and its short-term nature in general make it a bad form of finance for anything requiring funds for longer than a year. The behaviour of the UK banks in this respect is in marked contrast to that of banks in West Germany and Japan. Average formal terms of loans are two and a half years in UK, seven years in West Germany and 15 to 20 years in Japan. Not too surprisingly, bank loans to business averaged 15 per cent of gross national product (GNP) between 1974 and 1978 in Japan, 8 per cent in West Germany and only 3 per cent for the same period in UK. The differences between West Germany and UK are also apparent in respect of bank lending to small firms, as noted in an earlier section. Even when differences in population and GNP are taken into account, bank advances to small businesses in West Germany are still 50 per cent greater than in the UK. It has been argued that some of the reasons for this difference are over-centralization, lack of flexibility, failure to distinguish between the needs of individuals and small firms, and reluctance of UK banks to take risks compared with their counterparts in West Germany.[30] The case for a change in the banking system, from a bias towards short-term loans to consumers towards longer-term loans for firms, has been most forcibly argued by Lever and Edwards[31] as a means of lifting UK performance up to the level of West Germany and Japan. But the signs are not too hopeful, with clearing banks now competing more strongly with building societies in the provision of house purchase finance.

Differences in the use of bank credit by large and small companies may be discerned by examining table 7.5. Clearly, while smaller companies make extensive use of bank loans − 50 per cent of smaller firms in the Wilson Committee sample − far more reliance is placed on having cash-in-hand than in larger companies. This distinction has important implications for trade credit management, as we have seen.

Table 7.5   *Short-term liquidity of small and large firms compared, 1975*

Size firm	(1) Cash and short-term deposits (£bn)	(2) Bank overdraft and loans (£bn)	Ratio (1) ÷ (2) (%)
Smaller	1.2	1.3	96
Medium–small	0.6	2.0	31
Large	4.0	7.7	52

Source: Committee to Review the Functioning of Financial Institutions (Wilson Committee), *Evidence on the Financing of Industry and Trade*, vol. 3 (London, HMSO, 1978).

Hire purchase and leasing

Hire purchase is rarely used by large companies, but it is frequently a feature of small firms' purchases of plant and machinery. It is particularly used by small, rapidly growing concerns who may find it difficult to arrange a bank loan.

Some appreciation of the significance of hire purchase as a form of company finance may be obtained from an examination of table 7.6. First, it is clear that new hire purchase credit extended each year by retailers and finance houses for consumers is far greater than new credit extended to companies. Second, the role of retailers in providing hire purchase funds is probably overstated, since the figures for finance loans exclude agreements block-discounted with

Table 7.6   *Hire purchase agreements and bank loans compared (£ millions)*

Year	(1) Amounts out- standing	HIRE PURCHASE New credit extended (2) by finance houses to consumers*	(3) To companies	(4) By retailers to consumers	BANK LOANS Amounts outstanding (5) Persons	(6) Companies†	(7) Total
1978	6,336	2,156	1,419	2,435	5,848	29,306	35,154
1979	8,116	2,611	1,912	2,823	7,504	34,234	41,738
1980	9,209	3,006	1,794	2,939	9,074	41,298	50,372

* These agreements are regulated under the Consumer Credit Act 1974.
† Excludes financial companies and includes local government. Figures for gross amounts of bank loans extended are not available.
Source: Financial Statistics (August 1979; August 1981).

finance houses by retailers. (Block discounting arises when retailers take on small debts and handle the paperwork up to the point where the figure reaches a total of about £5,000, when the block of debts is taken over by a hire purchase company.)

When comparison is made with the amount of bank loans outstanding, it is seen that hire purchase is indeed a minority provider of short-term finance to companies. This is also confirmed by the survey of small firms in the service industry reported by the Wilson Committee.[32] Whereas 71 per cent of the 299 firms interviewed had bank loans, only 15 per cent had loans from hire purchase and leasing companies.

The lease-or-buy decision will be discussed in chapter 9. The decision to lease, say, equipment, which commits the firm to regular payments for a defined period, depends on an assessment of the advantages of capital economy and the possibilities of earning profit from the equipment weighed against the disadvantages of not owning the machinery. Although with rentals the total cost can be charged against tax, with leasing, since the leasing company owns the equipment, the lessee cannot charge wear-and-tear allowances. But leasing has the advantage of ameliorating the problem of obsolescence of machinery. This may be useful, for example, in the case of video-game machines, which rapidly change fashion. Other advantages are the freeing of bank overdraft and working capital for normal operating needs, easier budgeting, and the fact that assets earn their keep while the firm is paying for them.

Three other forms of short-term finance may be mentioned briefly: bills of exchange, borrowing from individuals, and sales of assets. Bills of exchange are fairly common in the export trade and in some domestic trades, where stock purchases are an important part of total costs, but are rarely used in manufacturing industries. Borrowing from individuals is a frequent source of finance in small firms and may be a way of easing short-term liquidity problems without affecting the controlling interests in the company. By subsequently converting the loan to equity, a director can increase his ownership stake in the company. Bank managers appear to be unhappy about the appearance of director's loans on a balance sheet, as they may present a misleading impression of the true liquidity position. Assets may be sold if they are no longer required, or sold and leased back if the company faces liquidity problems. It is necessary to assess carefully the advantages of raising cash in this way as opposed to other means. The method is largely restricted to buildings, since these are the most readily saleable. As mortgages on industrial property are not common and are often difficult to obtain, sale and leaseback may be more practical than attempting to finance the continued ownership of the property.

Case study
In order to appreciate the points that have already been made about the importance of short-term finance, consider the experiences of a small company.[33]

Company A is a two-man partnership employing three people in addition to the partners. The business is primarily involved in servicing equipment in certain sections of the motor trade in northern England. The firm was established in 1976 after both partners had been employees in the same field. Annual turnover in 1980 was approximately £75,000. The cost of the company's services are based on a call-out charge plus materials and labour costs payable if a minimum number of hours is exceeded. Terms for payment of invoices are 30 days with $2\frac{1}{2}$ per cent discount for prompt payment.

In 1980 the company faced cash flow problems which resulted from the difficulties in obtaining payments from customers, particularly large customers with many branches, who themselves were experiencing the effects of an economic recession. The company found it difficult to avoid having a trade-credit-given period longer than its trade-credit-taken period. This was the result of an inability to pass on increasing trade-credit-given periods to suppliers, since the major component supplier was able to exert pressure for payment. Also, payment for petrol, the largest single expense, was unavoidably on a very short-term basis.

The company was reluctant to use factoring to solve its problems because of the high cost and the possibility of driving customers away to competitors or driving them out of business altogether. The firm decided to try to pinpoint the worst offenders so as to deal with them severely.

Meanwhile, the extension of bank overdraft facilities, which were recognized as being expensive, was judged to be the most appropriate means of alleviating cash flow problems, particularly as the bank manager took a sympathetic view of matters. In addition to increasing working capital in this way, the company sought to reduce cash outgoings. This could be achieved either by reducing the miles travelled to service equipment or by revising the call-out rate structure. More detailed route planning could reduce wasted mileage, while differential mileage rates or demanding cash for call-out with the balance to be paid in the usual period could be an improvement.

A number of companies, not just this one, have argued for changes in the payment methods of value added tax (VAT) as a means of improving short-term finances. However, VAT assessments are based on invoice values. Assessments based on cash received would be open to widespread fraud and are thus administratively undesirable. There is also doubt whether extending the period of grace for VAT payments, which currently produces a 'VAT credit period' of about six weeks, would be administratively possible, but it may provide a 'once-and-for-all' alleviation from cash flow problems. As things stand an otherwise profitable business could be faced with liquidation owing to an inability to meet tax charges.

Possibly the most promising approach is the one requiring the most entrepreneurial skill: that is, to develop other options. Company A has achieved this by purchasing secondhand equipment, servicing and reconditioning it and then reselling it. By offering cash-only terms liquidity has been improved. The expansion of this side of the business is seen as important, since such machines have a competitive edge against new machines with increasingly cost-conscious customers. It also aids stock control through the incorporation of stock items into machines during the reconditioning process.

NOTES

1 For further discussion see J. Bates, 'Some problems in the interpretation of the accounts of unquoted companies', *Business Ratios* (Spring 1968).

2 B. Moore, 'Equity values and inflation: the importance of dividends, *Lloyds Bank Review* (July 1980).

3 G. H. Lawson and A. W. Stark, 'Equity values and inflation: dividends and debt financing', *Lloyds Bank Review* (January 1981).

4 Whether the firm is a sole trader, a partnership or a limited liability company really matters only in so far as it influences the sources of the funds. For a discussion of these different forms of company see, e.g., F. Wood, *Business Accounting*, vols 1 and 2, 3rd edn (London, Longman, 1980).

5 For further discussion of the different types of shares and loan capital see for example, R. J. Briston, *The Stock Exchange and Investment Analysis*, 3rd edn (London, Unwin, 1975), part II. For a more advanced treatment see G. A. Lee, *Modern Financial Accounting*, 3rd edn (London, Nelson, 1981).

6 See Briston, *Stock Exchange and Investment Analysis*, ch. 11, for an example.

7 Underwriting is simply a guarantee by a financial institution to take up any part of an issue that is not bought.

8 For a full discussion of the process of raising share capital see Briston, *Stock Exchange and Investment Analysis*, ch. 3.

9 Committee to Review the Functioning of Financial Institutions (Wilson Committee), *Evidence on the Financing of Industry and Trade*, vol. 3 (London, HMSO, 1978).

10 E. W. Davis and K. A. Yeomans, *Company Finance and the Capital Market*, University of Cambridge, Department of Applied Economics, Occasional Paper 39 (1974). The discount is calculated on the assumption that the 'correct' valuation of a company's newly issued shares is the average closing price of the first five dealing days after the issue. This price is then compared with the issue price after adjustment for any change in the general level of share prices in the industry to obtain the 'revealed market discount'.

11 R. Buckland, R. J. Herbert and K. A. Yeomans, 'Price discount on new equity issues in the UK and their relationship to investor subscription in the period 1965–75', *Journal of Business Finance and Accounting*, 8 (1981).

12 See S. Lumby, 'New ways of financing nationalised industries', *Lloyds Bank Review* (July 1981).

13 For a detailed discussion of the preparation of balance sheets see for example Wood, *Business Accounting*, vol 1, ch. 6, or for a more advanced treatment, G. A. Lee, *Modern Financial Accounting*, 3rd edn (London, Nelson, 1981).

14 Martin Binks, 'Finance for expansion in the small firm', *Lloyds Bank Review* (October 1979).

15 Strong evidence to support this view is contained in G. Meeks, *Disappointing Marriage: A Study of the Gains from Merger*, Department of Applied Economics, University of Cambridge, Occasional Paper 51 (1977).

16 See the classic work by E. Schumacher, *Small is Beautiful* (London, Blond and Briggs, 1973). The ideas have been developed further in G. McRobie, *Small is Possible* (London, Jonathan Cape, 1981).

17 P. S. Johnson, 'Policies towards small firms: time for caution', *Lloyds Bank Review* (July 1978).

18 Some examples are Technical Development Capital (TDC), Council for Small Industries in Rural Areas (COSIRA), National Research Development Corporation (NRDC), National Enterprise Board (NEB), Scottish Development Agency (SDA), and Welsh Development Agency (WDA). The Wilson Report also proposed the setting up of Small Firms Investment Companies (SFIC) and an English Development Agency (EDA). The reader is referred back to figure 7.1 for an indication of their lending patterns.

19 See N. Wilson and J. Coyne, 'Worker co-operatives and the promotion of co-operative development in Britain', *Industrial Relations Journal*, 12 (1981).

20 For a discussion of the operation of the US Small Business Administration see P. J. Hutchinson, 'Financial assistance to small firms: the American experience', *Nat West Bank Review* (November 1978).

21 See J. Shaw, 'The how and why of the USM', *Accountancy*, 92 (1981), 99–100.

22 Economists Advisory Group, *The Promotion of Small Business: A Seven-Country Study* (London, Shell UK, 1980).

23 These findings are reported in S. Goddard and S. Jay, 'Medium-sized companies and the cash discount trap', *Accountancy*, 91 (1980), 135–7.

24 R. A. Schwartz, 'An economic model of trade credit', *Journal of Financial and Quantitative Analysis*, 9 (1974).

25 The discussion that follows is based upon C. R. Myers, 'Comment: an economic model of trade credit', *Journal of Financial and Quantitative Analysis*, 12 (1977).

26 The company must do something by definition.

27 F. P. R. Brechling and R. G. Lipsey, 'Trade credit and monetary policy', *Economic Journal*, 73 (1963).

28 G. Whittington, *The Prediction of Profitability and Other Studies of Company Behaviour*, University of Cambridge, Department of Applied Economics Occational Paper 22 (1971).

29 E. W. Davis and K. A. Yeomans, *Company Finance and the Capital Market* (Cambridge University Press, 1974).

30 See, e.g., G. Bannock, 'The clearing banks and small firms', *Lloyds Bank Review* (October 1981) for discussion.

31 H. Lever and G. Edwards, 'Why Germany beats Britain', *The Sunday Times*, 2 November 1980.

32 Wilson Committee, *Evidence on the Financing of Industry and Trade.*

33 This example is taken from M. Wright and M. Jarrett, 'Will small be beautiful in the 80s?', *Accountancy*, 92 (1981).

8

Assessing Performance

The method used for assessing performance depends on the objectives of the various interested parties. While management is required to assess performance in order to exert internal control, shareholders want to know if it is still worthwhile holding shares in the business; employees need to know if they are likely still to have a job in the near future; the Inland Revenue need to calculate their tax demands; and society at large need to know about the company's progress because of consequences for employment, social services, rates revenue, balance of payments, etc., should it fail.

In this chapter the measurement of performance by outside interested parties is discussed, using illustrative data from the annual reports and accounts of Imperial Group Ltd. Internal assessment of performance and the associated control implications are covered in chapter 10. The Companies Acts require the publication of certain data which are intended to inform the owner of the company what has happened to the funds he has invested. The basis for this is the traditional stewardship function of accounting. It takes its form in the presentation and verification of the balance sheet and profit and loss account, which we examined in the previous chapter. However, in more recent years a need has become evident for more than just a straightforward recording function to be represented in the annual report. The emphasis has shifted to assessing how well the company has used the owner's funds, whether it will continue in business, and whether it is still worthwhile investing in the company.

The user of the accounts may obtain a picture of the state of the company by expressing information in the balance sheet and profit and loss account in ratio form; that is, for example, comparing the profits earned by the company with the resources used to produce the profits (the assets). The use of this technique is described in the next section, with a discussion of the problems of interpreting the ratios so obtained, in particular those related to inflation accounting and multiple products. While ratio analysis can be a very useful technique, it does not tell the whole story of company performance.

Many companies publish additional statements of value added and source and application of funds. The interpretation of these reports is discussed in subsequent sections. Once these various techniques for appraising the financial state of a company have been presented, it is possible to examine factors that determine corporate insolvency and company failure — a pertinent issue in current economic conditions. However, it must be remembered that not all information about a company's performance is quantifiable, for example, the state of industrial relations. Hence, a discussion of non-financial factors is included. The chapter ends with a consideration of the question of disclosure of information: what further information should be disclosed to enable interested parties to obtain a better view of the economic position of the firm, and what factors govern whether such information is published.

RATIO ANALYSIS OF COMPANY ACCOUNTS

If we are told that Imperial Group made a profit for some year of £100 million, this really says little about its performance. Apart from the problems of definition (which we discussed in the previous chapter), it is necessary to know what resources have been used to produce the profit, whether it is better or worse than in previous years, and how it compares with other firms in the same industry or with alternative opportunities for the shareholder to invest funds. In addition, as we also saw in chapter 7, profit is not the same thing as cash. The firm may appear to be highly profitable, but if it runs out of cash it may be forced into bankruptcy. Hence, in ratio analysis of company accounts we require systematic examination of both profitability and liquidity. These two sub-headings may be broken down further, into profitability of operations and profitability for the owner;[1] and into short-term and long-term liquidity. As a complement to the analysis of accounts on these bases, there is also the question of productivity — in particular, labour productivity.

Profitability of operations may be examined by use of a pyramid of ratios, as shown in figure 8.1. The rationale behind this is as follows. Starting from an overall view of profitability, at the top of the pyramid, which is defined as the ratio of operating profit to operating assets, a detailed view of the determinants of this figure may be built up. How far down the pyramid the external analyst will be able to go depends on the disclosure policy of the company. By using the supplementary notes to the accounts it should usually be

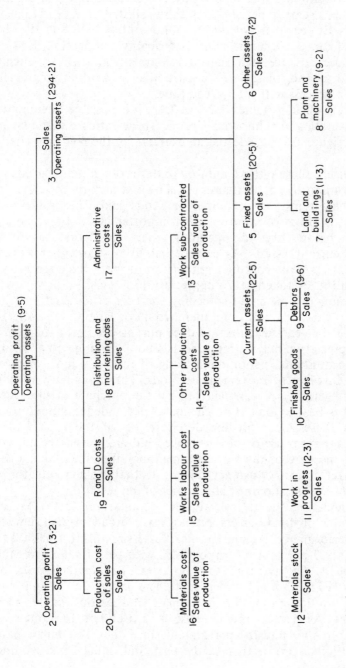

Figure 8.1   *An example pyramid of ratios. All figures in brackets are*
percentages and relate to Imperial Group Ltd for 1980.

Source: H. Ingham and L. Taylor Harrington, *Interfirm Comparisons* (London, Heinemann,
1980), pp. 20–1.

possible to obtain the first nine ratios (which are numbered on the chart). In the case of Imperial Group this is all that may be obtained. For Rolls Royce, it is possible to obtain ratios 1–12 and 19. The disclosure of this extra information is probably a reflection, first of the importance of research and development in the aero-engine industry and second, of the size, in particular, of work-in-progress in a production process with a long lead time.

By referring back to tables 7.2 and 7.11, it is possible to compute the relevant ratios for Imperial Group. These ratios are shown in brackets in figure 8.1. It is left as an exercise for the reader to check the figures.

In computing these ratios a number of definitional points needs to be borne in mind. First, all figures are shown at historic cost, that is, the cost when items were acquired or goods sold. The problem of historic cost in times of inflation is an important issue to which we shall return below. Second, operating assets are defined as fixed assets plus current assets less current liabilities – in other words, productive assets plus working capital.[2] Third, both fixed assets and operating profit are taken net of depreciation.

Depreciation is a means of spreading the cost of an asset over its useful life; if this were not done there would be large fluctuations in profit figures in years when assets were purchased. From this point of view, depreciation may be regarded as a bookkeeping entry, arising from the accountants' periodic matching of revenues and expenses. It does not involve the movement of funds. The funds have already been moved when cash was paid out on the purchase of the asset. However, it is best to look at profit figures net of depreciation provisions, since these allow for the deterioration of the capital of a business either from use or obsolescence, and are considered a more appropriate measure of the surplus remaining after 'maintaining the business intact'.[3] For consistency this means that the denominator in the profits-to-assets ratio must also be net of depreciation.

After calculating the ratios, we have to interpret them. As has been said, the profits-to-assets ratio gives a broad overall view of company performance. As one means of assessing this it is helpful to compare the 9.5 per cent return for 1980 with performance over the preceding years. The average return on assets for Imperial Group for the period 1971–80 is 11.4 per cent. The impression is that the company is not doing so well as in the past, and reasons for this need to be sought. As part of this exercise it is useful to find out how other firms in the industry performed, since they too might have experienced lower profits than in the past. Individual firms can find out about this by subscribing to Inter-Firm Comparisons, where, in exchange for supplying their own information, they receive comparative data for other anonymous companies in the industry.[4] It is necessary to compare performance within the same industry in order better to compare like with like. For the outside observer, unable to draw on the data provided by Inter-Firm Comparisons and incapable of constructing his own series, it is necessary to resort to other published sources, such as the data provided by Department of Industry, an example of which is shown in table 8.1. The problems with this method of comparison are, first, that the latest Department of Industry data available are three years old, because of the time taken to compile them; second, the industry groupings used may not be directly comparable with the markets in which the firm in question operates. The rate of return on assets in 1977 on the same basis as the data in table 8.1 for Imperial Group is 11.6 per cent. Comparing this figure with the Department of Industry data helps us to see how well the company was doing comparatively in that year, but it is of little use for 1980 and current decisions. However, there is another serious problem in that Imperial Group has interests in food, drink, tobacco and paper industries. Comparison of the Group's overall profitability figure with any of these four figures in the Department of Industry data would tell us little. What is required are data for the Group broken down by each division. The Group produces these data and they will be examined below.

Moving down the pyramid, the profits-to-sales ratio tells us something about the profit margin, that is the mark-up on costs. The sales-to-assets ratio (often termed the capital turnover ratio) gives some indication of the utilization of assets. On the tier below these two, the ratios of costs to sales help to pinpoint where costs are too high (or possibly sales revenue too low). On the other side, the balance of short-term and long-term assets to sales may be determined. Of particular importance here are the debtors-to-sales ratio (trade credit ratio) and the stock-to-sales ratio. The importance of the former has already been seen in the previous chapter and the points made there apply equally to the latter. In brief, these two ratios give some indication of the amount of cash that is tied up in relatively illiquid areas. If, in comparison with the past or with similar companies, these ratios are deemed to be too high, the management will wish to seek remedial action and the outside observer will be forewarned of possible liquidity problems.

The pyramid of ratios, therefore, provides a convenient starting point for a systematic examination of company performance. In

Table 8.1 Return on assets in quoted companies in the UK, 1977

Industry	Net income as % of average net assets*
Food	18.7
Drink	17.0
Tobacco	15.8
Chemicals and allied industries	17.5
Metal manufacture	13.7
Non-electrical engineering	18.9
Electrical engineering	22.6
Shipbuilding and marine engineering	8.6
Vehicles	12.5
Metal goods not elsewhere specified	13.9
Textiles	14.5
Leather, leather goods and fur	20.9
Clothing and footwear	9.5
Bricks, pottery, glass, cement	18.3
Timber and furniture	20.4
Paper, printing, publishing	17.4
Other manufacturing industries	15.4
Construction	19.0
Transport and communication (exc shipping)	19.0
Wholesale distribution	19.1
Retail distribution	20.2
Miscellaneous services	18.5
Manufacturing conglomerates	18.4
Non-manufacturing conglomerates	18.9
All manufacturing	17.5
All industries	17.9

* Net income is defined as gross trading profit (net of short-term interest) plus investment and other revenue income, less hire of plant and machinery and depreciation provisions. Average net assets are the average of opening and closing net assets (fixed assets + current assets — current liabilities) net of accumulated depreciation.
Source: HMSO, *Business Monitor MA3 – Company Finance,* 11th issue (1980), table 11.

addition to those shown in figure 8.1, a number of other ratios will be of interest to the outside observer. As some of the principal indicators of the size and equity of his dividend, the shareholder will be interested in the profits earned in relation to total shareholders funds (the return on equity ratio), the ratio of dividends paid to profit available for distribution (the pay-out ratio), and the ratio of profits available to ordinary shareholders to the number of ordinary shares (the earnings per share ratio).[5] These are what were earlier termed the profitability-for-the-owner ratios. They may also be called investment ratios, as to some extent they affect whether an individual or institution with funds to spare will wish to invest in the shares of the company.

In 1980 these ratios for Imperial Group were: return on equity, 8.5 per cent; pay-out ratio, 56 per cent; and earnings per share, 11.13 pence after tax. In making his decision whether to buy shares or not, the potential investor would compare these returns with those available elsewhere. He might well also be influenced by the dividend yield and price of share-to-earnings ratios reflected in the current stock market price of the shares.

More direct indicators of short-term liquidity than the trade credit and stock-to-sales ratios may be obtained by examination of the current and quick asset ratios. The current asset ratio is the ratio of current assets to current liabilities, and the quick asset ratio, the ratio of debtors plus cash to the same denominator. Both give an indication of the firm's ability to raise sufficient funds should creditors foreclose, although the latter is probably more accurate since it excludes stocks, which may be difficult to liquidate quickly. To be satisfactory, the quick asset ratio should take at least the value of 1, while the current ratio should be somewhat larger. In 1980 these ratios for Imperial Group were 0.6 and 1.4 respectively. On the face of it, these would appear to suggest liquidity problems. However, there is no hard and fast rule about the satisfactory sizes of these ratios; it depends on the industry. So, for a firm engaged in markets where customers pay in a shorter period of time than creditors demand payment, such as in food, drink and tobacco, lower current and quick asset ratios may be acceptable.

The simplest way of examining labour productivity is by using the ratios of sales to employees and profits to employees, both of which give some estimate of output per employee. At the end of the 1980 financial year there were 127,300 employees in Imperial Group. Using the figures for sales and profits incorporated in the preceding ratios produces a sales-to-employee ratio of £30,865 and a profits-to-employee ratio of £997. These ratios may be compared to those for the previous year, which were £37,543 and £1,342 respectively. From this we may conclude that labour productivity has decreased. However, care is needed in interpreting such ratios. Inflation, for example, would be expected to give rise to higher monetary sales in 1980 than in the preceding year. Correction for this would suggest an even greater deterioration in performance. It must also be noted that labour-intensive industries may have lower ratios than capital-intensive ones. Again, the extent to which part-time employees and different skills are present in the workforce may be significant. This last point means, among other things, that productivity bonus schemes must be based on more detailed information than changes in the aggregate figure.

The explanation for a particular level of performance may be derived from a number of sources: the efficiency with which inputs are combined to produce outputs (what is termed 'allocative efficiency'); whether the firm is using the best equipment available (technical efficiency); whether management control is as good as it might be (X-efficiency); and the market conditions in which the firm operates. The first three have been discussed in chapter 2, and it will be appreciated from there that they are difficult to measure. They cannot be assessed directly from the usual reports presented in the accounts. If we examine the fourth source of explanation, basic economic theory tells us that, at the one extreme, the monopolist will be able to earn supernormal long-term profits because, as the only producer, he can set his own price and is often able to engage in activities to prevent other firms from entering the industry. At the other extreme, in perfect competition, neither of these courses of action is possible and firms may earn normal profits only in the long run. For intermediate market structures the earning of long-run supernormal profits will depend on things like the elasticity of demand for the product, the possibility of entry into the industry, the numbers in the industry, and the reaction by producers to the activities of other producers. The point, then, is that, in interpreting performance figures, we should be aware of whether a certain level of profitability results from efficiency of resource use or the possession of market power. A number of attempts have been made to test the relationship between market power and profitability. Tests have focused on establishing the nature of the relationship between profit mark-up on costs (via the profits-to-sales ratio) and other economic factors that reflect market conditions; in particular, on the concentration ratio (which measures the proportion of total output of the industry produced by the largest firms); economies of scale (which measure the extent to which firms may be prevented from entering the industry); and the intensity of advertising (which establishes a degree of market power through product differentiation).[6] The general conclusion from studies of British conditions appears to be that the more highly concentrated the industry, the higher is profitability. The intensity of advertising tends to increase profitability but economies of scale are not always important. Large size in itself appears to be negatively related to the level of profitability, but it may allow a more stable pattern of profits over time.[7]

The level of profitability is considered in investigations by the Monopolies and Mergers Commission (MMC) because it may suggest over-charging by a dominant firm.[8] Such abuse may result in the firm operating against the public interest. This may take the form of higher prices and lower quality of products, higher costs, slower development of new techniques, and more adverse effects on employment than would prevail under competitive circumstances. Starting from a neutral view[9] about monopoly, the MMC uses a number of techniques to establish whether or not a dominant firm is operating against the public interest.[10] One of these techniques is to compare the firm's rate of return on assets with the average for manufacturing industry. The Commission then tries to assess whether the firm's level of return is due to greater efficiency, greater exposure to risk, or merely to the use of market power to increase mark-up. There have been quite acrimonious arguments at times between outside observers as to whether an appropriate rate of return has been chosen or whether another one would have made a difference to the Commission's final judgement.[11] The upshot appears to be that it is difficult to tell if different definitions would have changed the judgement reached as various other factors have to be taken into account. As illustrations of the flexible use made by the Commission of the rate of return criteria, consider the following. In the case of Hoffman La Roche,[12] manufacturers of tranquillizers, the Commission used the rate of return earned by the top quartile of manufacturing companies as the appropriate yardstick and argued that the level of profitability in the company was unjustifiably high; whereas in the case of Pilkington and Triplex[13] the Commission regarded its own indices as most appropriate but paid regard to the yardsticks submitted by the two companies in arguing that neither company's rate of return was excessive. In only a few cases has the Commission, in finding firms to be acting contrary to the public interest, recommended a reduction in the prices and profits of the dominant firm, and never has it recommended such a reduction to the point where the firm is earning a rate of return that is the average for industry as a whole. Price reductions have been recommended in the cases of Lucas and Champion, Kodak, Unilever and Proctor and Gamble, Hoffman La Roche and London

Rubber Co.,[14] but only in the last of these was the price reduction related to a recommended rate of return on capital.

We now turn to examine the two important factors, suggested above, that will affect the interpretation of performance data extracted from company accounts: the existence of multiple products and inflation.

MULTIPLE PRODUCTS

For the outside interested party, the publication of total profitability data in a multi-product firm provides an incomplete picture of the state of a company. All products are unlikely to be equally profitable, and overall company profitability may be seriously weakened by poor performance in one product area. Although, ideally, information on each product is required, in practice it may not be available. Company confidentiality often argues against the publication of product profitability data, in particular. There is also the problem of the assignment of overheads to products.[15] There is no economically unambiguous method of doing this in a multi-product firm. This problem can result in severe difficulties for government servants charged with assessing the extent of exploitation of a dominant position in a particular market. For example, in the Monopolies and Mergers Commission Report, *Colour Film − A Report on the Supply and Processing of Colour Film*, there was disagreement between the Commission and Kodak, one of the companies involved, over product profitability, because of different methods of apportioning overheads.

Multi-product information is presented in the annual report of Imperial Group, where data on sales and trading surpluses appear on a divisional basis. The results for 1979 and 1980 are reproduced in table 8.2. Taking this information together with the comments in the main body of the annual report, it is possible to gain a more detailed insight into the performance of the various parts of the company.

Of the four divisions of the company for which full details are available for both years, Tobacco and Brewery Divisions have increased their profits, while Paper, Board and Plastics and Food have fared less well. However, while all divisions have increased sales none has experienced an increase in profit expressed as a percentage of sales.

The improvement in the position of the Tobacco Division is seen by the company as a result of: two successful cigarette brand launches; trouble-free industrial relations; the beginning of a new technology

Table 8.2 Imperial Group Ltd, comparative divisional analysis of group sales and trading surplus, 1979, 1980

Division	Sales 1980 (£m)	Sales 1979 (£m)	Trading surplus* 1980 (£m)	Trading surplus* 1979 (£m)	Trading surplus as % of sales 1980 (£m)	Trading surplus as % of sales 1979 (£m)
(1) Tobacco	2,051.1	1,998.2	80.4	78.5	3.9	3.9
(2) Paper, board and plastics	87.0	84.4	(3.3)‡	1.5	(3.8)‡	1.8
(3) Food	1,172.0	1,081.7	10.3	24.5	0.9	2.3
(4) Brewery	539.9	481.7	42.4	38.6	7.9	8.0
(5) Howard Johnson†	107.5	–	11.5	–	10.7	–
(6) Total sales	3,957.5	3,646.0				
(7) *less:* Sales within the group	(28.4)‡	(25.0)‡				
(8) Total external sales and trading surplus	3,929.1	3,621.0	141.3	143.1	3.6	4.0

* Defined as profit after charging depreciation, profit on sales of properties, cost of hiring plant and machinery, auditors' fees, payments to Directors.
† New acquisition of restaurants and hotels company, included from 17th June 1980.
‡ Figures in brackets are losses or deductions.
Source: Imperial Group Ltd Annual Report and Accounts 1980, p. 15.

programme; and price increases, which more than offset the effect of lower sales caused by Budget tax increases. On the negative side, the division's overall market share was reduced owing to losses in sales for some existing cigarette brands, and price competition in the king-size cigarette market reduced profit margins.

The fact that the Brewery Division increased its sales when national beer consumption fell by 3 per cent helped to improve its profitability. Further benefits were derived from reductions in costs as a result of a rationalization programme. In the Paper, Board and Plastics Division as a result of the general recession no constituent company improved its position. The trading loss of the division was due entirely to losses in one company which was closed late in the year.

While the Food Division still earned a profit, its reduction in profitability was attributable mainly to problems in the company's poultry activities. The problems related to over-capacity, excess stocks and low prices. The catering section was adversely affected by weak demand, while other non-poultry business improved after having undergone a number of canning factory closures in the previous year.

Despite this additional information, serious inadequacies remain in the published accounts. For, as may be gleaned from the summaries of the activities of each division, there were marked differences between the performance of product lines within each product group. The extent of the possibility of misleading indications of performance being conveyed by the publication only of aggregate data may be appreciated when it is realized that *Who Owns Whom* lists almost 100 subsidiary operating units for Imperial Group.

INFLATION ACCOUNTING AND PERFORMANCE MEASUREMENT

We hinted earlier that the existence of inflation means that accounts based on historic cost valuations are misleading for purposes of evaluating performance. The problem of what should replace traditional accounts has exercised the minds of accountants and economists for at least a decade. At times the debate has generated considerably more heat than light. The extent of such disagreement may be gauged by the fact that since 1974 there have been no fewer than six attempts at a standard: Provisional SSAP 7, Sandilands Recommendations, ED18, Hyde Guidelines, ED24 and SSAP 16.[16] The debate continues; only one year after the introduction of SSAP 16 certain sections of the accounting profession were objecting that its proposals were too complex to implement and added little that was informative to the reader. Here is the crux of the whole matter. There is a seemingly unbridgeable gap between the demands of theory and what is acceptable in practice. We shall try to clarify the issues in what follows. However, it is a difficult area and some readers may prefer to skip this section.

To understand the problem, let us put aside for the moment the proposals contained in the Accounting Standard. The main concern in making adjustments for inflation is to ensure that sufficient provision has been made to maintain the business intact. The problem is that there are different views as to the meaning of the phrase 'maintaining the business intact'. In essence, the difference relates to whether the firm is seen as a source of income for the owner (the proprietary view) or as a collection of revenue-producing assets (the entity view). In the first case, we should seek to ensure, in making adjustments for inflation, that the owner is able to maintain his purchasing power over all items in general. In the second case, we want to be sure that the firm makes adequate provision for the replacement of its physical assets. In order to illustrate the contrasting effects of each of these views, a simplified example will be used of a hypothetical company that has only one asset – a house – which is financed by a loan.[17]

It is assumed that the house was bought for £20,000, of which £10,000 is borrowed and £10,000 paid by the owner, and that after one year the value of the house has risen by 20 per cent compared with an increase in the retail price index of 10 per cent. The results of taking differing views about the maintenance of the business are shown in table 8.3.

If, for simplicity, we assume that no loan repayments are made, then under conventional historic costs accounting the balance sheet and profit and loss account at the end of the year will be as shown in column (1), which are the same as at the beginning of the year.

If we now try to account for inflation from the owner's point of view, by using the current purchasing power method (as used in provisional SSAP 7), the end of year position is represented in column (2). Here only movements in the *general* price level are taken into account. The house now appears as £22,000 and owner's capital as £11,000, both derived by adding 10 per cent to the historic cost values. However, since the *money* value of the loan has remained the same, the company has gained by a fall in its *real* value of 10 per cent. Therefore, the profit and loss account shows a gain on monetary items of £1,000, which appears in the balance sheet under the profit and loss account reserve. But this procedure does not allow for the fact that the house has increased in value by £4,000. The current cost accounting procedure adopted by the Sandiland's Committee, and used in every proposal from then onwards, argues that what matters is the effect of inflation on the *specific* assets of the firm. Thus, the important profit figure is not that relating to the maintenance of the purchasing power of the *proprietor's* interest, as in current purchasing power accounting, but that relating to the replacement of the company's assets. As there is a need to replace physical assets, nominal holding gains, derived from an increase in the monetary value of the asset, are not treated as profit since, if they were to be distributed, the money would not be there to replace the assets. Instead, they appear in a statement of gains below the profit and loss account and

Table 8.3 *Effects of historic cost accounting and inflation accounting compared*

	(1) Historic cost		(2) Current purchasing power (CPP)	

(1) Historic cost

(a) Balance sheet

Liabilities	£	Asset	£
Owner's capital	10,000	House (cost)	20,000
Loan	10,000		
	£20,000		£20,000

(b) Profit and loss account

	£
Operating profit	nil

(2) Current purchasing power (CPP)

(a) Balance sheet

Liabilities	£	Asset	£
Owner's capital	11,000	House (CPP)	22,000
Profit and loss account reserve	1,000		
	12,000		
Loan	10,000		
	£22,000		£22,000

(b) Profit and loss account

	£
Operating profit	nil
Gain on monetary item (loan)	1,000
Total profit	1,000

(3) Current cost accounting

(a) Balance sheet

Liabilities	£	Asset	£
Owner's capital		House (current value)	24,000
	10,000		
Capital maintenance reserve	4,000		
Total equity	14,000		
Loan	10,000		
	£24,000		£24,000

(b) Profit and loss account

	£
Operating profit	nil
Statement of gains	
Nominal holding gain	4,000

(4) Real terms accounting

(a) Balance sheet

Liabilities	£	Asset	£
Owner's capital		House (current value)	24,000
	11,000		
Profit and loss account reserve	3,000		
Total equity	14,000		
Loan	10,000		
	£24,000		£24,000

(b) Profit and loss account

	£
Operating profit	nil
Real holding gain on the house	2,000
Gain on borrowing	1,000
Total profit	3,000

in the balance sheet as a capital maintenance reserve (table 8.3, column (3)).

This is an entity view of the firm, by which we mean keeping the firm itself intact in some way. It is a view that appears very attractive in the case of an asset that may not be readily saleable at the replacement cost price and which is seen to depreciate over time (for example, machinery). However, this view is erroneous and produces inconsistencies. Inconsistencies arise because, although appreciation in the value of assets is regarded as not giving rise to profit, any depreciation in the same assets would be deducted from profit at full replacement cost. In the words of one author, 'it registers death but not birth'.[18] The argument is erroneous in that it suggests that no benefit has been derived from holding the assets. But if prices are rising the company benefits from buying now rather than later as its money will go further. Holding gains reflect this benefit. Moreover, the implication of the argument that physical assets must be replaced since the firm is locked into its asset structure is not true. There are many examples to suggest that firms can change their asset structure considerably, for example by selling subsidiaries and buying others,[19] or by changing the nature of production activity, as British Gas did in moving from selling town gas to selling natural gas.

Unlike current purchasing power, current cost accounting (CCA) does not adjust the figure for the owner's capital in the balance sheet, since under this system general price movements are not recognized. In the original formulations of CCA there was also no separate recognition that borrowers gain when prices rise, thereby reducing the real cost of repayment; in effect, it was contained within the nominal holding gain on the company's assets. Here again was an inconsistency, since interest was charged against profit but the gain from borrowing was not added to profit. The Accounting Standard SSAP 16 incorporates an adjustment for the gain on borrowing, called the 'gearing adjustment'. This procedure starts by taking the ratio of long-term monetary liabilities (excluding share capital) to the same plus share capital and all reserves (i.e., the gearing ratio). This figure is multiplied by the total of the adjustments for inflation, that is for depreciation, cost of sales and monetary working capital. The resultant sum is added to current cost operating profit to produce current cost profit available for shareholders. We return to these terms below. It is sufficient to note at this juncture that the gearing adjustment is an unsatisfactory method of recognizing the owner's gain from borrowing. The reason for this is that it is derived from inflation adjustments based on *specific* changes in prices. The important price changes from the owner's point of view are *general* ones, since, as we saw with CPP, his purchasing power is assessed in these terms.

A theoretically more appropriate means of dealing with the problem of inflation accounting is seen in table 8.3, column (4), which takes into account general and specific price changes. In the example of the house, a real holding gain accrues to the firm as an entity of £2,000 which is the difference between its rise in value (£4,000) and the amount necessary to maintain its value relative to inflation (£2,000) (i.e.,the difference between CCA and CPP valuations). The gain on borrowing represents the difference between the amount necessary to maintain the original real value of the loan and its current monetary amount. The distributable profit figure includes both these gains. A clear and logical distinction is drawn between entity profit and proprietorship profit. The former is struck after the inclusion of real holding gains on assets, which recognizes the benefit from investing in that particular set of assets; the latter is arrived at after the addition of the gains on successful borrowing calculated by using price changes relevant to the owner rather than as in CCA.

This discussion should not just be seen as a rather esoteric academic debate. The distinction between the methods does matter. To take an example, consider the case of British Gas, which like most nationalized industries is set a performance target expressed as a rate of return on assets. This target is meant to guide the industry to performing effectively, and if it is set incorrectly the resulting actions by the industry may not produce the best results. In figure 8.2 rates of return on assets have been calculated using historic cost, CCA and real terms accounting.[20] Clearly, the effects of including holding gains are significant, particularly when compared with the CCA series. Hence, the implications of setting targets using different bases should be recognized by policy-makers.

In spite of the points raised in the foregoing discussion, the Accounting Standard SSAP 16 has adopted the CCA approach. The main reason for this is the accountant's traditional conservative view that replacement of physical assets should be provided for. The profit and loss account and balance sheet for Imperial Group on an inflation adjusted basis are shown in tables 8.4 and 8.5.

The profit and loss account contains four adjustments:

(1) depreciation
(2) cost of sales (COSA) ⎫
(3) monetary working capital (MWCA) ⎬ Operating adjustments
(4) gearing adjustment ⎭ Financing adjustment

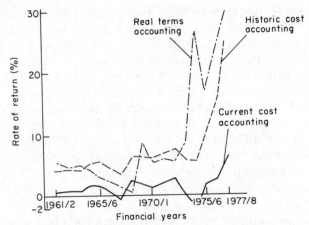

Figure 8.2   The effect of different methods of accounting for inflation on rates of return on assets: the case of British Gas.

Source: M. Wright, 'Real rates of returns on capital: some estimates for British Gas', *Journal of Business Finance and Accounting* (Spring 1980).

The first three are used to obtain profit on the productive assets of the business (group operating profit, line 7 in table 8.4); the fourth to obtain proprietary profit (group profit before taxation, line 12 in table 8.4).

The depreciation adjustment is arrived at by revaluing fixed assets using indices specific to each asset and then dividing the figure obtained by the life of each asset. The revalued assets and adjusted accumulated depreciation provisions are shown in the balance sheet (table 8.5, lines 1–5), with historic cost figures for comparison. The depreciation adjustment therefore reflects the increased cost of replacing assets. Similarly, the cost of sales adjustment is made for the difference between the current cost of stock at the date of sale and the amount charged in computing the historical cost result; and the monetary working capital adjustment is an extension of the cost of sales adjustment reflecting the burden to the firm of increases in prices arising from selling goods on credit. The MWCA should represent the amount of additional (or reduced) finance needed for monetary working capital as a result of changes in the input prices of goods and services used and financed by the business. As such, it can be positive or negative depending on whether debtors exceed or fall short of creditors. The MWCA is unsatisfactory as a measure of the effect of inflation on the real value of working capital, since under most circumstances it restricts itself to debtors and creditors and

Table 8.4   *Imperial Group Ltd, current cost profit and loss account, 1980*

	Historic cost (£m)	Current cost (£m)	(£m)
(1) Sales	3,929.1		3,929.1
(2) Group trading surplus	141.3		141.3
(3) *less:* Current cost operating adjustments:			
(4) Depreciation		(43)	
(5) Cost of sales		(22)	
(6) Monetary working capital		5	
			(60)
(7) Group operating profit	141.3		81.3
(8) Share of profits of associated companies	5.0		4.0
(9) Investment income	33.5		33.5
(10) *less:* Interest charges	(52.9)	(52.9)	
add: Gearing adjustment		17.0	
			(35.9)
(12) Group profit before taxation	126.9		82.9
(13) *less:* Taxation	(46.1)		(46.1)
(14) Group profit after taxation	80.8		36.8
(15) Minority interests	(0.3)		–
(16) Extraordinary items	11.6		(66.0)
(17) Group profit/(loss) attributable to parent company	92.1		(29.2)
(18) Dividends	(51.8)		(51.8)
(19) Profit transferred to/(from) reserves	40.3		(81.0)
(20) Earnings per share after taxation, excluding extraordinary items	11.3p		5.2p

Note: Figures in brackets are negative.
Source: Imperial Group Ltd Annual Report and Accounts 1980, pp. 22 and 42.

excludes other important components of monetary working capital such as cash and short-term deposits, a curiously narrow view of working capital. It seems logical to argue that a firm will hold monetary items to finance regular transactions in a situation where receipts and expenditures are not synchronized and where, also, other unexpected transactions arise from day-to-day activities. Under such

Table 8.5   Imperial Group Ltd, current cost balance sheet, 1980

		Historic cost (£m)	(£m)	Current cost (£m)	(£m)
	Assets				
	Fixed assets				
(1)	Land and buildings	506.2		1,072.0	
(2)	*less:* Depreciation	(60.4)	445.8	(222.0)	850.0
(3)	Plant and machinery	627.0		1,115.0	
(4)	*less:* Depreciation	(267.4)		(679.0)	
			359.6		436.0
(5)	Net fixed assets		805.4		1,286.0
	Current assets				
(6)	Stocks	483.3		491.0	
(7)	Debtors	378.5		378.5	
(8)	Cash and bank balances	20.9		20.9	
		882.7		890.4	
	less: Current liabilities:				
(9)	Creditors	(604.3)		(604.3)	
(10)	Proposed dividends	(32.2)		(32.2)	
(11)	Net working capital		246.2		253.9
(12)	Goodwill arising on consolidation		353.2		–
(13)	Interest in associated companies		18.8		18.8
(14)	Investments		265.0		280.0
(15)			1,688.6		1,838.8
	Financed as follows:				
(16)	Issued ordinary shares		178.7		178.7
(17)	Reserves		911.6		1,414.9
(18)	*less:* Goodwill arising on consolidation		–		(353.2)
(19)	Shareholders' funds		1,090.3		1,240.4
(20)	Minority interest in subsidiaries		2.7		2.7
(21)	Loan capital		263.0		263.0
(22)	Short-term borrowings		309.4		309.4
(23)	Future taxation		23.2		23.2
(24)			1,688.6		1,838.7

Note: Figures in brackets are negative.
Source: Imperial Group Ltd Annual Report and Accounts 1980, pp. 23 and 43.

circumstances a firm will normally have some flexibility in the combination of trade credit, cash, overdrafts, etc., it chooses to hold. The actual combination chosen will reflect the relative costs of such items. For example, as we have already seen, trade credit is not usually free. There are often discounts for prompt payment or surcharges for late payment, and overdrafts carry interest burdens. Hence, more than just debtors and creditors should be included in MWC. The choice of definition and the index used in the calculations can have a dramatic effect on the size of the MWCA. For example, in the case of British Gas it has been shown to vary by as much as £18 million or 100 per cent in 1976.[21] The most appropriate method appears to be to define MWC as current assets (less stocks) less current liabilities and to adjust by the retail price index.

The gearing adjustment has been dealt with already. Notice that taxation is calculated on historic cost profit.

The profit left after distributing dividends (line 19 in table 8.4) is added to the reserves in the balance sheet (line 17 in table 8.5). These reserves include the current cost reserve, which comprises the revaluation surpluses on assets and stocks, and the monetary working capital adjustment, offset by the gearing adjustment. It is necessary to include these items here to reflect that this aspect of the increase in owner's equity is considered unavailable for distribution, being purely nominal holding gains. Notice another difference between the historic cost and current cost balance sheets. Goodwill arising on consolidation, which measures the excess of the purchase price of a subsidiary over its historic cost book value, appears in the historic cost balance sheet (line 12 of table 8.5) but is excluded from that for current cost since inflation-adjusted accounts remove this difference in value. If the figure were not excluded, double-counting would result. Readers are invited to calculate a pyramid of ratios on the current cost basis and to compare the result with the historic cost figures.

Inflation accounting is obviously a complex subject, as the extent of disagreement signifies. Extreme care is required in interpreting what the various adjustments mean. As we have seen, it is often difficult to reconcile the adjustments used in practice with any coherent theoretical rationale. It thus seems necessary to be clear about the requirements of the different users of accounts and to prepare inflation-adjusted statements to meet each need, rather than to try and satisfy everybody with a rag-bag of adjustments that please no one.

We now examine two more statements presented in the annual report and accounts, which provide evidence on performance.

VALUE ADDED STATEMENTS

Value added is the difference between the value of goods produced and the cost of materials consumed in manufacturing those goods. It represents the sum available to cover all wages, salaries, expenses and profit. For the economist it should, in theory at least, provide a more appropriate measure of the firm's contribution to the wealth generated in the economy during a particular period than does trading profit. The *Corporate Report* (1975)[22] recommended that companies should include in their annual report and accounts a statement of value added. This statement for Imperial Group is shown in table 8.6. Two methods of calculating value added are shown. First, there is the subtractive method, whereby the costs of inputs are deducted from sales revenue and the share of profits of associated companies are added (lines 1–5). In the second method the applications of the value added, such as employee payments, taxation, dividends, depreciation and retained profit are summed to produce the total figure for value added (lines 6–15).

A number of advantages are often claimed for using a value added statement.[23] It is a useful tool for identifying trends in labour and other costs. Second, it is argued that it improves worker motivation, as they obtain a better sense of achievement than from seeing a high profit figure. Whether such behavioural effects exist or not is very difficult to test. But it may lead to higher wage demands if increases in value added are used as indicators of increased performance, a view that may be misleading, particularly if figures are uncorrected for inflation.

Two of the main difficulties in the calculation and interpretation of value added are as follows.

The first difficulty arises in relation to the stage in the production and distribution process at which value added is recognized. The economist would prefer value added to be recognized at the point of production, whereas the principles observed by the accountant would lead him to prefer recognition at the time of sale. The problem here, for the economist, is that it would be necessary to establish a market value for closing stock. For the accountant an under-estimate of value added will occur if sales are not adjusted for any increases in closing stock. Even if sales are so adjusted, under-estimation still occurs as the convention of valuing stock at the lower of cost or market value excludes the profit element.

The second problem concerns depreciation. We have seen that depreciation is an allocation of the cost of an asset over its useful life

Table 8.6 Imperial Group Ltd, value added statement, 1979 and 1980

		1980 (£m)	(£m)	1979 (£m)	(£m)
(1)	Sales		3,929.1		3,621.0
(2)	*less:* Cost of materials, services purchased and customs and excise duties paid		(3,224.2)		(3,014.3)
(3)			704.9		606.7
(4)	Share of profits of associated companies*		5.0		17.3
(5)	Value added by manufacturing and trading operations		709.9		624.0
	Distribution of value added				
	Employees				
(6)	Wages, salaries, pensions and social security contributions, etc.		509.0		423.0
	Taxation				
(7)	Taxation on profits and investment income		46.1		13.3
	Dividends, interest, minorities and investment income				
(8)	Interest on borrowings	52.9		37.7	
(9)	Minorities share of profits	0.3		0.5	
(10)	Dividends to shareholders	51.8		51.4	
(11)		105.0		89.6	
(12)	*less:* Investment income	(33.5)	71.5	(19.6)	70.0
	Reinvestment in the Group's business				
(13)	Depreciation	54.6		40.6	
(14)	Profit retained	28.7	83.3	77.1	117.7
(15)			709.9		624.0

Note: Figures in brackets are negative.
* Defined as those companies of which the parent owns a maximum of 30%.
Source: Imperial Group Ltd, Annual Report and Accounts 1980, p. 40.

(chapter 7). Hence, it should be deducted as a cost before arriving at value added. The purchase of fixed assets, on the other hand, is a use of value added created. Failure to make this distinction could lead to double counting. Notice that Imperial Group treats depreciation as an allocation of value added.

As with profits, the usefulness of the value added figure is enhanced when it is related to the resources used to create it — the employees or the assets of the firm. But this reintroduces the problems that we have already discussed. In particular, there are difficulties with skill differences between employees and the revaluation of assets in times of inflation. Value added itself, like profit, may be an inappropriate reflection of efficiency as it may contain elements of monopoly rent.

FLOW OF FUNDS STATEMENTS

In an earlier section of this chapter company performance in terms of both profitability and liquidity was examined by the use of ratios. Flow of funds statements permit further analysis of a company's liquidity. They may be of two types, budgeted and historic. Both concentrate on movements rather than on the position at any one time. Since this chapter is concerned primarily with the external user of accounts, budgeted statements are left until chapter 10, as this information is rarely available to anyone other than internal management.

As we have emphasized already, liquidity is of paramount importance, since if a firm is unable to meet the demands of creditors it may go out of business, even though it appears to be profitable.

At its broadest, a funds flow statement examines the sources and uses of funds to explain changes in the company's working capital. In the narrowest sense, the statement may be used to analyse changes in cash during the year. The latter statement is not usually shown in published accounts, since it is often said to give too much information to competitors in the nature of cash received from customers, cash paid to suppliers and cash overheads. We focus on the Source and Application of Funds statement, an example of which is shown in table 8.7 for Imperial Group. It may be derived from the changes in the company's balance sheet from one year to the next. From the balance sheet equation, assets equals liabilities; thus by definition changes in assets must equal changes in liabilities.[24] As may be seen from table 8.7, the primary source of funds is trading activities. Money earmarked to make good depreciation does not involve the movement of funds and can be added back to give total funds from trading operations available for the company's use (line 3).[25] To this figure is added funds obtained elsewhere, so enhancing the sums disposable (line 6). Other sources of funds include the proceeds of any share issues and proceeds from the sale of assets.

Table 8.7 Imperial Group Ltd, source and application of funds statement, 1980

		£m	£m
	Sources of funds		
	Funds generated by operations		
(1)	Group profit before taxation	126.9	
(2)	*add:* Back decpreciation	54.6	
(3)		———	181.5
	Other sources		
(4)	Extraordinary items	9.6	
(5)	Currency amounts	(17.2)	
(6)		———	(7.6)
	Application of funds		173.9
(7)	Fixed assets (purchases less sales)	289.0	
(8)	Stocks (decrease/increase)	(17.4)	
(9)	Associated companies	(46.7)	
(10)	Goodwill	64.7	
(11)	Dividends paid	51.6	
(12)	Taxation paid	41.0	
(13)	Investments (purchases less sales)	19.4	
(14)	Loan capital (decrease)	6.7	
(15)	Debtors (increase)	29.8	
(16)	Creditors (increase)	(89.7)	
(17)	Others	(23.7)	
(18)			324.7
	Difference represented by:		
	Movement in net liquid funds		
(19)	Increase in short-term borrowings		(159.2)
(20)	Increase in cash and bank balances		8.4
(21)	(line (6) − line (18))		(150.8)

Note: Figures in brackets are negative.
Source: Imperial Group Ltd Annual Report and Accounts, 1980.

Such funds are applied in various ways (lines 7–17), thus leaving the movements in net liquid funds, which includes short-term borrowings and changes in bank balances, as the residue (line 21). The application of funds includes such things as purchases of stocks and assets, payments of dividends and taxes, purchases of investments and the redemption of loan capital. They also include items like the increase/decrease in debtors/creditors. These are applications of funds, since by extending credit to debtors or paying off creditors we are prevented from using these funds elsewhere.

In interpreting Source and Application of Funds statements, increases in net liquid funds indicate an increased ability to meet short-term obligations while a decrease has the opposite effect. An increase in liquid funds seems preferable, but the observer must be mindful of the distinction between the firm being too illiquid or too liquid. The former is unhealthy, as too many funds are tied up in non-productive assets such as stocks and debtors. However, the latter is also undesirable, as it means too many funds are lying idle. The fall in liquid funds of £150.8 million for Imperial Group appears, *prima facie*, to be unsatisfactory, particularly when linked with the low acid test ratio calculated earlier.

COMPANY FAILURE

The discussion so far has allowed us some insight into the performance of companies. By using ratio analysis, and value added and funds flow statements, it is possible to gain a fairly reliable picture of the company's health. Although it is a continual feature of economic life, it seems particularly appropriate in current circumstances to examine one extreme aspect of performance: that of company failure. For present purposes this will be taken to mean both instances of a company going out of business because it cannot pay its debts (liquidation) and occasions when a company is sold by its owners as they see opportunities for obtaining a better return on their investments elsewhere (divestment). The extent of both these aspects of failure is seen in table 8.8. Both types of liquidations, compulsory and creditor's voluntary,[26] display something of a rising trend, with total liquidations rising from average of 3,925 per year up to 1976 to almost 7,000 in 1980 in a period of recession. Divestments provide a means for a parent company to adjust to failure by selling a part of its business to another party who believes he can obtain a better performance from the subsidiary. Whether the purchaser is correct in his judgement depends partly on his own managerial skills but also on two other factors. If the buyer does not have all the information about the company, he may realize, too late, that he has bought a 'pig in a poke'. The realization of this possibility will result in the purchaser making allowances via the price he is prepared to pay. The other factor relates to the market conditions in which the subsidiary

Table 8.8 Company liquidations, divestments and management buyouts

	Company liquidations			Divestments	
Year	Compulsory	Creditors voluntary	Total	Management buyouts	Other non-financial
1969-1976	12,039	19,361	31,400	43*	1,434
1977	2,425	3,406	5,831	13	110
1978	2,265	2,821	5,086	23	125
1979	2,064	2,473	4,537	52	120
1980	2,920	3,956	6,876	107	101

* 1967-76.
Sources: as shown in B. Chiplin and M. Wright, 'Merger activity and sales of subsidiaries between company groups: a note', University of Nottingham, Department of Industrial Economics, mimeo, September 1981, table 1.

operates. If the market is in decline, the parent may have sold the subsidiary, often reducing investment in it over a number of years, in order to invest in more profitable ventures.[27] In this case the acquirer may have an uphill task. Of course, it is not all bad; the subsidiary may be sold because it is successful and provides the only means by which a parent company facing liquidity problems can ease its difficulties. Management buyouts have already been mentioned in chapter 7. Their growing importance in relation to other non-financial divestments, i.e., those subsidiaries acquired by other companies, is clear from table 8.8. The reason for this may be that in current circumstances firms are less willing to take on unknown quantities, while for the management the buyout may present the only alternative to redundancy or becoming subservient to an unwelcome outsider. These reasons certainly applied in the cases of Panache Upholstery and Progress Foundry (redundancy) and Expro (unwelcome outsider).[28]

Having distinguished the forms that failure may take, we need to discuss the characteristics and causes of failure, since this may enable management, owners and government to recognize the signs early enough to take action. Three paths to eventual failure may be distinguished (see figure 8.3). In type I, the company never really gets off the ground; growth and performance are poor, so the company is unlikely to last for more than about eight years. The main reasons for failure may be delineated as: an inaccurate analysis of the product's potential; poor planning and control of the product's financial

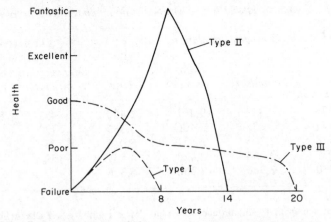

Figure 8.3   Paths to company failure.
Source: adapted from J. Argenti, *Corporate Collapse, the Causes and Symptoms* (New York, McGraw-Hill, 1976).

requirements and of the production process; and an initial high gearing level. The prediction of whether a young company will fail or not requires analysis of the company's relative strengths and weaknesses in these areas. Much of this information is unlikely to be available to the outside observer, but for banks contemplating providing loan facilities it may be worthwhile obtaining such data. There is some evidence from plant closures in Scotland to suggest that companies in the first few years of their lives are particularly susceptible to this type of failure, though once past this stage the probability of failure falls significantly. According to the study by Henderson,[29] 6.15 per cent of new plants that opened between 1960 and 1974 ceased production within one year, 4 per cent had closed by their tenth year, and only 1.2 per cent closed after 15 years.

Type II failures are fairly unusual, even though the few there are may feature prominently in the media. Their rapid rise to success depends on the outstanding performance of the product and the attributes of the proprietor. However, the companies usually falter at the consolidation stage when they fail to find new products and maintain adequate returns from their original one. Decline is often rapid. Notable examples of this type of failure are John Bloom's washing machines, Cyril Lord's carpets and Sir Freddie Laker's 'Skytrain'.

Possibly the most frequent kind of failure is that of type III, where in mature companies management become complacent with the result that product profitability, product investment requirements and general financial matters are neglected. The company eventually realizes what has happened, and launches new projects or diversifies in order to remedy the position. But, as the management has lost touch with the market, the chances of success are slight. Couple this with increasing financial commitments, undertaken to fund the new products, and it is hard to avoid failure. Henderson's study, which demonstrated high vulnerability to failure in young firms, shows that 59 per cent of all failures are of mature firms (over 15 years in production) compared with only 23 per cent of closures being in plants less than six years old.

We can use the sort of profitability and liquidity ratios that we discussed earlier to give us an indication of whether a company is likely to fail or not. But other factors, which cannot be picked up in these ratios, may give important warning signals. For example, in the study by Henderson, already discussed, companies supplying capital goods were most vulnerable. Locational aspects should also be considered. Henderson showed that firms in Glasgow had a higher failure rate than those in other areas. Characteristics of management, which are difficult to quantify, may also have an important role to play. The mechanism of company failure is therefore a complex one, which as yet is not particularly well understood. But certainly, important differences in failure rates between industries are not due to variations in profitability.[30]

NON-FINANCIAL PERFORMANCE

Domestically, the state of industrial relations in the company is of great importance. Although references to industrial disputes may be found in the Chairman's Report, they are likely to be very much muted so as to avoid unnecessarily upsetting creditors, customers and employees alike. In a small company, where the managing director is the only person responsible for controlling the business, the state of his physical health can have paramount importance for the firm's survival. However, the outside observer is unlikely to be aware of the likelihood of serious illness resulting from liquidity problems pertaining to the drinks cabinet.

The imminent expiry of patents and licences and the losses of markets and source of raw materials may also be impossible to adduce. The latter may be important if the firm depends to a great extent on politically unstable countries in Latin America and Africa for its supplies of raw materials.

Some further non-financial items which it may be desirable to disclose are discussed in the following section.

Disclosure of information
As the discussion in the previous sections of this chapter has indicated, for outside interested parties, published accounts present an incomplete picture of the health of the firm. The original stewardship function of accounts merely portrayed where the owners' funds had been used. However, since the 1940s a number of measures have been taken to improve the disclosure of company information. The Companies Act 1948 provided for the disclosure of the extent of secret reserves and the revelation of directors' interests, so helping to protect shareholders' interests. The publishing of data relating to turnover, exports, number of employees, political donations, directors' emoluments and to subsidiary companies was enabled by the Companies Act 1967. Despite these changes, there has continued to be disquiet over the contents of published accounts. There have been a number of company failures that were quite unexpected by outside readers of the accounts, for example Slater Walker Securities in 1975.[31] There have also been a number of Department of Trade investigations into the behaviour of the directors of certain companies, with the behaviour of one company being referred to by a Conservative prime minister, Edward Heath, as 'the unpleasant and unacceptable face of capitalism'. A subsequent Companies Act in 1976 dealt with disclosure of share dealings and filing of accounts, and the Accounting Standards Steering Committee[32] produced a discussion document entitled the *Corporate Report* in 1975. However, the most comprehensive recommendations were contained in the Green Paper, *The Future of Company Reports – A Consultative Document* (Cmnd 6888), published in mid-1977, and it is on these proposals that the discussion here will focus.

The proposals relate to large companies, which are rather arbitrarily defined as employing more than 500 people or having a turnover in excess of £5 million. Leaving aside this shortcoming, the specific proposals are for the publication of the following to be made legally compulsory:

(1)   Statement of Added Value
(2)   Employment Statement
(3)   Statement of Sources and Application of Funds
(4)   Short-term borrowings
(5)   Leasing commitments

(6)   Pension commitments
(7)   Transactions in foreign currencies
(8)   Research and development expenditure
(9)   Disaggregation of information by product group and geographical area
(10) International trade
(11) Statement of Future Prospects
(12) Social accounting
(13) Energy usage

For some of these items the legal requirement for publication already exists, but it has so far proved unsatisfactory. In other cases there are recommendations to publish statements (e.g., Added Value Statements), but not all companies comply.

The question of whether or not these proposals, if implemented, would satisfy the requirements of interested parties, such as employees, shareholders, society at large and government agents of competition policy, needs to be answered.

Statements of Added Value and Sources and Applications of Funds are already widely published and provide useful information on how the firm has performed, as we have seen. Their publication does not appear to be a contentious issue.

It is proposed that the Employment Statement should include numbers joining and leaving the company during the year, with details of school-leavers, retirements and redundancies; education and training policies; unions recognized by the company for collective bargaining purposes; man-days lost through industrial disputes; pension and sick-pay arrangements; and numbers of disabled people employed. Unfortunately, nothing is said about details of qualified manpower in the firm, which is arguably of greater importance in assessing performance. This statement should be seen as attempting to incorporate social accountability into the law. However, the concept of social accountability is as yet under-developed, so that any move here should be a cautious one.

Expenditure on research and development (R and D) is clearly an important ingredient in the future growth of the firm. The absence of any information relating to R and D causes difficulties in assessing future prospects; but it also produces problems in determining the profitability of the firm, since R and D is deducted before the declaration of accounting profits. Such procedures may cause profits to be unnecessarily deflated, particularly when it is remembered that the benefits from R and D expenditure may be felt for a number of years. Two related items here are the number of patents taken out by the firm and the extent of royalty transactions. These provide a better insight into the benefits accruing to the firm from R and D than broad figures of expenditure. Quite apart from performance measurement *per se*, disclosure of this information may provide insights into the extent of competition restriction through holding patents and the extent to which multi-national companies can transfer profits between countries through royalty payments.

As has already been discussed in the case of Imperial Group, the provision of disaggregated information on turnover, profits, etc., provides a better indication of the performance of multi-product companies. The suggestions in the Green Paper to extend this disaggregation to the Standard Industrial Classification 'Order' level may be criticized for not going far enough. The suggestion has been made[33] that gross margin on sales broken down by product should be reported. Companies may object to this on the grounds that it discloses too much to competitors. This objection also applies to disaggregation by geographical area of the world, particularly if overseas competitors are not forced to do the same.

It would be expected that a Statement of Future Prospects would incorporate such indicators for the future as orders in hand (particularly important for companies, such as Rolls Royce (Aero-engines), with long lead-times; new investment projects; R and D expenditure; short-term borrowing changes; expiry of patents; and other factors likely to affect significantly the future of the company. Such requirements appear reasonable, but any attempt to extend these to the publishing of financial forecasts would probably be undesirable since it would be open to abuse by the company.

The remaining suggestions contained in the Green Paper appear to be desirable and uncontentious. However, there remains a number of areas upon which the Green Paper is silent.[34] First, there is the case of advertising expenditure, which can significantly affect profits in both favourable and unfavourable ways and can influence the extent and nature of competition in the industry. The inclusion of information relating to advertising appears justifiable on the same grounds as for R and D expenditure. Second, in order to facilitate comparability with other companies and to enable the benefit of assistance to be assessed, it is essential that companies receiving government financial subsidies (e.g., British Rail and the Public Service Obligation Subsidy) should disclose separately the extent of such assistance and the conditions attached. Third, it would be desirable for multi-national companies operating in UK to disclose information relating to the manner in which their overseas activities affect their UK business.

Finally, the extent to which interlocking directorates exist should be disclosed since, if they operate among companies in the same market, competition between companies may be seriously weakened.[35]

In general, the disadvantages of further disclosure than presently exists are the increased costs, the possibilities of providing competitors with too much information and the risk that capital markets may interpret the data wrongly, especially that relating to the future. However, these disadvantages may be overstated, since much information is available internally already and its publication may have offsetting advantages in the form of reducing uncertainty, helping to promote competition, etc.

In the absence of further legal requirements, the extent of disclosure is likely to depend on a number of characteristics of the firm. These characteristics relate to size, stock market listing, auditors and the philosophy of management. In a study of four firms, Mitchell *et al.*[36] conclude, after interviewing 33 managers and 77 employees, that extending disclosure of information was seen as an evolutionary process which did not depend on commercial criteria. Management did not expect significant improvements in productivity to occur, nor was it expected, by either side, that disclosure should be part of the collective bargaining process. Almost half the employees interviewed in this study appreciated that there were certain items of information that should not be disclosed (e.g., individual salary details, items relating to commercial secrecy, etc.). However, this study highlighted another aspect of disclosure: very few employees were able to comprehend financial data presented to them. The easiest solution to this problem seems to be to incorporate an appreciation of accounting information in company-based shop-steward training courses, as part of a general programme to meet the changing needs of employees for further information.[37]

At a more aggregate level of analysis, the relationship between voluntary disclosure of items and the size of firm, whether or not it is quoted on the stock exchange and the firms auditors has been examined by Firth.[38] Using a list of 48 items likely to be voluntarily disclosed, suitably weighted by financial analysts' judgement as to their explanatory importance, paired samples of 40 large listed and unlisted companies and 100 stock exchange companies were analysed. It was found that disclosure was significantly increased the larger was the firm, and if it had a stock market listing. The auditing company made no difference to disclosure levels.

So far very little has been done to tighten up the legal requirements on disclosure. Indeed, for one category – private companies – the need to disclose information has been reduced by the Companies Act

1981. It is possible that the need for compliance with the Fourth Directive of the EEC on Company Law will improve the quality of information disclosed and create harmonization with other European companies, where the disclosure of information on the length of order books, the size of future capital expenditure, etc., is already widespread.[39] The same is true of companies in the USA. For example, a comparison of two competing firms in the aero-engine industry, Rolls Royce (UK) and General Electric (USA), reveals that the latter provides detailed information on divisional profitability, turnover, costs of goods sold and selling and administrative expenses, which are not provided by Rolls Royce. However, it is fairly clear that any developments are likely to be slow. For example, even after reaching agreement on a Statement of Standard Accounting Practice (SSAP 16) on inflation accounting, there is still some resistance to the publication of accounts adjusted for the effects of inflation.[40] The widespread separation between ownership and control, with the company itself (and not the shareholders) the legal institution owning productive assets, militates against any rapid change in the area of disclosure of information.

CONCLUSIONS

A comprehensive discussion of performance assessment from the points of view of outside observers has been presented in this chapter. A number of reports are published in a company's accounts, and from these a detailed appraisal of progress may be compiled. However, a number of shortcomings have been pointed out which must qualify any interpretation of accounting data.

NOTES

1 In the jargon, the former may be termed 'entity' profitability and the latter, 'proprietary' profitability. To the extent that the management of the firm has the discretion to invest funds other than in productive assets within the business, 'entity' profit may include income from non-trading sources.
2 Operating assets and operating profits are defined on the wider entity basis so as to be comparable with the figures in table 8.1. A detailed definition is given in the note to that table.

3 This is an area where accountants and economists part company, as we shall see when we discuss inflation accounting. However, for present purposes, maintaining the business intact shall be taken to mean the maintenance of physical assets or productive capacity.

4 For a discussion of this method see H. Ingham and L. Taylor Harrington, *Interfirm Comparison* (London, Heinemann, 1980), ch. 3.

5 As we have already seen in chapter 7 the gearing ratio is a complementary ratio to those mentioned here. The efficacy of the ratios will be affected by factors that distort the reliability of earnings figures because of their uncertainty, in particular, deferred taxation and transactions made in foreign currency. See N. Taraporvala, 'The reliability of earnings per share as an indicator of growth', *Accountancy*, 89 (1978) for discussion.

6 Empirical research in this area is fraught with problems as the variables for market power cannot be measured directly. Such measurement problems need not concern us here. For a discussion and also a review of the main studies see M. C. Sawyer, *The Economics of Industries and Firms* (London, Croom Helm, 1981).

7 See G. Whittington, 'The profitability and size of United Kingdom companies', *Journal of Industrial Economics*, 28 (1980).

8 A dominant firm is considered to be one with at least a 25 per cent market share in a particular product. This size of market share is the triggering mechanism for investigations by the Monopolies and Mergers Commission. For a discussion of the working of the MMC see D. Swann, *Competition and Consumer Protection* (Harmondsworth, Penguin, 1979). Since the passing of the Competition Act 1980 it is now possible for the Director-General of Fair Trading to instigate enquiries when he considers a firm to be pursuing a course of conduct which may amount to an anti-competitive practice, irrespective of market share.

9 There have recently been arguments that the MMC should look for positive public interest benefits, not just whether a firm operates against the public interest. See Swann, *Competition and Consumer Protection*.

10 In the jargon this is termed the 'structure–conduct–performance' approach and is based on the proposition that there is a causal link between these factors and whether the firm operates in the public interest.

11 See for example C. K. Rowley, 'The Monopolies Commission and the rate of return on capital', *Economic Journal*, 79 (1969) and the subsequent exchange with Sutherland in the June and September 1971 issues of that journal; also see O. Bello, 'The firm, investment, rate of return and the Monopolies Commission', *Journal of Business Finance and Accounting*, 4 (1977) and the exchange with Grant in the Winter 1978 issue of that journal.

12 Monopolies and Mergers Commission, *Chlordiazepoxide and Diazepam*, HC 197 (London, HMSO, 1972/73).

13 Monopolies and Mergers Commission, *Flat Glass*, HC 83 (London, HMSO, 1968).

14 The relevant MMC Reports were as follows: *Chlordiazepoxide and Diazepam*; *Colour Film*, HC 1 (London, HMSO, 1966/67); *Contraceptive Sheaths*, HC

135 (London, HMSO, 1974/75); *Report on the Supply of Electrical Equipment for Mechanically Propelled Land Vehicles*, HC 21 (London, HMSO, 1963/64); *Household Detergents*, HC 105 (London, HMSO, 1966/67).

15 For a discussion of this problem see any basic management accounting textbook, for example, T. Horngren, *Cost Accounting: A Managerial Emphasis* (Englewood Cliffs, NJ, Prentice Hall, 1977).

16 SSAP stands for Statement of Standard Accounting Practice. ED stands for Exposure Draft, which means the proposals are open to discussion.

17 This example is adapted from G. Whittington, 'Inflation accounting: why the debate has gone off-course', *The Times*, 10 March 1980.

18 W. T. Baxter, 'Accountants and inflation', *Lloyds Bank Review* (October 1977.

19 Approximately one-fifth of all acquisitions are of divested subsidiaries; see B. Chiplin and M. Wright, 'Divestment and structural change in UK industry', *Nat West Bank Review* (February 1980).

20 Gains on borrowing are excluded since in the nationalized industries in general, and in the case of gas in particular, all finance is loan finance from the government so that the gearing adjustment would be zero.

21 See I. Papps and M. Wright, 'The use of an MWCA: an example from British Gas', *Accountancy*, 91 (1980).

22 Accounting Standards Steering Committee, *The Corporate Report* (London, ICAEW, 1975).

23 For a discussion of the advantages and disadvantages of value added statements see M. F. Morley, 'The value added statement in Britain', *Accounting Review*, 54 (1979). See also B. A. Rutherford, 'Published statements of value added: a survey of three years' experience', *Accounting and Business Research*, 41 (1980).

24 Clearly, liabilities in the balance sheet may be regarded as total sources of funds and assets as total applications thereof.

25 An alternative presentation is to start with retained profit, in which case dividends and taxes paid would not appear under applications.

26 Compulsory liquidation involves the issuing of a court order, while voluntary liquidation follows agreement at a meeting of creditors. There is an important distinction between liquidation and receivership; liquidation is usually final, whereas receivership may mean the continuation of the company, particularly if more could be realized from sale of the business as a going concern. Often continuation is possible only after the sale of a substantial part of the business and the reconstruction of the company's debt (termed 'hiving-down'). For an excellent discussion of the practical aspects of corporate failure see, 'Corporate insolvency', *Bank of England Quarterly Bulletin* (December 1980), 430–6.

27 See K. R. Harrigan, *Strategies for Declining Businesses* (Lexington Books, 1980).

28 For a discussion of these cases see R. V. Arnfield, B. Chiplin, M. Jarrett and M. Wright, *Management Buyouts: Corporate Trend for the 80's*, Proceedings of the First National Conference on Management Buyouts (University of Nottingham, Industry and Business Liaison Office, 1981).

29 R. A. Henderson, 'An analysis of closures amongst Scottish manufacturing plants between 1966 and 1975', *Scottish Journal of Political Economy*, 27 (1980).

30 For further discussion see S. Dev, 'Ratio analysis and the prediction of company failure', in H. Edey and B. S. Yamey (eds), *Debts, Credits, Finance and Profits* (London, Sweet and Maxwell, 1974).

31 See D. Bosworth, M. C. Flemming and W. P. J. Maunder, 'The accountability of companies from the viewpoint of the industrial economist: thoughts on the Green Paper', *Journal of Industrial Affairs* (Winter 1979) for a number of examples.

32 The Accounting Standards Steering Committee is a body made up of leading practitioners and academics in the field of accounting. Its aim is to establish standardized procedures for accounting, based on sound principles and consensus.

33 Bosworth, Flemming and Maunder, 'The accountability of companies'.

34 Ibid.

35 See P. S. Johnson and R. Apps, 'Interlocking directorates among the UK's largest companies', *Antitrust Bulletin*, 24 (1979), for a discussion of the extent of this phenomenon among large firms in the UK.

36 F. Mitchell, I. Sams, D. Tweedie and P. White, 'Disclosure of information: some evidence from case studies', *Industrial Relations Journal*, 11 (1980).

37 The nature of these changes and how the needs may be met have been discussed in a case study by J. Coyne and M. Wright, 'The changing needs in company-based shop steward training', *Industrial Relations Journal*, 13, (1982).

38 M. Firth, 'The impact of size, stock market listing and auditors on voluntary disclosure in corporate annual reports', *Accounting and Business Research*, 36 (1979).

39 The extent of disclosure by the West German company Siemens has been discussed in 'Not just a lot of stupid foreigners', *Accountancy Age*, 1 May 1981.

40 D. Keymer and M. Haslam, 'Boycott SSAP 16', *Accountancy Age*, 24 July 1981, p. 8.

9

Investment

In the simplest terms, the investment decision is concerned with the question of whether adding to capital now will increase the profit that can be earned in the future sufficiently to justify the expense.

Investment decisions are not easy. Since they involve the calculation of costs and revenues into the future they must involve some degree of uncertainty. We are not yet able to forecast the future perfectly. Great care is therefore needed in assessing the best place to invest before any finance is committed. After the decision is taken and money is sunk into buildings and machinery, there may be little chance of recovering it for many years. If the investment decision then turns out to have been mistaken, the consequences for the firm may be serious.

When so much has been written about the UK's poor investment performance compared with its competitors, the need to make correct investment decisions has further significance. On such decisions depends ultimately the ability of firms to compete, the provision of employment, and the growth in living standards.

In this chapter we first examine the opportunities for investment and the factors influencing the level and type of investment. We then discuss the mechanics of the investment decision, using illustrative examples. The discussion incorporates the various techniques available to assess the suitability of investment projects, their relative merits and how the problems of uncertainty and financing may affect the decision. The problem of whether to lease or buy is also considered. In the final section the importance of investment in the public sector is dealt with. In particular, consideration is given to the problems of choosing investment projects in such a way as to avoid distortion with the private sector. Attention is also paid to cost-benefit analysis of projects that may not be worthwhile when only strict commercial criteria are used, but which may be acceptable when their effects are seen from the viewpoint of society as a whole.

OPPORTUNITIES FOR INVESTMENT

In simple terms, firms invest to take advantage of apparently profitable opportunities that may arise in three main ways:

(1) the need to replace existing equipment;
(2) the growth of new markets and products;
(3) the development of new production methods.

The, need to replace existing machinery may arise simply because it is old and worn out. Hence, if profits are to be maintained and maintenance costs reduced, investment should take place. But the firm need not necessarily buy the same equipment; it may have the opportunity to purchase more productive machinery.

However, the decision to purchase new machinery when the old is wearing out is not automatic. The firm must first of all ask itself whether it wants to continue producing the same products. If the market is declining, investment in new equipment may be unwise. Alternatively, in growing markets, the need to replace equipment may be crucial to maintaining market share and competitiveness, since more efficient firms may otherwise capture the new demand. In both cases there is a danger that excess capacity, will result. In a rapidly growing market, free entry may lead to an increase in capacity, by both new entrants and from retaliatory action by existing firms, which outstrips the increase in demand. Low profits in general come to be earned as firms indulge in price competition in order to maintain their market share. Although some firms will go bankrupt and leave the industry, others will stay until equipment is worn out, so long as the return they can earn by staying in the industry exceeds the return they could obtain elsewhere. This opportunity cost return will be influenced by the price that can be obtained for the assets, which, if assets are specific to one product in a declining market, is unlikely to be high enough to encourage mobility. Such exit barriers prolong the existence of excess capacity. The experiences of the dry cleaning industry from the late 1950s to the early 1970s were very much along these lines.[1] A firm may also invest purposely in excess capacity in order to secure its position of dominance in the industry. The excess capacity acts as a barrier to new entrants, since the firm has the potential to increase production quickly should a new entrant appear on the scene. The new entrant may thus be deterred as he sees little possibility of gaining a significant market share.[2] Restrictive trade practices may lead to excess capacity by means of price-fixing and information agreements keeping in business inefficient producers who, under competitive conditions, would be bankrupt. The passing of the 1956 and 1968 Restrictive Trade Practices Acts did a great deal to remove such agreements, with a consequent increase in competition and a reduction in excess capacity.[3] The Acts have often been blamed for reducing profits, by causing price competition, and hence reducing investment, as fewer internal funds were available to undertake such ventures. However, this argument would appear to be untrue. Reductions in profit since the passing of the Acts are attributable mainly to general macroeconomic factors. Much competition took the form of discounts or extensions of trade credit rather than direct price competition. Any fall in investment may have helped reduce under-utilization of assets in declining markets.[4]

The more investment is undertaken with the object of exploiting new markets or new products, the more uncertain the results of it are likely to be. The uncertainties surrounding such decisions will have to take into account the qualities of the articles to be produced, the potential market for them, the feasibility of the production processes that are proposed, and the intentions of actual and potential competitors. Investment in export markets is probably more uncertain than in the home market, and business would accordingly require the prospects of higher yields in order to undertake such investments. Particularly vulnerable are investments in plants in politically unstable countries. Despite the use of special tax remissions to encourage investment, there may be a serious danger of expropriation without compensation if the government suddenly changes. If, on the other hand, the decision is taken to export to overseas countries rather than to establish production there, sales are at the mercy of import duties, import restrictions and competition from both inside and outside the country.

Investment in new products is often related to the development of new production techniques. The process can be two-sided. On the supply side, science may push new products forward that customers could not previously have envisaged. On the demand side, the market may demand new products and pull research and innovation along. New products and techniques can be considered under the general heading of 'innovation'. Innovation is the commercial exploitation of an invention. The successful firm will be the one that can link together the technological and market possibilities.

Of course, the best way for a firm to exploit such opportunities will not be the same for all firms and markets. The appropriate method depends on the type of product market, the relative dynamism of the market, the market power of the firm and the expertise of the entrepreneur. The combination of these factors will be an important determinant of the innovation strategy to be followed and hence of the size and pattern of investment.

The offensive innovator – that is, one seeking to be first in the field – needs large in-house research and development expertise and some protection from competition, at least in the short term, during which time monopoly profits can be obtained as a reward for undertaking risky ventures. A successful example of this type of firm and its associated innovation is the float-glass process developed by Pilkington's.

The opportunist really possesses little or no research and development expertise, but depends for success on finding a gap in the market. The flexibility in operations that this requires makes it likely that firms undertaking such investment are small enterprises set up to exploit an opportunity that the larger firms may have missed or may not be interested in.[5] The extent to which existing firms provide the opportunity for such innovations, that is, act as 'incubator plants', is a function of the industry in which the firm is operating[6] and the qualities of their employees.[7] One example of this type of innovation is shown in the case of General Electric in the USA. Owing to its large organizational structure, it may not be worthwhile for GE itself to enter certain new markets. Instead, new techniques developed, such as microfiltration, are turned over to a newly formed company of ex-employees who are able to exploit the product. The essential ingredients for success are the existence of a definite niche in the market and the willingness of GE to maintain supportive links. In addition to the benefits gained by the new entrepreneurs, General Electric also gains through its ability to enter indirectly markets that, if it entered directly, it would dominate and incur the effects of anti-trust legislation.[8]

Imitative innovators aim to follow the market leader but to gain a substantial market share by producing the new product at a lower price and more efficiently. Success for such a strategy depends on the firm's possessing the ability to adapt new techniques quickly. The success of many Japanese firms in entering European markets is often attributed to their use of this type of innovation strategy.

Component producers and other sub-contractors are the type of firm dependent on the innovations of other companies. As such, their success depends on the ability to produce to the new specifications of the innovating firm.

In oligopolistic markets, defensive innovation may be undertaken in order to keep up with the market leader, while at the same time being able to learn from his mistakes. Often it takes the form of product differentiation. The large-volume car market is probably one of the most familiar examples of activities in which defensive innovation takes place. The market is highly competitive, with investment in new products being necessary every few years if firms are to stand a chance of surviving. The investment by BL in the Mini Metro was essential for the company to maintain a significant share in the UK market. The original Mini, which had been a market leader, was losing out to the newer models marketed by Renault, Peugeot, Volkswagen, etc. Here was a case of a company failing to invest soon enough to keep its position of market leader. In the event, the investment had to be financed by government as part of a programme to rescue the company from liquidation. This programme included the introduction of new robot-controlled production lines, in order to increase productivity and reduce costs in line with competitors.

When products and production techniques change little, innovation may tend to take the form of straight replacement.

In addition to the above mentioned innovation strategies, which relate primarily to revenue-earning projects, many firms will be required to undertake new types of investment of a non-revenue nature, such as those relating to compliance with health and safety at work regulations.

In practice, investment by many firms does not fit neatly into one of the above categories. For example, Rolls-Royce (Aero-engines) operates in a market where strong competition exists between three main producers and investment in a large amount of research and development is essential and risky. The long development periods of highly technical products mean that the firm must be an offensive innovator and carry a great deal of risk, without the guarantee of earning supernormal profits at the end of it. This is particularly illustrated by the development by Rolls-Royce of the RB211 engine. Rolls-Royce obtained an order to supply this engine to Lockheed in the USA, while the engine was still being developed. In order to gain the contract it was necessary to offer financial terms that left little room for significant increases in development costs — otherwise Pratt and Whitney or General Electric would have moved in. Unfortunately, the delays caused by the necessity to overcome unforeseen technical problems led to the triggering of penalty clauses in the contract, and the company, its cash flow seriously impaired, was forced into liquidation in 1971. As an indication of the magnitude of the sums involved, the development costs, which were initially estimated at £60 million, had increased to £135 million as early as November 1970, long before development was complete. The government was forced to ensure financial support for the project. The engine is now regarded as an important revenue-earner for the company; but the company's profits are low, and the nature of the market still requires government financial support in order to ensure that the company can carry out sufficient investment to be able to continue to compete.[9]

The case of Imperial Group is an illustration of a firm holding a dominant position in a market – tobacco – where sales are slowly declining, owing partly to the effects of health education and partly, in the short term, to periodic increases in excise duty. Product differentiation is important in maintaining market share, as is price competition in some market sectors. For such reasons the ability to maintain low-cost production is an important factor in staying competitive. To this end, the company embarked on a programme of investment in new high-speed cigarette making and packing machinery in 1980. The company is thus in a different position to BL and Rolls-Royce, as it is investing from a position of financial and market strength. Moreover, the element of uncertainty and the necessity for huge research and development expenditure is probably relatively low.[10]

Clearly, the implications for investment opportunities of each strategy are very different, involving greater or lesser uncertainty, the requirement for more or less finance and the earning of greater or lesser returns over shorter or longer periods.

From what we have said, it would appear that a number of investment opportunities can present themselves to the firm. However, in order to narrow the range of possibilities down to a small number to which detailed consideration may be given, the firm requires some kind of filtering device. One such technique is an investment project classification table,[11] for example, as shown in table 9.1. Along the top of the table are the broad opportunities for investment, as we have seen in this section. Down the left-hand side the firm can classify projects by the degree of choice they have as to their adoption and the degree of risk involved. The categories shown are by no means rigid, merely illustrative of the use of the method.

In addition to the microeconomic factors affecting investment so far examined, the general level of investment will be influenced by macroeconomic conditions. If both domestic and international

Table 9.1 An investment project classification table

	Replacement investment Same capacity	Extra capacity	New production techniques	Non-revenue-earning
No choice	Machinery worn out and wish to stay in industry	If new entrants threaten	If competitors are innovating	If required by govt regulation
Choice	Machinery worn out and can obtain better return elsewhere	If wish to grow but there are options elsewhere	If the firm is the market leader	If are perquisites for employees and management
Risk	Fairly low if same product, but depends on state of market	Fairly low if product market is growing	High risk if the products are new and development has to be done	Cost of fines, industrial action or loss of personnel if do not comply

economies are generally experiencing a recession, there will be little incentive to invest in new plants, since there will be little demand for the product. Of course, in some sectors of the economy demand may remain buoyant even in a general recession. Otherwise, companies will seek to survive until an increase in demand returns, by reducing costs and destocking. If a company believes that an upturn is at hand it may start to invest ahead of the increase in demand, with the intention of gaining a lead over competitors. But there is the danger that forecasts of a resurgence in demand are premature and the company will then have to cope with more idle capacity.

The existence of other factors may make investment in manufacturing generally unprofitable, relative to alternative avenues for placing funds. For example, it has been argued that the effect of North Sea oil exports on the exchange rate has been to make manufacturing exports less competitive and imports cheaper.[12] Hence, manufacturing industry is made less profitable and it may be more worthwhile to invest funds overseas until revenues from oil begin to decline and their effect on the exchange rate is removed.

Since the firm is likely to be stuck with an investment for a number of years, or may even be forced into liquidation through making errors in its investment planning, great care is needed in assessing the opportunities for investment. The discussion in the next section focuses on the use of techniques to choose between the options highlighted in this part.

THE INVESTMENT DECISION

A number of techniques for appraising projects are in use, some of them representing convenient and first approximations to more refined analysis. In order to examine how investment decisions may be made with these techniques we shall make use of the following hypothetical example.

Let us assume that Imperial Group, as part of its regular corporate planning procedure, has to decide on an investment programme to obtain the best return in the light of economic conditions which it generally sees as continuing to be unfavourable for a number of years. For the sake of simplicity, let us also assume that the range of possible projects has been reduced to two, only one of which may be undertaken because of a limit on the amount that can be borrowed.

The alternatives are:

(1) to invest £100 million in its Tobacco Division, in which market it has traditionally held a dominant position;
(2) to invest £300 million in a new venture involving hotels and restaurants, of which it has little experience.

Investment in the Paper, Food and Brewery Divisions is to remain unchanged, since growth prospects here are thought to be relatively poor.

If it makes the investment in either option, the company has estimated that the extra profits from each, over an expected ten-year life before further investment will be required, would be as shown in table 9.2. The company will borrow the funds required for the project it chooses at a fixed rate of interest of 15 per cent.

Given this information, which project should be chosen? We can examine a number of the techniques available to make this decision.

The most familiar of the simpler approaches is the accounting rate of return method, which expresses the average annual net cash flows from the investment as a percentage of the capital invested. Using the data in our example, the accounting rate of return is calculated

Table 9.2   Forecast cash flows from alternative investment projects

	Cash flows for years into the future (£m)					
Project	0	1	2	3	4	each of 5-10
Invest more in tobacco	−100	+29	+27	+22.5	+20	+20
New venture	−300	+30	+28	+60	+75	+90

Table 9.3   Accounting rate of return method

Project	Total net cash flows over life (£m)	Average net cash flows per year (£m)	Accounting rate of return (%)
Invest more in tobacco	218.5	21.85	21.85
New venture	733	73.3	24.43

as shown in table 9.3. With this criterion, investment in the new venture is preferred to further investment in tobacco. A major problem with this method of appraisal is that it fails to take into account the time value of money. However, it has been shown that, under quite reasonable assumptions, the accounting rate of return is a good approximation to the more sophisticated internal rate of return that we shall discuss shortly.[13]

The payback method differs from the accounting rate of return approach by simply working out how many years will elapse before the cost of the investment is met out of the net expected receipts.

In our example, five years is the minimum payback period; the investment in the Tobacco Division will pay back the outlay with an inflow of £118.5 million in this time. But the new venture requires one year longer to cover the initial costs. Hence, the investment decision based on the quicker payback period would be to invest further in the Tobacco Division. This method is simple and is widely used, but it has serious analytical defects. Indeed, its use by the banks for assessing whether to lend to companies has been blamed as one of the contributory reasons for Britain's poor investment performance.[14] The major problems are these: the method pays no attention to what happens after the payback period has been completed; it attaches no weight to the pattern of earnings within the payback period itself; and it ignores the fact that an investment project with large earnings in the first few years but smaller earnings over its total life is to be preferred to one for which the reverse applies. In addition, it may not even provide a safeguard against accepting unsound projects since safe options in practice are unlikely to earn high returns immediately.

The reason for the continued use of this method as an investment appraisal technique is that it may suffice as a quick method of filtering out non-starters, concentrating attention on the need to make money turn over quickly in times of financial stringency and avoiding long payback periods where risk of obsolescence is an important element.

The internal rate of return and the net present value methods are both approaches designed to deal with the problem, neglected by the previous two methods, that money in the future is worth less to us than money in our pockets today. Money received some time in the future is worth less than the same amount received today, since in the meantime it can earn interest. The opportunity cost of holding money is, therefore, the interest that could be earned in the period in which it is held. The process that takes account of this is called 'discounting', and is most easily understood as the reverse of the process of accumulating money at compound interest. If we have a sum of money, A_0, and we put it in a deposit account at the bank for a year at a rate of interest r, where r is expressed as a proportion rather than a percentage (0.10 rather than 10 per cent, for example), it will grow to:

$$A_0 + (A_0 \times r) = A_0(1 + r)$$

at the end of the period, assuming interest is paid at the end of the year. If the principal (A_0) plus accrued interest is left to accumulate for a further year, the total sum invested will increase to:

$$A_0 + (A_0 \times r) + (A_0 \times r) + (A_0 \times r \times r) = A_0(1 + r)^2.$$

This process may be continued for as many years as we like, until we decide to withdraw the money. In general, the sum that will be available at the end of each year can be expressed in the form

$$A_0(1 + r)^n$$

where n is the number of the year we are considering. In other words,

Future value = Present value $(1 + r)^n$.

Now, suppose we think that at the end of year n we shall have a sum of money A_n and we want to find its present value. All we need do is rearrange the above by dividing both sides by $(1 + r)^n$ so that

$$\text{Present value} = \frac{\text{Future value}}{(1 + r)^n},$$

that is,

$$A_0 = \frac{A_n}{(1 + r)^n} = A_n \times \frac{1}{(1 + r)^n}.$$

The expression $1/(1 + r)^n$ is called the present value factor. Thus, whenever we have a future value we can establish a present value by using a rate of discount r.

The net present value method takes r as given. It is either the cost of borrowing the money to finance the investment, or the alternative yield that could be obtained from lending the company's money to outsiders. If, in using this discount rate, the sum of the discounted future cash flows from each year of the project's life are equal to or greater than the initial outlay, it is worth undertaking the project. The internal rate of return method works the other way round, by requiring us to find that value of r that makes the sum of the discounted future cash flows equal to the outlay now.

Consider again the data in our example. We can use these figures to illustrate the workings of each technique in turn. From what we have said above, the net present value (NPV) rule may be shown generally as follows. If

$$A_0 < \frac{A_1}{(1 + r)} + \frac{A_2}{(1 + r)^2} + \ldots + \frac{A_n}{(1 + r)^n}$$

then the project is profitable. Rearranging the equation, we could express it as follows. If

$$-A_0 + \frac{A_1}{1 + r} + \frac{A_2}{(1 + r)^2} + \ldots + \frac{A_n}{(1 + r)^n} \equiv NPV$$

is positive, then the project is profitable.

In the second case, $-A_0$ represents money paid out now to buy the investment, the machinery or whatever. Given the data in our example and the fact that the discount rate is 15 per cent, since this is the cost of borrowing money the net present value is worked out as follows. The investment decision, using the data in table 9.4, would be too choose both projects, as both have positive net present

Table 9.4   *The net present value method*

				Present values	
		New	Present		New
	Tobacco	venture	value	Tobacco	venture
Year	(£m)	(£m)	factor*	(£m)	(£m)
0	−100	−300	1.000	−100	−300
1	+29	+30	0.870	25.23	26.1
2	+27	+28	0.756	20.412	21.168
3	+22.5	+60	0.658	14.805	39.480
4	+20	+75	0.572	11.440	42.900
5-10	+20	+90	2.163†	43.260	194.670
Net present value				15.147	24.318

* The present value factor is $1/1 + r$ in year 1, $1/(1 + r)^2$ in year 2, etc.
† This figure is derived from the sum of the present value factors in years 5–10 inclusive.

values. However, since we have limited funds available, we can choose only one project. We choose that with the highest net present value: that is, the new venture.

The general expression for the internal rate of return (IRR), following from what we have said, is: set the net present value to 0 and solve the following for r:

$$NPV = 0 = -A_0 + \frac{A_1}{1 + r} + \frac{A_2}{(1 + r)^2} + \ldots + \frac{A_n}{(1 + r)^n}.$$

If the value of r required to solve this equation is greater than or equal to the cost of borrowing the money for the project, there is a case for accepting the project.

In order to solve the equation we make use of the technique of linear interpolation. For a discount rate of 15 per cent we obtain the net present values above. If we take a discount rate of 25 per cent, we obtain net present values of −15.62 and −87.8 for the investments in tobacco and the new venture, respectively. Somewhere between these two values lies a value of r for which the net present value is 0. The linear interpolation formula is as follows:

Internal rate of return = Lower discount rate

$$+ \left[\left(\frac{\text{Minimum } NPV}{\text{Range of } NPV} \right) \times \text{Difference between discount rates} \right].$$

Substituting in the relevant values, we obtain the internal rates of return for each project, which are 19.9 and 17.2 per cent respectively. The decision is then to choose the first project, that is, to invest further in tobacco.

Notice that, with a minimum acceptable rate of return of 15 per cent, determined by the cost of borrowing, each method tells us to accept both projects, if sufficient funds can be obtained. However, when we have to choose one project, the methods give us different answers. The reason for this is that the NPV method gives greater weight to cash flows in the later years of the project's life than does the IRR, since the rate of discount that gives a positive NPV is less than that required to obtain a NPV of 0. This point is illustrated in figure 9.1, where the present values of £100 at future dates using various discount rates are shown. Clearly, £100 in year 10 is worth more now with a 15 per cent discount rate than with a 25 per cent discount rate. So, the higher the discount rate, the more the profitability of the project depends on what happens in the earlier years. In our example, we can see this point illustrated. The investment in tobacco receives returns in the earlier years that are at a level similar to those of the new venture.

The solution to the problem of inconsistent answers is to use the following approach. The incremental rate of return is the return

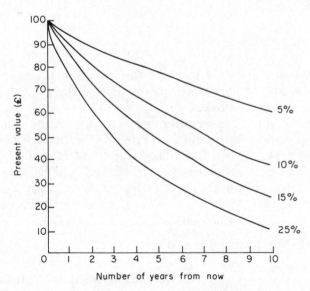

Figure 9.1   Present value of £100 at future dates using various discount rates.

yielded by the extra outlay on one project over an alternative project. If the incremental flows earn an IRR greater than the cost of funds, it would pay to invest in the more expensive project, and there will be consistency between the two methods. The result of computing the IRR for the extra £200 million outlay on the second project is an IRR of 16.1 per cent. Since this figure exceeds the cost of borrowing, it is worth investing the extra funds. If the NPV of the second project is greater than that for the first project, the incremental rate of return must be greater than the cost of borrowing. Hence, the net present value method is more appropriate since it leads us directly to the correct solution.

From our discussion, we may note a number of reasons why the NPV is to be preferred to the IRR. First, as we have just seen, the IRR tells us to prefer the project with the highest percentage rate of return, rather than one with a higher absolute rate of return. In other words, it measures profitability, not total profits. Second, differences in the ranking of projects may also occur with identical initial outlays, but with different patterns of cash flows, because of the different weighting of earlier and later cash flows by each method. A third problem is caused when projects produce cash flows that vary between positive and negative over their lives. In such situations, the IRR may produce multiple solutions. This problem may be dealt with, particularly if negative cash flows occur at the end of the life, by discounting the negative cash flows back until, when subtracted from the next positive year, they are positive. The IRR is then recomputed for the new profile of cash flows.

It might be suggested that Imperial Group would do better to accept the further investment in tobacco, as this has the highest internal rate of return, but to do so by investing £300 million rather than £100 million if this amount can be borrowed. In this way a higher net present value could be obtained. However, we cannot assume that further investment in tobacco would yield cash flows at the same level as the first £100 million. The reason for this lies in the market conditions faced by the company – the demand may just not be there to take the increased output. It would be foolish to have to pay storage costs, tying up cash unproductively, or to cut prices to such a level that losses are incurred.

A final point of comparison concerns the reinvestment of funds generated by projects. It is often argued that the IRR technique implies the reinvestment of funds at the internal rate of return, while the NPV method implies reinvestment at the discount rate used in the calculation. Since alternative investment projects may not be available at the internal rate of return, the net present value is the more appropriate method. However, the rate of return from reinvestment is really the subject of another investment decision at a later date, and is not relevant to the current decision. What is relevant is the return on some alternative investment forgone, which sets the opportunity cost of capital, the appropriate discount rate under conditions of capital rationing.[15]

UNCERTAINTY AND FORECASTING CASH FLOWS

Accurate estimates must be made of costs and benefits over the life of each project. Here is the crux of the whole problem, since, if the exercise is badly carried out, the final decision will be meaningless. As regards costs, increases in overheads will have to be taken into account, as will purchases of raw materials, wage payments, fuel costs, amounts of scrap, etc. Depreciation of the capital equipment is not included as a cost in making these estimates because it is accounted for in taking the difference between revenues and outlays. As we have already noted in chapter 7, depreciation is merely a device to spread the cost of the project throughout its life; it is a bookkeeping entry, and does not involve any movement of funds. Since we already have the cost in the equation, it would be double-counting to include depreciation. Against running costs it is necessary to set receipts, which may be a difficult task if the product is an intermediate good.[16] The difference between costs and receipts will give us the net cash flows for each year. They will not always be positive, as losses may be made or, for example, restitution of land at the end of an open-cast mining operation will involve a net cost of considerable magnitude. Costs and receipts may be fairly easy to estimate in the case of replacement investment or new investment in a familiar activity. But, when investment is to be made in very new ventures, such as new products or the acquisition of subsidiaries, serious problems may arise. In the former case, there may be difficulties in estimating costs of production, the market size, the effects on industrial relations (particularly if it involves new technology and the threat of redundancies) and the time-pattern of cash inflows. In the case of acquisitions, there is the danger that a price may be paid based on limited and inaccurate information about the subsidiaries' prospects. The result may be that the investment does not fulfil the expectations held by management, producing what has been called a disappointing marriage.[17]

Uncertainty may be accommodated in a number of ways. One way is to use sensitivity analysis, which consists of computing a number of discounted cash flow options, each with a different assumption about the way in which future costs and revenues will arise. By this means, a range of possibilities is obtained. The investment decision may then be considered in relation to the worse result that it is thought could materialize, bearing in mind that this view may prove to be pessimistic.[18]

In choosing between risky projects, a strategy may be followed such that projects with the risk of serious loss might be rejected even if there were the opportunity, in favourable circumstances, of large gains. Another approach may be to accept projects involving high risks only if the prospect of gain were substantially higher than average. In many respects, risky investments may be regarded as being in the same category as investment decisions made when interest rates are high. As we have seen, the effect of high interest rates is markedly to discount the future; uncertainties about the outcome can be seen as having the same effect as the heavy discounting of future returns. A further means of examining uncertainties is to attach probabilities to the future cash flows, such that the earlier ones may be more certain and carry a higher probability of occurring while the later ones may be less certain and hence carry a lower probability.

FINANCING AND THE DISCOUNT RATE

So far we have simply said that the rate of discount to be used in net present value calculations is the cost of borrowing the funds. But we have said nothing about the choice of funds and how this affects the discount rate. We have examined the various sources of funds in chapter 7. The costs of each were considered and the effects of using a combination of sources were seen in the discussion of the capital gearing ratio. We now examine these points a little more.

First, consider the use of shareholders' funds only in financing investment. Theoretically, the cost of such capital is the net of tax return that shareholders can earn elsewhere on share investments of comparable risk. Hence projects should be required to earn at least this rate of return if equity finance is to be forthcoming. But there are problems with this line of argument. The use of such historically achieved rates of return implies that the required rate of return has not changed. It also assumes that this was the desired return. Neither of these assumptions may be true. Moreover, past rates of return may not continue into the future. There is also the problem that returns available elsewhere are the average returns from a number of projects. The investment decision is concerned with marginal returns. The return that shareholders would be paid by the company would also be based on the average from all investments, since we must pay all shareholders the same dividend per share. Existing shareholders, however, may gain through an increase in the share price arising from the capital market adjusting for the expected increase in future dividends occasioned by the new project. This market capitalization will be affected by the degree of risk attached to future dividends. The greater the perceived risk, the higher the discount rate used to capitalize future dividends and the lower the market capitalization. The equity cost of capital will thus be the minimum rate of return, after allowing for risk, that must be obtained from a project to ensure the maintenance of the value of the existing equity.

While retained earnings may have no accounting cost, they do have the opportunity cost of the return that the shareholders could have earned elsewhere if all profits had been distributed. In financing projects by retained earnings, it is necessary to accept only those projects whose expected future dividends at least cover these forgone opportunities.

In a perfect world, the cost of raising finance by means of equity, internal or loan finance would be the same. However, in practice long-term loans and debentures are normally expected to have a lower cost than equity shares. The reason is that their interest payments are fixed and thus fairly certain. The cost of loan capital is not the contractual rate, since such funds may sell at a premium or discount on the nominal price. The correct rate is the effective rate of interest – found by equating the market price of debt to the present value of the interest per year plus any final amount due on the date the loan matures. Risk may be accounted for by including a risk premium in the discount rate.

For all three sources, the discount rate has been discussed in terms of opportunity costs external to the company, that is, returns elsewhere forgone by providers of capital. When funds are scarce, the use of capital may have an internal opportunity cost, in terms of projects whose returns exceed the cost of borrowing but cannot be chosen since funds are not available. A discount rate may be estimated which is deemed to measure forgone internal opportunities, which can then be used in net present value calculations.

When more than one source of finance is used, the calculation of the discount rate becomes very complex. If the proportions of debt and equity capital are to remain unchanged, the appropriate cost of capital, and hence the discount rate, is the weighted average of each source with market values of each providing the weights. Any project earning more than the weighted average rate would be acceptable. However, there are problems with using such a discount rate, primarily because it assumes that the acceptance of any project does not change the general riskiness of the firm. This may not be true, and the cost of capital would need to be changed to account for this. In addition, we have seen that the cost of capital will be affected by the use of book or market values, in the same way as the gearing ratio was in chapter 7.

If the proportions of debt and equity funding change, the financial risk of the business as seen by debt or equity holders may change. The effects of this on the cost of capital are the subject of much debate in the academic literature. As often is the case, the problem reduces to one of a conflict between theoretical purity and practical applicability. There are two main views. The first is that as the gearing ratio rises the cost of equity will also rise in order exactly to offset any advantages flowing from the lower cost of loan finance relative to equity. This is based on the argument that the market discounts a company's total returns independently of the pattern of financing. The argument implies that the best estimate of the cost of capital is the simple weighted average method, which will remain constant. But this approach relies to a great extent on the assumption of perfect capital markets. As we have seen in the context of share issues, the market may not be so perfect.

The alternative view is that, above a certain gearing ratio, the uncertainty felt by equity providers increases. The reason is simply that, the more fixed interest commitments are taken on by increasing the proportion of debt-financing, the more likely it is that there will be no dividend for shareholders, and the more likely that bankruptcy will occur. The cost of equity will thus rise until, eventually, any advantage from debt-financing is offset. The cost of debt finance also rises with the increase in the amount of debt finance used, as the market demands increased returns to compensate for the increased risk of profits being inadequate to cover interest commitments. The average cost of capital will thus be affected by the gearing ratio.

In essence, the two arguments disagree as to the effects of gearing on the valuation of the firm by the market. The first contends that the total value is unaffected, while the other says that it is. As yet, neither theory has been absolutely proved or disproved. What is important to note is that the acceptance of one view may produce a different investment decision than if the other view were preferred.[19]

We have seen that in general the overall cost of capital is the rate at which the company's future earnings are discounted by the capital market in valuing the sources of finance on which the earnings will be obtained. The cost of capital, in short, is the discount rate at which this financial valuation equals the present value of future earnings. A problem, though, is that expectations of future earnings are impossible to observe. It is possible to obtain a simplified, but practicable, estimate of the real cost of capital. Let us assume that expected future earnings on the existing capital stock in all future years are equivalent to earnings in the current year. The ratio of current earnings to the market valuation of the company is an approximation to the cost of capital.[20] This ratio has been used, in conjunction with the ratio of profits to assets valued at replacement cost, to calculate a valuation ratio. This ratio measures the incentive for firms to invest as it relates the cost of capital to the likely profitability of projects. There will be an incentive for the firm to invest when the value of this ratio is greater than 1, since effectively the returns from the project are greater than the cost of purchasing the assets. The valuation ratio is published regularly by the Bank of England and has been found to be a reliable indicator of the incentive to invest, at an aggregate level. For individual firms it would be necessary to calculate a specific valuation ratio.

It is worth noting that the general effect of company taxation on the cost of capital is upwards, so depressing investment. Allowable deductions may reduce taxable profits to zero in a period of high nominal interest rates. The company thus loses out on capital allowances. This problem has been a contributory factor to the increase in asset leasing, which we examine in the next section. The effect of taxation is that, at the extreme, if corporation tax is 50 per cent, the relevant cost of capital is doubled.

To return to our investment example, it may be worth seeing what investment decisions Imperial Group actually made. In fact, the company invested over £100 million in all of its existing divisions. In particular, a new technology programme was started in the Tobacco Division. But, unlike the constraint we imposed in our example, the company was also able to spend £280 million to acquire the hotel and restaurant business of Howard Johnson Company in the USA. The group also divested itself of certain unprofitable and incompatible parts. Implicitly, the investment in the new subsidiary accounted for uncertainty, to some extent, by the payment of a price well below the current value of its assets. The acquisition was funded by the realization of holdings in government securities ('gilts'), which suggests the use of the return on gilts in determining the discount rate to be used to assess whether the new venture was worthwhile. Obviously, many other factors would be examined, but if the return from the new investment were not significantly above the return on gilts, it would hardly be profitable to make such a decision.

FURTHER APPLICATIONS OF DISCOUNTED CASH FLOW TECHNIQUES

It is possible to use discounted cash flow to assess the price to be paid for a firm. The basic approach to be followed is to ascertain the value of future discounted cash flows and to compare these with the purchase price contemplated. A number of factors peculiar to each firm may need to be taken into account, such as existing contracts with employees, whether previous losses can be offset against future profits to obtain tax savings, whether certain assets are not required and can be realized to provide funds for different uses.[21] The purchaser may also use discounted cash flow techniques to ascertain whether the price that may be obtained for the parts to be sold off and the return from the reinvested funds exceeds the returns that may be obtained from continued ownership.[22]

The techniques may also be used to decide how large a plant to build when demand is increasing. Large plants may cost less to build per unit of capacity than small plants, but if they are not fully utilized for some time surplus funds will be tied up unproductively. There is a need to balance the increased costs of construction against the reduced unit cost of capacity. Too much excess capacity to begin with represents a waste of capital; too little means that the possibilities of reducing unit capital costs of output will not be fully exploited. Such an approach applies to most cases of 'lumpy' investments, that is, where indivisibilities in plant size mean that it is impossible to increase capacity precisely in line with demand. One example is the construction of electricity power stations. The task is to ensure that sufficient capacity is available at all times to prevent power failures. Capacity is required to cope with peak daytime and winter-time demands and to allow for breakdowns. But at other times the capacity is left idle. Given that it takes a number of years to construct a power station, it is difficult to forecast accurately the appropriate amount of capacity to meet demand. The pattern of demand at times of the day and at various seasons of the year is fairly stable, but the growth in demand is affected by growth in the economy, the price of electricity relative to other fuels, the price of inputs, etc. All of these factors are difficult to forecast five to ten years ahead. The Monopolies and Mergers Commission, in their examination of the efficiency of the Central Electricity Generating Board, recognized these problems.[23]

A familiar problem to many businesses is whether or not to buy or lease a building or piece of capital equipment. Buying involves an immediate cash payment; leasing involves a succession of cash payments over the period for which the building or equipment will be used. Discounted cash flow techniques can be used to help make the decision. The company will wish to know at what rate of interest it becomes beneficial to lease rather than buy, in other words, the discount rate that equates the present value cost of the lease payments with the cost now of purchasing the same equipment. This discount rate may then be regarded as the maximum borrowing rate for purchasing the equipment. If the firm can obtain finance at a higher rate it would pay to lease the equipment.

Consider an example. Let us assume that the firm has decided that it must replace a certain machine. The alternatives are to purchase a replacement machine for £10,000, or to lease it for five years with a fixed annual rental, payable in advance, of £2,700. Table 9.5 indicates that, if the company can borrow at a rate of 18 per cent, it is just worthwhile to buy the machine (the net present value is positive). If the firm can borrow only at rates above this level, the preferred decision is to lease the equipment.

This is a simple example of the lease or buy decision; in practice, it would be necessary to take account of tax allowances or capital

Table 9.5 The lease or buy decision

Year	Lease payments (£)	Purchase cost forgone (£)	Discount factors (18%)	Present value (£)
0	−2,700	10,000	1.000	7,300
1	−2,700		0.847	−2,287
2	−2,700		0.718	−1,939
3	−2,700		0.609	−1,644
4	−2,700		0.516	−1,393
Net present value				+37

grants that may be obtained from buying equipment but not from leasing it. The ability to obtain capital allowance against tax depends on the existence of sufficient profits against which to set the cost of purchasing equipment. In times of a recession, the size of capital investment projects may exceed taxable profits, such that companies cannot obtain the full advantages from capital allowances. When high interest rates are taken into account it becomes beneficial, subject to the availability of leasing finance, to lease rather than buy.[24] The existence of this situation brings into question the appropriateness of the current system of taxable allowances for encouraging investment in manufacturing industry. It means that tax incentive schemes are likely to be ineffective. It also means that some of the financial benefits from investing accrue to the financial institutions leasing the equipment, since they gain the tax advantage from buying the equipment. It is they who, by making a profit from leasing, may have sufficient taxable profits to take full advantage of capital allowances. The response of a number of companies to this problem has been to set up separate financing subsidiaries, who buy the capital equipment and lease it to the parent company. In this way, it is possible to ensure that the benefits of capital allowances are kept within the firm.

INVESTMENT IN THE PUBLIC SECTOR

Investment projects carried out for the government or in the nationalized industries should, in theory at least, be based on the same criteria as those we have examined for private business. If not, distortions may occur such that a project that would be regarded as unsatisfactory in the private sector may be undertaken in the public sector or vice versa. In either case there is a misallocation of resources. It was partly to overcome this problem that the 1967 White Paper on the control of the nationalized industries[25] introduced the test discount rate (TDR). This discount rate was based on the real pre-tax rate of return sought on low-risk projects in the private sector, and was set at 10 per cent. In other words, the TDR was an opportunity cost measure determined by what the resources were expected to earn if they were invested in the private sector. As we have seen, the discounted cash flow rate of return on an investment is that discount rate required to equate the present value of its stream of future cash flows with the present value of the capital outlay. To assess the validity of a project in the nationalized industries, the present value of the project is set to 0 in our equation for the internal rate of return, so that the equation becomes:

$$0 = -A_0 + \frac{A_1}{(1+r)} + \frac{A_2}{(1+r)^2} + \ldots + \frac{A_n}{(1+r)^n}.$$

The value of r, the internal rate return, required to satisfy this equation, is compared with the TDR. If it is greater than or equal to the TDR the investment project is worth undertaking.

In practice, only a small proportion of nationalized industries' investment was appraised after 1967 using the TDR. A study in 1976 by the National Economic Development Office (NEDO) examined investment appraisal in the gas, steel, rail and telecommunication industries.[26] Only in the steel industry were discounted rates of return calculated. The other industries used techniques that involved the choice of investment projects that had the lowest discounted costs. The argument for this approach is that much investment is essential, inescapable, unavoidable or necessary to provide a satisfactory level of service. For example, in the case of British Gas, about three-quarters of investment was undertaken as an unavoidable consequence of the decision to exploit natural gas.

As a solution to this problem, the 1978 White Paper[27] introduced a new investment criterion, the 'required rate of return' (RRR). This rate is also intended to equal the real opportunity cost of capital to the nationalized industries. The approach to investment appraisal will be that individual industries will agree their own discount rate with their sponsoring[28] department, subject to the demand that, on new investment as a whole, they earn a RRR of 5 per cent. While this may mean that more investment is subject to a full appraisal, the RRR has a number of shortcomings. We have seen that discounted cash flow investment appraisal techniques are based on the marginal costs and benefits from a project. By concerning itself with the real return earned on investment as a whole, the RRR is an average measure. Moreover, by using achieved returns it contradicts the *ex ante* nature of investment appraisal. There are also difficulties raised by allowing each industry to use a different marginal discount rate. The result is that there will be no unique combination of projects that will be consistent with earning the RRR; there will be cross-subsidization of less profitable projects; and there will be distortions as industries within the same sector (e.g., energy) use different tests of the acceptability of projects.

There is clearly a conflict between the theoretically more appropriate TDR and the practically more feasible RRR. However, for both there is also the problem of how they relate to the cost of borrowing. In fact, since both are 'shadow prices' (i.e., measures of opportunity cost), they do not relate to the cost of borrowing. The nationalized industries are able to borrow from the National Loans Fund at less than the RRR. By lending to the industries at the RRR, this problem could be avoided, with the attendant benefit that misleading surpluses arising from favourable financing rather than higher prices would be removed.

The problem of capital rationing imposed by the external financing limits, discussed in chapter 7, can be accommodated into the investment criterion by measuring the discount rate with reference to the best public sector investment forgone, rather than with respect to the private sector.[29]

In recognition of the problems discussed in this section, there have recently been increasing arguments that the nationalized industries should be subject to the pressures of the market by a requirement to borrow at least part of their finance from the private sector. We have examined these arguments in chapter 8.

It was mentioned above that the nationalized industries often claimed that it was not possible to subject individual investment projects to the TDR since they followed unavoidably from other decisions. In such cases it is necessary to examine the extra benefits and costs to society of undertaking these large projects. The technique of cost–benefit analysis is an attempt to quantify the social effects of undertaking certain projects which, on strict commercial lines, may not appear worthwhile.

There have been a number of cases where cost–benefit analysis has been employed in public sector decision-making. Some examples are: the building of the Victoria Underground Line in London,[30] the Channel Tunnel,[31] the decision on where to build the third London airport,[32] the decision on whether or not to close the Cambrian Coast Railway Line in Wales,[33] etc. In addition, a number of studies have been undertaken internally by public organizations, but remain unpublished. In all these cases attempts were made to examine the wider repercussions of the investment decision.

The basic idea behind cost–benefit analysis is that, if it is necessary to decide whether to undertake a project or not, it should be accepted only if the benefits exceed those of the next best alternative. The benefits of the next best alternative are the opportunity costs of undertaking the project. Hence, it is in this way that costs and benefits are compared. The problem arises in measuring these costs and benefits. In particular, there is the difficulty of dealing with externalities, which are the effects of courses of action for which there is no market transaction. Thus, for example, airline operators do not have to pay for the inferior noise quality that they impose on the affected population.

In order to discuss cost–benefit analysis we shall take as an illustrative example the case of the third London airport,[34] which involved the most detailed cost–benefit study ever undertaken. The Roskill Commission were charged with the task of inquiring into 'the timing of the need for a four-runway airport to cater for the growth of traffic at existing airports serving the London area' and 'to consider the various alternative sites and to recommend which site should be chosen'.

The Commission concentrated on the latter part of the reference. Preliminary examination produced a short-list of four sites: Cublington, Foulness, Nuthampstead and Thurleigh. For each site the cost–benefit analysis examined six main factors that would arise from construction of an airport: planning, noise, aviation issues, airport design and construction, surface access and defence issues. For each it was necessary to measure the impact of the airport, to forecast how the people affected would react, and thence to assess the costs and benefits associated with their reaction. The value of costs and benefits are, respectively, what the person adversely affected by the airport would just be willing to accept in compensation, and what the person benefiting would just be prepared to pay for it.

The costs of airport design and construction are fairly straightforward. The planning issues involve costing site acquisitions. Difficulties arise in assessing the effects of agricultural land lost, in measuring the effects of fixed access links, in determining the effects of any resultant urban and industrial growth, and in estimating the prices that individuals put on relinquishing their property through compulsory purchase.

The noise generated by an airport is perhaps the major externality. However, there are major difficulties in quantifying it and assessing compensation. An approach to the problem is to draw ordinal noise contours around an existing airport, with the highest noise nearest to the airport and the lowest furthest away. It is then possible to compare the observed depreciation in house prices with these contours. The relationships so obtained can be applied to each potential site. By multiplying the fall in house prices in each contour band by the number of houses affected, it is possible to quantify the noise effect. But, to the extent that individual preferences are ignored, this method produces inaccuracies.

Surface access issues are very important. The dilemma that arises is whether to build the airport near the people and accept the noise or away from population centres at the expense of poor access. Leaving aside the possibilities for using 'science fiction' modes of transport, since travel at such speeds is impractical over short distances, it is necessary to estimate the extra facilities required to cope with the increased traffic flow in the relevant catchment areas. In addition to the problems of assessing what the increase in traffic will be, subsidiary issues, such as evaluating the cost of travellers' time, are involved.

In evaluating air access costs, traffic flow simulations under varying circumstances are needed in order to balance the benefits accruing from the reduction in congestion at one airport against the costs involved in flying greater distances to land.

Defence costs relate to the costs of finding new sites for displaced defence establishments and of interference with the operation of military airfields.

Since all the costs and benefits will not be incurred at the same time, it is necessary to express them in some common form that facilitates comparison. In the case of the third London airport, the 10 per cent test discount rate was used, with 1982 as the base year, since this was more representative of the time period when resources would be committed to the project. In particular, it was seen as being important for easing the task of comparing measured costs and benefits with unmeasured items, such as the effect on wildlife. Many of these effects would not start until after the airport was in operation. If a much earlier base date were chosen, the effect of the discounting process would be to make it appear that any inter-site differences after the mid-1980s would be negligible, when in fact this would not be the case.

The results of the Commission's exercise are shown in table 9.6. It is worth noting that these figures were revised in order to take into account criticisms of earlier estimates, so emphasizing the difficulties in undertaking cost–benefit analysis. For each item, costs/benefits are expressed as differences from the lowest-cost site, mainly because of the difficulty of estimating the absolute magnitudes of each option. This is acceptable since, if it is agreed that an airport is required, the only important figures are the differences between each option. The aggregate figures for each site are based on the estimated effects of the assumption of a median noise level and, by taking into account the highest and lowest values placed on time saved or lost, provide a range of possible costs. It is sensible to express figures in

Table 9.6   Cost–benefit analysis of the third London airport – excess over lowest-cost site (£ million at 1982)

	Cublington			Foulness			Nuthampstead			Thurleigh		
	a	b	c	a	b	c	a	b	c	a	b	c
(1) Airport construction		18			32			14			0	
(2) Extension of Luton		0			18			0			0	
(3) Airport services	23		22	0		0	17		17	7		7
(4) Meteorology		5			0			2			1	
(5) Airspace movements	0		0	7		5	35		31	30		26
(6) Passenger user costs	0		0	207		167	41		35	39		22
(7) Freight user costs		0			14			5			1	
(8) Road capital		0			4			4			5	
(9) Rail capital		3			26			12			0	
(10) Air safety		0			2			0			0	
(11) Defence		29			0			5			61	
(12) Public scientific establishments		1			0			21			27	
(13) Private airfields		7			0			13			15	
(14) Residential conditions (noise, off-site)		13			0			62			5	
(15) Residential conditions (on-site)		11			0			8			6	
(16) Luton noise costs		0			11			0			0	
(17) Schools, hospitals and public authority buildings (incl. noise)		7			0			11			9	
(18) Agriculture		0			4			9			3	
(19) Commerce and industry (incl. noise)		0			2			1			2	
(20) Recreation (incl. noise)		13			0			7			7	
Aggregate of inter-site differences (costed items only)*	0		0	197		156	137		128	88		68

Key to columns: a = based on assumption of high value placed on time saved
b = based on median noise level assumption
c = based on assumption of low value placed on time saved.
* Aggregate derived by taking Cublington as lowest cost and summing differences between this and each other site respectively.
Source: Commission on the Third London Airport, *Report* (London, HMSO, 1971), p. 119.

terms of a range because of the process of estimation inherent in the exercise.

In the table, row 2 refers to the effect on costs of extending Luton airport. Only in the case of Foulness being chosen would Luton continue to operate. In row 4 the effects of different weather conditions at each site are estimated. Row 5 reflects the fact that each site will have a different pattern of air traffic. In rows 6 and 7 the estimates of the relative inconveniences of each site for passenger and freight are shown, while in rows 8 and 9 the costs of providing the surface links to cater for the expected traffic changes are calculated. Notice the very high surface access costs at Foulness. Row 10 is simply an estimate of the cost of bird-strike damage at Foulness. Row 11 involves costs of redeployment of defence establishments. Thurleigh in particular, is a problem in this respect. Row 12 reflects the greater conflict of Nuthampstead and Thurleigh with government research establishments, and row 13 shows the effects on the operations of private airfields. As regards noise, notice that row 14 shows a very high cost penalty against Nuthampstead. Row 15 represents the compensation that should be paid to those living in the areas covered by the airport sites, including an element to reflect the sentimental value that residents attach to their homes for which they would receive no compensation. Row 16 shows airport noise costs relative to Luton, with only Foulness significantly higher. Rows 17, 19 and 20 estimate the effects on non-residential factors, while row 18 shows the effects on agricultural land of the airport development.

Clearly, from the final row Cublington is the lowest-cost site and Foulness the highest. However, in spite of all the evidence weighed by the Commission in reaching their verdict, the government decided, mainly on political grounds, to choose Foulness. As yet, the construction of the third London airport is not underway, questions are still being raised about the timing of the need for it, to which the Commission devoted little attention, and the appropriate siting of it.[35]

A number of general problems with cost–benefit analysis are highlighted by our discussion of the case of the third London airport. In particular, there are problems of uncertainty, correctly assessing need, accounting for unquantifiable items, assessing compensation and the appropriate discount rate. While uncertainty may be dealt with by sensitivity analysis, the question of need, especially in the London airport case, is often inadequately assessed. If this were remedied it might appear that the project is not justified for a number of years.[36] Unquantifiable items are difficult to account for, and it is unlikely that planning, while drawing attention to the available options, is able to provide a rule for finding that solution which contributes the maximum net benefit.

Cost–benefit analysis is often regarded with scepticism because many of its estimates of compensation are merely notional. While it is proper to incorporate such items in arriving at the overall effect on society of the decision, cost–benefit analyses may be better understood and accepted if the losers from such decisions were fully compensated, even if it were only on a rather rough basis. The discount rate chosen heavily discounts the future; that is, it implies that society does not value the future very highly. Conservationists would certainly argue that the future should be valued more highly. But it is notoriously difficult to estimate society's time-preference rate. The test discount rate, as we have seen, is more appropriate as a reflection of the returns on private investment displaced. Indeed, it ignores social time-preference entirely. For the ways in which it is possible to deal with these considerations, readers are referred to a specialized text.[37] It is sufficient to note at this point that there are circumstances that would cause society to take a more favourable view of the future. This may be so if the growth of incomes is expected to fall, and if investment in a project subject to cost–benefit analysis is likely to displace less private investment than investing an equivalent sum in a nationalized industry.

NOTES

1 For an interesting discussion of the experiences of this industry see R. W. Shaw, 'The dry cleaning industry', *Journal of Industrial Economics*, 22 (1973).
2 The possibility of the use of excess capacity as a barrier to entry is illustrated in the case of Spillers in the Monopolies and Mergers Commission report, *Cat and Dog Food*, HC 447 (London, HMSO, 1976/77).
3 See D. Swann, *et al.*, *Competition in British Industry* (London, George Allen & Unwin, 1974).
4 See D. P. O'Brien, *et al.*, *Competition Policy, Profitability and Growth* (London, Macmillan, 1979).
5 As a proportion of total new-firm formation, the number of innovators is probably quite small. For example, in one study of new-firm formation only 9 of the sample of 55 new firms could be classed as innovators. See P. S. Johnson and D. G. Cathcart, 'New manufacturing firms and regional development', *Regional Studies*, 13 (1979).
6 See Johnson and Cathcart, 'New manufacturing firms', and J. R. Firn and J. K. Swales, 'The formation of new manufacturing establishments in the Central Clydeside and West Midlands conurbations, 1963–1972: a comparative analysis', *Regional Studies*, 12 (1978), for discussion. For US experience see A. C. Cooper, 'Spin-offs and technical entrepreneurship', *IEEE Transactions on Engineering Management*, EM 18 (1971).
7 See E. B. Roberts and H. A. Wainer, 'Some characteristics of technical entrepreneurs', *IEEE Transactions on Engineering Management*, EM 18 (1971).
8 This example is discussed in S. Sabin, 'At Nuclepore, they don't work for GE anymore', *Fortune* (December 1973).

9   A summary of this example is in N. Innes, 'The Rolls-Royce crash', *The Listener*, 22 January 1981.

10   Some further examples of innovations are contained in C. Layton, *Ten Innovations* (London, George Allen & Unwin, 1972).

11   For a discussion of this method see J. A. Piper, 'Classifying capital projects for top management decision making', *Long Range Planning* 13 (June 1980).

12   See J. Forsyth and J. A. Kay, *The Economic Implications of North Sea Oil*, (London, Institute of Fiscal Studies, 1980).

13   J. A. Kay, 'Accountants, too, could be happy in a Golden Age', *Oxford Economic Papers* 28 (1976).

14   H. Lever and G. Edwards, 'How to bank on Britain', *The Sunday Times*, 13 January 1980.

15   B. Carsberg, *Analysis for Investment Decisions* (London, Accountancy Age, 1974).

16   This is a case in which transfer pricing could be used.

17   See G. Meeks, *Disappointing Marriage: The Gains from Merger*, University of Cambridge, Department of Applied Economics, Occasional Paper 51 (1977).

18   For a full discussion of the use of sensitivity analysis see R. A. Brealey and S. C. Myers, *Principles of Corporate Finance* (New York, McGraw-Hill, 1981).

19   See M. Bromwich, *The Economics of Capital Budgeting* (Harmondsworth, Penguin, 1976), chs 6–8, for full discussion of the arguments.

20   See J. S. Fleming, L. D. D. Price and S. A. Byers, 'The cost of capital, finance and investment', *Bank of England Quarterly Bulletin* (July 1976), for an exposition of the method.

21   A discussion of this method is contained in A. J. Merrett and A. Sykes, *The Finance and Analysis of Capital Projects*, 2nd edn (London, Longman, 1974).

22   For a method of assessing this see A. Quintart, 'Pour une politique financière du désinvestissement', *Annales de Sciences Économiques Appliquées*, 36 (1980).

23   Monopolies and Mergers Commission, *Report on the Central Electricity Generating Board* (London, HMSO, 1981).

24   For an illustration of the lease or buy decision under such circumstances see J. R. Franks and S. D. Hodges, 'The role of leasing in capital investment', *Nat West Bank Review* (August 1979) 20–31.

25   *Nationalised Industries: A Review of Economic and Financial Objectives*, Cmnd 3437 (London, HMSO, 1967).

26   NEDO, *A Study of UK Nationalised Industries* (London, HMSO, 1976).

27   *The Nationalised Industries*, Cmnd 7131 (London, HMSO, 1978).

28   The sponsoring department is simply the department of the civil service dealing with the particular industry.

29   This method is outlined in M. G. Webb, 'United Kingdom policy for nationalised industries', in B. M. Mitchell and P. R. Kleindorfer, *Regulated Industries and Public Enterprise* (Lexington Books, 1980).

30   See M. Beesley and C. D. Foster, 'The Victoria Line: social benefit and finances', *Journal of the Royal Statistical Society*, 128 (1965).
31   See E. J. Mishan, *Cost-Benefit Analysis* (London, George Allen & Unwin, 1975).
32   Commission on the Third London Airport, *Report* (London, HMSO, 1971).
33   K. Richards, 'The economics of the Cambrian Coast Line', *Journal of Transport Economics and Policy*, 6 (1972).
34   The Roskill Commission Report is summarized in A. D. J. Flowerdew, 'Choosing a site for the third London Airport: the Roskill Commission's approach', in R. Layard (ed.), *Cost-Benefit Analysis* (Harmondsworth, Penguin, 1972).
35   See P. J. Forsyth, 'The timing of investments in airport capacity: the case of London Airport', *Journal of Transport Economics and Policy*, 6 (1972).
36   See A. A. Walters, 'Airports – an economic survey', *Journal of Transport Economics and Policy*, 12 (1978).
37   See Layard, *Cost-Benefit Analysis*.

10

Control

The discussion in this chapter will focus on the internal control of the company by management, rather than external control by shareholders or government.

To direct and co-ordinate any set of activities one must be clear about its purpose. As we have seen in chapter 1, most companies have stated aims, some of which appear in their annual report. For example, in Imperial Group the 'objective is by careful and constructive allocation of resources and by energetic and enterprising management to sustain a steady growth in earnings per share'. Aims such as these require refining into practical objectives. The refinement of broad aims into more specific ones and then into detailed planning is itself an important activity and will be dealt with in chapter 11. Physical work by people and machines follows planning, and the measurement of actual output provides an opportunity to measure differences between what happened and what was intended to happen. These deviations can be taken into account in future plans. If this is done well, achievement should more closely approximate intention and the aims of the company are most likely to be fulfilled.

The above description contains the four essential elements of a controlled system. They may be identified as:

CONTROL SYSTEM = AIM + PLAN + ACTION + FEEDBACK.

A system of activities will be out of control if any of these elements is missing. This does not mean it will cease to function, but it does indicate that it is vulnerable and any change could cause it to collapse. In simple terms, luck rather than judgement sustains an uncontrolled system. In such circumstances, X-inefficiency would exist. We return to this problem below.

This chapter will be concerned with what is required to ensure that aims and plans are fulfilled. The main requirement here is for information. Information for control needs to be both backward-looking (*ex post*) and forward-looking (*ex ante*). Control exerted by outside parties, as we saw in chapter 8, has to rely on published information, which by its nature is backward-looking. This information is insufficient for internal control purposes. Management need detailed information on how the firm has performed in the past so as to be able to evaluate the achievement of plans. They also require information about the future to enable action to be taken to achieve future plans. The type of information required is not the same for forward or backward-looking control. To see the difference, we can relate each to the management structure of the firm. Figure 10.1 shows a typical management organization chart. At the top, senior management is concerned mainly with making long-term decisions, over a period of months to years. We may term this *strategic control*. For this type of control, forward-looking information is needed – for example, about the future pattern of demand for the product, predictions about the performance of the economy in general, etc. As such, the information will be required less often and in less detail than for shorter-term control. The essential need is for broad trends to be available.

Middle management, at the *tactical level of control*, are concerned with ensuring that the aims and plans laid down by senior management are put into operation and achieved. The relevant time-span is in terms of weeks and months. Information is required on what each department expects to happen (costs, outputs, etc.) over the coming months and on what did happen. Control is exercised by comparing actual with expected performance and taking corrective action.

At the lower management level, *operational control*, information required is the most detailed. Control involves co-ordinating productive activity. Not only does this mean information on delivery dates, materials availability, machine capacity, etc.; it also concerns the organization of employees - who will produce goods. As such, attention needs to be given to payment systems, overtime scheduling, skills availability, etc. Much of this is forward-looking information. Backward-looking information is provided by past production records.

We shall examine in detail below the gathering and use of information for these control requirements. The production decision has already been discussed in chapter 3. Here we deal simply with the information co-ordination problems and highlight the X-inefficiency difficulties that might arise at the operational level. This leads us into tactical control, where we shall consider how well the firm has performed given its targets. Budgetary control is the main tool

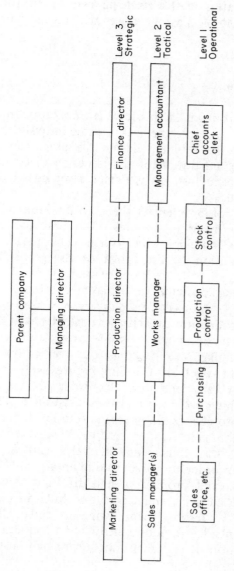

*Figure 10.1   Typical organization chart, showing control levels and communica-
tion links. Solid lines represent the usual management hierarchy
channels of communication; broken lines, the channels of cross-
communication between departments at the same level.*

available here. Having looked back to see how we have done, it is then necessary to look forward to see what the future holds and what action needs to be taken. Forecasting techniques can provide the required information at this strategic level of control. Corporate planning in the light of these forecasts will be the subject of the following chapter.

OPERATIONAL CONTROL

One of the major problems at this level is the ability to co-ordinate resources in order to achieve the best possible output. In many cases the key to solving the problem lies in the use made of available information. As an illustration of the issues involved consider the co-ordination of production in two steel companies,[1] only one of which was successful.

The crucial control problem is the co-ordination of selling and productive activity in order to make the best use of available capacity. In the first company, which was not successful, the aim was to make a contribution to the profit of the group to which it belonged, by supplying rolled sections of steel of a quality that other manufacturers found difficult to achieve. Customer orders were accepted by sales on the basis of a delivery promise of three to six weeks. Available production capacity was calculated at about 5,000 tonnes per week. The order was passed to production, who placed it with orders for similar specifications. A steel rolling cycle was arranged with a three-week span, rolling progressively from larger to smaller sections. At any one time the order book contained six weeks' work, of which half was in arrears. Customer pressure led to production having to change the machine setup in order to meet the priority (an eight-hour shift was required to change the rolls of steel). Effective capacity was thus reduced. Sales continued to offer delivery promises in order to attract and maintain custom. Problems arose because sales and production had different views about the extent of available capacity and lead-times. Such incompatibilities, and the inability to resolve them owing to personality conflicts between departments, led to poor control and a consequent low level of capacity utilization. It is perhaps not surprising that the company closed not long after the reported study was undertaken.

We may compare this company with another steel company which, through better understanding between sales and production, was able to achieve a compatible view of capacity. As a result, 90 per cent of orders were delivered on time and capacity utilization was as much as 66 per cent, close to full capacity within the constraints of the rolling programme. In this company the aim was to make a profit by providing a reliable supply of high-quality products to the home and exprt markets. Figure 10.2 illustrates the operational activity to achieve this aim. As before, orders were received in sales, who booked the order on to the rolling programme at a point on one of the future three-week rolling cycles using a computer which holds order book and production information. Unlike the previous company, each cycle covered a predetermined set of roll changes with approximate periods and hence capacity at each roll size. A daily report showing the load, including arrears, resulting from previous orders and the expected spare capacity, assisted sales with this decision. Sales also estimated the lead-time needed for the

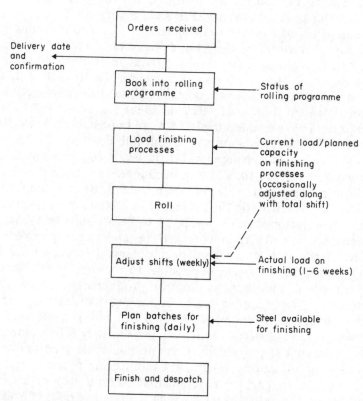

Figure 10.2   Operational information in a steel company.

various finishing processes. Reports of total load by finishing process for each week assisted this decision. These reports were up-to-date, as of the previous day. This timeliness was achieved by the use of the computer.

The total load by process for the next six weeks was used as a guide in allocating shifts or workers to particular processes. There was thus some provision for the adjustment of basic capacity. Control was achieved through the use of feedback reports of the degree of lateness in production to modify the amount of available capacity which it was the aim of sales to sell.

Quite clearly from this example, good control depends very much on the use of information on the available machines and materials. But poor control may also result from problems with labour. The improvement of information on productivity levels may help to pinpoint problem areas.

This aspect of control is illustrated by the case of the Inner London letter post.[2] As the postal system is very labour-intensive, its success depends to a great extent on the level of labour productivity. As we saw in chapter 8, there are difficulties in measuring productivity, but it is possible to establish trends in available figures. The Monopolies and Mergers Commission were able to establish that, while productivity in other postal regions had remained fairly constant between 1968 and 1979, in Inner London it fell by some 25 per cent. This was due mainly to a fall in postal traffic by 30 per cent when related man-hours worked fell by only 10 per cent. Although with small changes in traffic levels the number of man-hours worked will be fixed, for a decline of this magnitude a large reduction in hours worked would be expected. Rather than blaming the fall in productivity on the decrease in business, working practices and payment systems were considered to be at fault. In the former, overmanning, inflexibility in work patterns and stopping work before the end of the shift were the main problems. However, because of union opposition, it was not possible to measure traffic levels in sufficient detail and thus to monitor productivity. Hence, it was difficult to revise manning levels in the light of changed circumstances. In addition, payment systems did not provide sufficient incentive for the individual to increase productivity. The Commission saw as a vital first step to solving these problems the need to establish the means of measuring traffic and monitoring productivity. This would need to be part of a system that continuously reviewed the operations of the postal service. Such a system would provide the necessary key information to enable managers to set realistic targets and provide the information on which performance could be assessed against regional manpower budgets. We turn to examine budgetary control in the next section, as a part of tactical control.

One of the main tools of tactical control is the annual budget. It is not the only means of control at this level; for example, production control is also important, as we have seen in an earlier chapter. The value of the budget lies in its attempts to integrate all aspects of the business. Narrowly defined, a budget is a plan showing how resources are to be acquired and used over a specific period. However, in a modern large-scale organization, a budget may be better regarded as an activity designed to help ensure the achievement of strategic organizational objectives.

The master budget is a set of interlocking accounts for each part of the business for the coming financial year, often broken down into monthly periods. It should contain, for each department, estimates of the levels of expenditure and output. Often a total output figure for the firm will be determined with the budgeted figures for each department reflecting this level of capacity utilization. Departmental budgets will be drawn together to produce the budgeted profit and loss account and balance sheet for the company.

In a large company, the budget may be drawn up for each operating division or production unit. Hence, for Imperial Group, we would expect there to be separate budgets for the Tobacco, Food, Brewery, and Paper, Board and Plastics Division. Control focuses on the deviation of actual from budgeted performance in each division. However, problems can arise in some companies because the use of divisional data may give a misleading view of where responsibility lies. Divisions may be more or less centralized. For budgetary control to be effective, managers must have some independence in their actions and be clear as to what are their responsibilities. A second problem in such multi-product firms relates to the assessment of the profitability of individual products. This difficulty arises when one division obtains some of its inputs from another division. The internal pricing policy of the company may mean that the price to be paid is not a true reflection of the costs of the inputs.

In the case of a fairly small company, budgets will focus on each part of the firm's trading activities. The budget for the sales department should specify the value of sales required. Underlying this figure will be estimates of the quantities of various products that can be sold and the prices that will be realized. Expenditure by the sales department will also be budgeted; the figure allowed being a function of the number of salesmen, the average salary and commission earned and the selling expenses. For the production department, output will take the place of sales, and expenditure will be based on the supposition that production programmes are adhered to.

Table 10.1 shows how the budgeted expenditure for a production department compares with actual outgoings after nine months of the current year. Column (1) is the total budgeted expense for the year and column (2) gives the budget for nine months, which is simply three-quarters of the annual total. The advantage of monitoring performance against budget each month is that it should allow 'fine-tuning' to take place and so give a better chance of achieving

Table 10.1   Budgetary control in the production department

	(1) Budget for year	(2) Budget for nine months (1) × ¾	(3) Actual for nine months	(4) Deviation from budget (3) − (2)
	£	£	£	£
Direct production department costs*				
Basic labour	152,417	114,313	152,890	+38,577
Overtime	60,404	45,303	31,875	−13,428
Materials	90,495	67,871	66,248	−1,623
Heat, light, etc.	23,005	17,254	21,750	+4,496
Indirect production department costs†				
Basic labour	45,844	34,383	36,472	+2,089
Overtime	12,487	9,365	7,275	−2,090
Materials	8,215	6,161	6,312	+151
Heat, light, etc.	3,868	2,901	3,400	+499
Total production Department costs	396,735	297,551	326,222	+28,671

* Direct costs are those incurred in manufacturing the product.
† Indirect costs are incurred other than in manufacturing; e.g., labour includes maintenance, administration, etc.; materials include maintenance materials, stationary, etc.

the budget at the year's end. In the table negative deviations occur in column (4) when actual costs are less than those budgeted for; positive deviations arise when they are higher.

In general, variations from the budget may arise for a number of reasons and we should adjust the information given in the table to obtain adequate data for control purposes. For example, the level of output may be greater than the budget assumed. If we do not recast the table for different output levels, we cannot say whether the department has done well or not. We may also have to make allowances for the effects of having to pay higher prices for items and having to use greater quantities of inputs. In the case of raw materials, we may have to pay more per unit because of an increase in world prices or perhaps because our buying policies are not as good as they should be. We may have used more material per unit because of increased wastage through using inferior inputs. Labour costs may be raised by taking more man-hours to produce the product as labour productivity has fallen. Expenses like electricity may cost more if the electricity board raises prices faster than we expect. Clearly, the information as presented hides a number of effects that may cancel each other out. For many firms, though, this is probably the typical budgetary control statement.

The standard costing method of budgetary control provides a more detailed approach. This approach starts by specifying the input prices and quantities of materials, labour, etc., that the process should incur if it is in control. Budgetary control then consists of comparing these desired prices and quantities with those actually incurred. In this way, it is possible to isolate whether deviations from budget are due to the use of too much material, the payment of too high a price, or both. For further details readers are referred to a specialized management accounting text.[3]

But not every departure from the intended costs and inputs is necessarily bad. In some cases the differences may be fairly minor. Management have to decide whether it is worth investigating such variances. The first question to be asked is whether or not the variance is controllable. If management cannot do anything about it, there is little point in carrying out an investigation. If it can do something about it, we need to know whether the difference is significant or not. Should the difference be significant, then the question is whether the costs of investigation outweigh the likely benefits to be derived from correcting the variance. If they do not, it is worth pursuing the matter.

In the case of the quantity of materials used per unit of product, the firm may be able to exercise some degree of quality control and proceed as follows. The standard amount of materials that should be used may be determined by taking the average amount per unit over a number of months, or perhaps years. A control chart may then be constructed by setting limits either side of this average, within which performance would be regarded as acceptable. An example of such a control chart is that shown in figure 10.3. The diagram shows the average as the standard to be attained, with upper and lower control limits. Outside the control limits, the probability of the process being in control is very low. Observations 1–12 are the average quantities of inputs in each period. Observations 5, 6, 7 and 10 lie outside the control limits and should be investigated. With the first three of these, too much material is being used. Is it faulty? Is there a lot of waste owing to inattention by operators? Observation 10 may need to be investigated as it may mean that production costs have been increased in order to save material or alternatively that the goods produced will be of poor quality because too little material has been used. Great care is needed in setting control limits because if they are set too generously there is a danger that the process will not be investigated when it is out of control; and if they are set too severely we may investigate when the process is still in control.

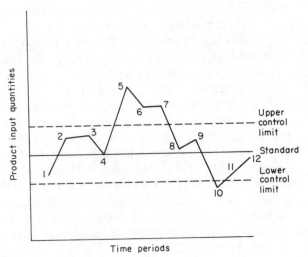

Figure 10.3   A control chart.

Clearly, in all the above cases, the problem of the interpretation of performance will be complicated if the firm produces more than one product. Particularly when it is possible to vary the input proportions of raw materials or labour, it will be necessary to ascertain whether the company has produced the best product mix.

Investigation of input costs and control decisions based on these will be affected by the existence of inflation. Inflation means that prices of raw materials, labour and overheads will rise. If our target was set some time ago cost variances are likely to appear significant. But the difference may not be due to management performance. It is necessary in such circumstances to adjust the target to take account of inflation. With high levels of inflation, raw material buying policies, energy conservation and labour productivity take on greater importance, since small errors in quantities used may be associated with large financial effects. Hence, the cruder comparison of aggregate actual and budget figures may be inadequate for ensuring accurate budgetary control.

The use of inflation-adjusted information for management control was found by the Sandiland Committee, reporting in 1975, to be fairly insignificant.[4] However, more recent case study experience,[5] after companies have been exposed to high levels of inflation for a number of years and have acquired greater awareness of the benefits of accounting for inflation, indicates a far higher utilization of inflation-adjusted management information. We have discussed inflation accounting in chapter 8. As regards the adjustments discussed there, management control is more interested in the use of specific changes in the prices of assets and stocks; with taking account of the change in the price of stocks possibly being seen as more relevant than using replacement cost asset values to calculate depreciation because of uncertainty about when or whether the asset would be replaced. Experience in the USA of inflation-adjusted management accounts shows that about half of companies utilize them in some form, reflecting the recognition that inflation would continue to be a significant feature of the US economy.[6] This was reinforced, by the publication of an inflation accounting standard, as also happened in Britain. However, it was argued by the authors of both studies that greater education was required to alert managers to the advantages of inflation-adjusted data for internal control purposes.

Traditionally, budgets have been prepared without consulting employees. However, more recently there have been arguments for their participation in the setting of budget targets. When this is the case, budgets are likely to take into account the needs, aspirations, etc., of the budgetees. If this is not done, employees may not be motivated to achieve the budget target.[7] However, we must be careful about the way in which participation in the budgeting process is achieved. A study by Lowe and Shaw shows very clearly how participation in the preparation of budgets may have adverse effects if it encourages those concerned with executing them to act in their own interests, in conflict with the interests of the company.[8] The process of sales budgeting was examined in a retail chain of over 300 shops. The nine area managers of the company formulated their own sales budgets for the coming year, for each shop in their area, prior to a meeting with the senior marketing officer at which results were finalized. It was found that the benefits from using detailed local knowledge possessed by the managers were outweighed by bias in the budget forecasts. As the company reward structure was based on a league table of performance against budget, there was every incentive for those responsible for sales to set a low target so as to be fairly sure of achieving it. Second, as company policy included an implicit norm that sales would continue to grow by 5 per cent per year, this tended to be built into forecasts, in order to please head office. But clearly, in those shops that were declining it was impossible to achieve this target. Finally, the desire by unsuccessful managers to gain job security by forecasting high performance, which could clearly not be achieved, also produced biased budgets. All three of these reasons led managers to behave rationally, by defending their own aims, although these were in conflict with the aims of the company.

Our discussion in this section has shown that the success of the budgetary control process depends not only on the degree of sophistication in the tools used to forecast and analyse results, but even more on achieving a satisfactory balance of conflicting pressures.

Cash flow forecasting
There is a need to forecast cash flows into the long-term future and to examine sources of finance when investment decisions are being considered. We have discussed these aspects in previous chapters. For tactical control purposes, it is also necessary to forecast cash flows for the coming year. This should be carried out as part of the annual budgeting procedure. The statements thus produced are forward-looking. This contrasts with the use of source and application of funds statements, balance sheets, and profit and loss accounts, which as we saw in chapter 8 are essential backward-looking.

The cash flow forecast is a useful tool for management since it enables them to assess whether the company will obtain sufficient funds from sales to pay for outgoings. Should there not be enough funds, management are forewarned of the need to reduce costs or to seek external financial assistance from the bank. The cash flow forecast is particularly important when we recall the distinction between profitability and liquidity. The budgeted profit and loss account may show a healthy profit for the year, but unless the company is able to meet the demands of creditors, it may not reach the end of the year.

Consider the example in table 10.2, which consists of a budgeted profit and loss account and a cash flow statement, for a company which buys materials one month, and packages and distributes them the next month. The starting point for preparing these figures is to forecast sales for the coming year, using one of the techniques we discuss in the next section. In our example, sales are forecast to increase steadily throughout the year. Given the sales forecast, we can estimate the cost of selling the goods (the expenses), in order to obtain the forecast profit or loss. The monthly expenses here are wages, cost of materials sold and one-third of the quarterly rent. Line 3 of the table shows a steadily improving monthly profit, producing a total profit of £4,140 for the year.

Contrast this with the cash flow forecast. The company starts the year with £3,000 in cash. Each month it pays wages in cash and pays cash to its suppliers, so that it receives no trade credit. In the first month of each quarter it pays the rent. Notice the different effect rent has on the cash flow forecast and the profit forecast. All goods bought in January are sold in February, all goods bought in February are sold in March and so on. Customers pay one month after receiving the goods (i.e. a trade credit taken period of 30 days), so that the sales figure of £1,450 in February (line 1), for example, becomes the cash received figure in March (line 5). The effect on the cash balance at the end of each month of all these factors is shown in line 9, which becomes line 4 in the following month.

Clearly, the company will need bank overdraft facilities to tide it over most of the year until it achieves a positive cash balance in December. Alternatively, it could try to collect debts faster, pay creditors more slowly, reduce the workforce or try to find a cheaper source of materials.

Although the cash flow forecast provides an early-warning device, it is only as good as the forecasts on which it is based. While the firm may have a satisfactory knowledge of the market in which it operates, it will be able to predict the future only within certain

Table 10.2   *Fauché Ltd, budgeted profit and loss statement and cash flow forecast, 1982*

	Jan.	Feb.	Mar.	Apr.	May	June	July	Aug.	Sept.	Oct.	Nov.	Dec.	Total
	£	£	£	£	£	£	£	£	£	£	£	£	£
(1) Sales	—	1,450	1,700	1,950	2,200	2,450	2,700	2,950	3,200	3,450	3,700	3,950	29,700
(2) Expenses*	480	1,280	1,480	1,680	1,880	2,080	2,280	2,480	2,680	2,880	3,080	3,280	25,560
(3) Profit/(loss)	(480)	170	220	270	320	370	420	470	520	570	620	670	4,140
(4) Cash balance at 1st of month	3,000	1,560	160	10	(330)	(380)	(380)	(570)	(470)	(320)	(360)	(110)	
(5) *add:* Cash received from customers		—	1,450	1,700	1,950	2,200	2,450	2,700	2,950	3,200	3,450	3,700	
	3,000	1,560	1,610	1,710	1,620	1,820	2,070	2,130	2,480	2,880	3,090	3,590	
(6) *less:* Wages	400	400	400	400	400	400	400	400	400	400	400	400	
(7) Rent	240			240			240			240			
(8) Cash paid to suppliers	800	1,000	1,200	1,400	1,600	1,800	2,000	2,200	2,400	2,600	2,800	3,000	
(9) Cash balance at end of month	1,560	160	10	(330)	(380)	(380)	(570)	(470)	(320)	(360)	(110)	190	

* Monthly expenses are wages, cost of materials sold and one-third of quarterly rent.

limits. Hence, sales volume and prices may not grow as fast as expected or in the pattern expected; costs of materials may rise faster; debtors may pay more slowly; a bigger wage rise may have to be conceded so as to avoid a strike; etc. If allowance can be made for the possibilities of errors, the cash flow forecasts should provide a useful means for minimizing the dependence on expensive bank finance.

In the case of a limited public company, paying dividends and corporation tax, such statements may also help to highlight the adverse effects of these items on liquidity.

While those backward-looking cash flow statements serve a particular purpose, it is too late to do anything about the cash that has been paid out. Budgeted cash flow statements may alert management to the need to modify dividend payments and to examine means of tax avoidance.

STRATEGIC CONTROL

As we have seen, strategic control is concerned mainly with forming a view about the future.

It may be an optimistic view, a pessimistic view, one based on hunch or a simple assumption that the future will be rather like the past. All of these views require some kind of forward-looking information. When action has to be taken and resources committed, the accuracy of forecasts may make a great deal of difference to the fortunes of the company.

Some of the most important forecasts in business are connected with sales. Most production is carried out in advance of sales; to produce too much is expensive, to have too little on hand may be to miss substantial profits if demand proves to be unexpectedly high. In addition, uncertainty about the course of demand vitally affects investment decisions. An unexpected turn of events can make past decisions appear wrong in retrospect. Mistakes of this kind can be costly, and it is worth seeing whether techniques can be developed to give greater accuracy of prediction. The decision to spend money on forecasting should be based on the following considerations. If the use of forecasting techniques increases the accuracy of assumptions made about the future for planning purposes and improves the quality of managerial decisions in consequence, forecasting may be worthwhile. But it will do so only if the increase in profits that results from improved foresight exceeds the cost of making the forecasts. If profits can be increased by greater accuracy in fore-casting, it will be worthwhile increasing expenditure on the prepara-tion of forecasts up to the point that the additional cost just offsets the increase in returns that results.

Methods of forecasting
The method of forecasting used will depend very much on the objective. Some things are appropriate for a business to forecast, others are not. All businesses are affected by the rate of growth of the economy, but few businesses have the resources to devote to estimates of this kind. In most cases it may be best to rely on fore-casts made by those specializing in this field – although, as we shall see below, there then becomes a problem in choosing which forecast to believe. For most businesses the interest is in forecasting demand for their particular product range.

Non-mathematical methods of forecasting use interview techniques to obtain a view about the expectations of potential customers or businessmen. The industrial trends survey carried out by the Con-federation of British Industry in Britain asks businessmen about the changes they anticipate in business conditions and whether, for example, they anticipate increasing the level of their investment in some future period or whether it will fall or remain unchanged. In this way, fairly accurate short-term forecasts of investment patterns may be derived. But care is needed in this type of forecasting.

It is safer to ask what businessmen intend to do rather than what they think will happen, since opinions may be affected by what has been said in the media.

Consumer attitude surveys are also used as short-term forecasters of demand, by asking in a general way either about consumers' financial expectations in the coming year or about what they intend to buy. But what consumers actually spend may be different from their declared intentions, because of problems in obtaining the goods they want, owing to deficiencies in the production and distribution network or the inability to raise finance. Hence, other factors need to be taken into account, such as changes in the distribution of income, changes in disposable incomes, changes in the savings ratio, changes in inflation, changes in relative prices, etc.

In addition to making forecasts on these bases, qualitative techniques may be used, particularly where little historical data are available. For their success they depend on the judgement of manage-ment. In order to reduce the element of judgement, more sophisti-cated methods of forecasting are employed in suitable cases where data are available and accuracy can be improved sufficiently to justify the costs involved. This may involve the use of mathematical methods. Time-series and causal models are the two main types of mathematical forecasting method.[9] Time-series models, which we examine first, involve establishing patterns and trends in a historical series of data. On the assumption that the pattern will continue, extrapolations may be made into the future. Since they rely on past trends continuing into the future, such methods are more likely to be better for short-term forecasting, where trends are less likely to change.

Figure 10.4 illustrates typical forms that trends may take. Curve (i) represents a rising linear trend. Rising trends simply show an increase in the value of a variable over time; for example, sales may display a trend similar to curve (i) perhaps because of the effects of inflation. Of course, the trend need not be linear; it could, for example, display a logarithmic form (i.e., rising by the same percentage over time). Curve (ii) is a constant time-series there is no systematic change in the data over time. Curve (iii) displays a seasonal pattern; that is, in addition to the rising trend, peaks in sales appear at certain times of the year. For example, sales in off-licences

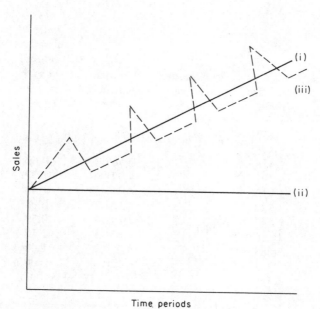

Figure 10.4   Time-series trends.

increase significantly at Christmas time. Cyclical patterns differ from seasonal patterns in that regular fluctuations in the time-series occur over a number of years rather than within a year.

Classical decomposition analysis provides a means for breaking down any time-series into its constituent parts. Forecasting is carried out based on the components found to be present in the data. Random and seasonal elements are smoothed out by taking moving averages of the series. This smoothed series contains only the trend component. The ratio of the raw data series to the smoothed series provides a seasonal index, which, when multiplied by the trend factor, can be used to obtain the forecast for any future period.

To see more clearly how the technique works, let us take an example. The information in table 10.3 relates to quarterly gas sales for the period 1978–80. The raw data are shown in column (1). Seasonalities in gas sales are quite clearly shown when the data are plotted, as in figure 10.5: peak sales occur in the first quarter (the winter quarter) of each year.

Table 10.3 Gas sales trend

(million therms)

Year and quarter	(1) Raw data series	(2) Four-quarter moving average	(3) Centred moving average	(4) Ratio of actual to centred moving average (1) ÷ (3)	(5) Average seasonal index
1978 (1)	5,257				
(2)	3,344				
(3)	2,416	3,827.0	3,908.7	0.62	0.60
(4)	4,291	3,990.3	4,021.9	1.07	1.09
1979 (1)	5,910	4,053.5	4,057.5	1.46	1.47
(2)	3,597	4,061.5	4,104.7	0.88	0.84
(3)	2,448	4,147.8	4,169.4	0.59	0.60
(4)	4,636	4,191.0	4,151.5	1.12	1.09
1980 (1)	6,083	4,112.0	4,097.3	1.48	1.47
(2)	3,281	4,082.5	4,120.0	0.80	0.84
(3)	2,330	4,157.5			
(4)	4,936				

Source: Energy Trends (various issues).

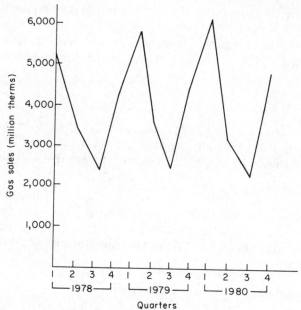

Figure 10.5   Seasonal effects in gas sales.

If we take a moving average over the period of seasonality of the series, the seasonality is removed and we are left with the trend in the data. In the table, the first number in column (2) is derived by taking the average of the first four observations: $\frac{1}{4}(5{,}257 + 3{,}344 + 2{,}416 + 4{,}291)$. The second number is obtained by dropping the 1978 (1) observation and substituting that for 1979 (1) in the above calculation. In this way a series of moving averages is obtained (col. (2)). As each moving average falls between two quarters, it is necessary to centre it on the relevant quarter by taking the average of the two moving averages that straddle that quarter. Hence, for 1978 (3) the centred moving average is given by: $\frac{1}{2}(3{,}827 + 3{,}990.3)$.

Column (4) is derived by dividing the raw series observations by the centred moving averages. This gives the ratio of actual to centred moving average – the seasonal index. But it contains random elements, and to remove these it is necessary to take the average of the figures in column (4) for the same quarter in each year. Hence, for the first quarter the average seasonal index is $\frac{1}{2}(1.46 + 1.48) =$ 1.47, and similarly for the other three quarters (column (5)). Clearly, the longer the data series, the more it should be possible to remove random fluctuations. We may obtain a de-seasonalized, smoothed data series by dividing each observation in the raw data series by the appropriate index.

If the trend in the moving average data is linear, we can 'explain' the smoothed series by solving the equation for a straight line, in general:

$$S_t = a + bt$$

where S_t = sales in a particular period; a = constant; b = slope of the line; t = time period. Using the data in table 10.3, and the regression technique outlined in chapter 1, we can estimate this equation to be:

$$S_t = 3,960.9 + 26.22t.$$

If the third quarter of 1978 is $t = 1$, then the first quarter of 1981 is $t = 11$. Thus, by extrapolating the trend (i.e. by substituting $t = 11$ into the above equation) we can forecast gas sales in this quarter to be:

$$S_{11} = 3,960.9 + 26.22 \times 11 = 4,249.3.$$

We noted that the average seasonal index for the first quarter in any year was 1.47. So, the forecast is $4.249.3 \times 1.47 = 6,246.5$ million therms of gas. This may be compared with the actual sales in that quarter of 5,862 million therms, a margin of error of just over 6 per cent. Differences between the forecast and actual figures may to some extent be the result of basing forecasts on a short series of data. This is important, because gas sales are very sensitive to temperature changes. Fluctuations in seasonal temperatures from year to year may not be ironed out in such a short data series. The usual solution is to undertake the calculations over a longer series, which has the advantage of reducing the influence of any one quarter on the estimates of seasonal factors. The disadvantage is that, the further back over time we go, the less appropriate may be the figures used. Thus, if winter sales of gas are becoming more pronounced because of an increasing use of gas central heating systems, the longer time-series will introduce a bias into the estimation. The method that we shall now consider provides a better means of ironing out random fluctuations.

An alternative to the use of moving averages is *exponential smoothing*. The logic underlying this technique is that future values of some variables are related to past values, with the more recent observations exercising greater influence than those taken earlier; hence the technique may be more accurate than the simple weighted average method, which gives equal weight to all observations. The value for some variable, such as sales, is based on an average of previous values, weighted in an exponential manner. Exponential means that the weights diminish as we look backwards in a constant proportion, as we shall see when we consider an example below.

If previous values of sales are S_t, S_{t-1} and S_{t-2} where t is the present time and $t-1$ and $t-2$ are earlier periods, an exponentially weighted average is calculated according to the formula:

$$A = (1-a) S_t + (1-a) aS_{t-1} + (1-a) a^2 S_{t-2}.$$

The value of a is chosen so that the sum of the weights equals 1. a itself, of course, is less than 1 and the weight given to earlier observations thus diminishes progressively, with remote observations contributing very little to the average. The 'best' value for a can be determined from past observations in such a way as to minimize the difference between the actual observations recorded over the same period and the values given by the exponentially weighted moving average system. This process is simpler than might seem, because once some average is accepted as an approximation to the first exponentially weighted average of a system, subsequent moving averages incorporating more recent observations are easily calculated. In fact, the new average is the old average plus $(1-a)$ times the difference between the new value of sales and the old average. This follows from the form of the geometric progression. If necessary, the best value of a can be determined by a process of trial and error. When a has been determined, forecasting may consist of no more than taking the value of the latest exponentially calculated mean as the expected value for subsequent periods. While such procedures may work, and have the advantage of smoothing out chance variations in the data for recent months, they suffer from the defect that they make inadequate allowance for any trend that may be present. If an upward trend is present, the moving average will always be less than the most recent value recorded, while it will be greater for a declining trend. Thus the base from which forecasts are made really represents the situation at some earlier time and moving averages may therefore require adjustment when a trend is present if they are to serve as forecasts. This is easily carried out, as Holt and Winters have shown, by utilizing estimates of both level (at time t) and trend.[10] The forecast n periods ahead is then given by:

$(level)_t + n \times (trend)_t.$

An interesting example of the use of exponential smoothing is shown in the estimation of gas demand in North West Gas.[11] A high level of accuracy is required in forecasting gas sales in order to avoid being unable to meet demand. (This remains necessary with the advent of natural gas, even though the method described here was developed for town gas, as it is not possible to meet peak demands directly from the North Sea.) Sales of gas are to a great extent affected by temperature. While a seasonal pattern, using average long-run temperatures, to some extent reflects the effects of temperature on demand, such a method is not good enough to give accurate demand forecasts on a weekly or day-to-day basis. This is particularly the case in periods of abnormally bad weather: although consumers' behaviour tends not to be affected by a few days of unusually cold weather, it is affected if the same temperature as in previous years has been preceded by a prolonged period of abnormally severe weather. The use of exponentially smoothed previous temperatures provides a way of taking into account the effect of these on demand. The most appropriate weights were found in the study to be:

$$T_e = 0.70W_t + 0.22W_{t-1} + 0.06W_{t-2} + 0.02W_{t-3}$$

where T_e is the exponential temperature effect; W_t is the average temperature in the week for which gas demand is to be estimated; W_{t-1} is average temperature in the previous week, etc. The initial value of 0.70 was chosen as it enables the exponential rates to decay relatively quickly, restricting the temperature analysis to only four weeks. The fit of the weekly gas demand relationship was found to be good, with a standard error of only 1 per cent, compared with 2 per cent for the long-run average temperature method. An increase in the amount of temperature-sensitive load can be allowed for by an increase in the slope of the straight line relationship between the logarithm of gas demand and the exponentially weighted temperature, with the weights remaining constant.

In addition to these forecasting methods, which rely on the past performance of the variables being examined, there are causal methods. These techniques use an underlying economic rationale to specify a causal relationship between the variable to be estimated (the dependent variable) and a number of explanatory variables (independent variables). By using a past series of data, with sufficient observations, the relationship can be quantified and the power of the model as a forecasting device indicated.

As an example, we may take forecasting the demand for wines and spirits in the study by Deaton, referred to in chapter 4.[12] It was postulated that consumption of these products was a log-linear function of income of the consumer and the relative price of the products. An equation of the following form was estimated using publicly available data for 1954–70:

$$\log Q = \alpha_i + (\beta_i^0 + \beta_i^1 \theta) \log \frac{\mu}{\pi} + \gamma_i \log \frac{P_i}{\pi}$$

where the terms are as described in note 11 to chapter 4. Note one difference from the equation shown there; the time trend for price elasticities (represented by the γ_i coefficient) was removed for projection purposes, because it was found in the study that the presence of a time trend in price elasticities was giving poor results. The resulting equation was estimated as:

$$\log Q = -19.794 + (3.7633 - 0.0054\theta) \log \frac{\mu}{\pi} - 0.3978 \log \frac{P_i}{\pi}.$$

The use of this equation to estimate observations over the period 1954–70 and to project forward to 1975 are illustrated in figure 10.6. The 1975 projection was obtained by substituting into the

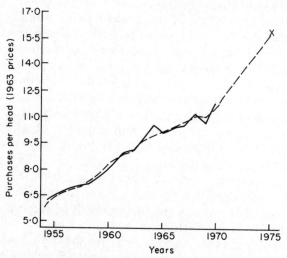

Figure 10.6   Comparison of actual and forecast demand for wines and spirits.
Source: A. Deaton, *Models and Projections of Demand in Post-War Britain* (London, Chapman & Hall, 1975), p. 118.

equation values of θ, $\log \mu/\pi$ and $\log P_i/\pi$ for 1975. The solid line represents actual data. The dotted line to 1970 and projected to 1975 shows the estimated observations. Although this is a rather simplistic causal model, and the study by Deaton examines more complex ones, it was found to perform reasonably well when compared with these other models.

Accuracy of forecasts

The accuracy of forecasts depends on a number of factors, including the accuracy of the data being used, the appropriateness of the forecasting method utilized, the assumptions that are made about the future and about the relationships between variables, and the way in which the forecasting technique is used.

The inaccuracy of data may arise simply from clerical errors in its compilation. But where it is necessary to employ sampling procedures to obtain data, other errors may arise. Sampling is undertaken in order to avoid the cost of asking everyone in the population their views on what they intend to buy, etc.;[13] if carried out correctly it is possible for the losses in accuracy necessarily incurred to be more than offset by the gains in reduced expenditure. However, the results obtained may be unrepresentative of the views of the population as a whole, and any decisions based on the information would then run the risk of being incorrect. The sample may become biased if some of those asked to fill in the questionnaire do not respond; if non-respondents have different characteristics from respondents, adjustments need to be made. Non-response bias may be checked by making efforts to interview a sample of those not responsible initially. A second request for the completion of a questionnaire may sometimes improve response rates. In general, personal interviews are better methods of obtaining information than mailed questionnaires, but the extra information obtained has to be balanced against the higher cost of obtaining it. Response rates may be affected by the organization carrying out the survey. For example, the response rate to the government's census is high because of legal penalties for failing to comply; in other cases companies may have to rely on the goodwill of respondents, which may diminish as survey techniques are increasingly used. Responses to mail questionnaires may be affected by the day on which mailing occurs, whether the envelope appears to be official or just a circular, and so on.

Even if the sample has been drawn correctly and a respectable response rate achieved, the size of the sample in relation to the population is important. The smaller the sample, the more likely errors are to occur. For example, a survey of 200 housewives over the whole of England may provide a reasonable sample on which to base forecasts of demand for a product; but if we wish to try and pinpoint how much will be bought in each of our sales regions, we have problems. If we have ten sales regions, we have on average only 20 respondents per region, which may produce misleading indications of likely demand in a particular area of the country. Errors due to biased samples can be estimated by statistical methods within certain limits.[14]

Instead of using large sample surveys, it is possible to use carefully chosen consumer panels of up to about 20 people. By using more detailed interviewing techniques than are possible with questionnaires, it may be possible to obtain information that is sufficiently accurate on which to base forecasts. But such techniques are expensive. For many firms it may be preferable to use published information of trends in consumer expenditure, or to compile information from their own historical records. Both these sources of information relate to the past. How far past information is capable of prediction depends on the extent to which economic relationships established in the past will continue into the future. If there were no relation between the past and the future there would be no basis for forecasts, and a guess would be just as useful. One simple way of dealing with uncertainty about past trends continuing into the future is to express forecasts in terms of a range, between the extremes of which the actual result will fall with a certain level of probability. But this is likely to under-estimate the effects of any break from the past trend.

Business forecasters may utilize predictions of macroeconomic factors in their assessment of the future prospects for their particular product. To the extent that macroeconomic forecasts are in error, there will be an adverse effect on the decision by the individual firm.

Some of the available macroeconomic forecasts are shown in table 10.4. The accuracy of these forecasts depends partly on the way the forecasting model is constructed, the view taken about the way the economy works and how variables are interrelated. If government policy or external factors never changed, the forecasting procedure would be fairly straightforward and past trends would continue. However, one of the main problems is fitting into the forecasting model assumptions about changes in government policy. But even if all the forecasters shown in table 10.4 managed to quantify the effects of any changes in exactly the same way, the predicted

Table 10. 4 *Forecasts of economic objectives compared*

					Forecaster						
	(1) *NIESR* *(Feb.)*	*(2)* *LBS* *(Feb.)*	*(3)* *HG* *(Mar.)*	*(4)* *CE* *(Mar.)*	*(5)* *EIU* *(Mar.)*	*(6)* *P & D* *(Mar.)*	*(7)* *OECD* *(Dec.)*	*(8)* *ITEM* *(Jan.)*	*(9)* *CBI* *(Nov.)*	*(10)* *Treasury* *(Mar.)*	*(11)* *Range*
Gross domestic product	−1.3	−1.2	+0.8	−1.8	−2.5	−3.5	−2	−3.7	−2.4	−2	4.5
Inflation	9.6	10.6	10.1	12.4	12.6	11.2	12.0	13.7	11.3	10.0	4.1
Unemployment ('000)	2,670	2,415	2,600	2,550	2,500	2,680	2,893	2,632	2,500	2,500	478
Balance of payments on current account (£m)	5,100	3,026	4,960	1,030	3,200	3,000	1,800	2,337	−500	1,500	5,600
Consumer spending	1.0	0.2	1.1	−2.8	−0.9	−1.2	−0.5	−1.6	0.8	−1.0	3.9

Notes: 1 All figures percentage change between 1980 and 1981 unless otherwise stated.
2 Key to forecasters: NIESR, National Institute of Economic and Social Research; LBS, London Business School; HG, Hoare Govett; CE, Cambridge Econometrics; EIU, Economist Intelligence Unit; P & D, Phillips and Drew; OECD, Organization for Economic Co-operation and Development; ITEM, Independent Treasury Economic Model Club; CBI, Confederation of British Industry.
3 The month in which the forecast was published is given in brackets.

Source: The Times, 12 March 1981, compiled from original sources.

results would vary, because each forecaster has a different view about the way in which the economy works. These differences present problems for the business decision maker.

The forecast of whether the economy is likely to grow or not will affect decisions about the need to increase capacity or to take on more employees. The expected level of inflation will affect decisions about cost control, sources of materials and prices of saleable goods. The level of unemployment and consumer spending will give some indication of the demand for the product, and the balance of payments may provide the basis for estimating the effects of import competition and export possibilities. The business forecaster will have to build in knowledge about his particular industry in formulating his own forecasts, but he cannot ignore macroeconomic factors. In deciding which forecast to choose, it may be better to consider how accurate the forecasters have been over a number of years, not just one year. An illustration of forecasting accuracy in the context of forecasting the demand for a particular product may be seen in the case of the Central Electricity Generating Board. This example also illustrates the problems involved in forecasting in practice, which the wines and spirits case we discussed previously did not have to deal with.

The CEGB's forecasts of electricity demand are built up around three broad sectors: domestic, industrial and commercial. It examines the likely total energy demand for sub-sectors within each of these and then considers what electricity's share might be. This is because electricity faces competition from other fuels in each market in which it operates. In the domestic market the board has used relationships between demand and useful energy and consumers' expenditure in preparing forecasts, based on data since 1954; this has been modified recently to take account of consumers' reaction to higher energy prices by installing additional insulation. The effect of changes in the composition of the housing stock are also taken into account. In the industrial sector, the link between output and demand for useful energy is estimated in ten main groups of industries, based on the Board's own estimates of increases in industrial production in each sector. Relative prices are not considered to be as important in determining demand as in the domestic sector. In the commercial sector the estimating procedure is more approximate as the diverse nature of customers makes accurate information difficult to obtain. Using these methods, the Board prepares forecasts each year of total sales in each sector for the seventh year ahead. For investment planning it is also necessary to estimate the peak winter demand in the seventh year ahead, since in order to avoid power cuts extra capacity may need to be constructed, which can take a number of years. While the above approach has been developed since 1974, prior to this date forecasts were made for six years ahead by extrapolating past trends of demand. It is too soon to see if this development will improve their forecasting record, but we can see the success rate under the previous system in table 10.5, which compares forecast and outturn of maximum electricity demand in a number of years. In all years, CEGB has over-estimated the demand for electricity. There are a number of reasons for this. First, the importance of North Sea gas was under-estimated. Second, there has been a significantly higher degree of optimism about general economic conditions built into the forecasts than has actually been the case. Third, the estimates of future energy demand were too high. Its record on estimating the market share of electricity has been fairly good. Over-forecasting the demand for electricity has affected the Board's costs, through inducing the ordering of plant to support a load that in the end did not materialize. In fact, given the power stations that were ordered in. the 1960s and did not come on stream until the 1970s, and allowing for plant taken out of service, the Board could have met actual demand in the 1970s without needing to place any further orders, and would have kept within the operating reserve margin (the margin of excess capacity necessary to allow for the effects of breakdowns of plant). If it could have forecasted without error it would have avoided these costs. The fact that it did not do so

Table 10.5   Comparison of CEGB forecast of electricity demand with outturn

Date when forecast made	Forecast for demand in:	CEGB forecast (Gwatts)	Outturn (Gwatts)	Percentage over forecast
March 1969	1974–75	54.1	41.9	29.1
March 1970	1975–76	57.1	41.1	38.9
March 1971	1976–77	58.7	42.0	39.8
March 1972	1977–78	60.6	42.4	42.9
March 1973	1978–79	56.8	43.8	29.7
July 1974	1979–80	58.2	44.1	32.0

Source: Monopolies and Mergers Commission, *Report on Central Electricity Generating Board* (London, HMSO, 1981), p. 46.

suggests some poor performance by the forecasters, but also indicates the difficulty in forecasting in practice when many interrelated factors have to be quantified.

We noted above the need for the CEGB to forecast ahead for a number of years, from which many of the problems derived. This point suggests that the accuracy of forecasts is likely to be higher the shorter is the forecast period. Trends are less likely to change in the short term. However, there are other reasons to suggest that, even these forecasts should be treated with caution. In their study of the budgeting procedure in a retail chain, Lowe and Shaw found that annual sales forecasts for each shop, produced by the area manager, were affected by past performance and a number of organizational factors. These latter influences included the company's sales growth norms and the need to take into account declining shops. In other words, managers' forecasts of sales were affected by the need to appear to be successful. If they were not successful, the reward system in the firm punished them, even if lack of success was beyond their control.

In addition to the problems we have noted, errors can arise from fundamental reasons, inherent in the methods of forecasting in use. Many forecasts begin with the assumption that some variable can be expressed as a linear relationship of some other variables; that sales, for example, will vary proportionally with income. This relationship, however, may not emerge from a consideration of past data if there are errors in the data, or if the data series is not sufficiently long for it to be perceived. In addition, it may not emerge from the data if the relationship postulated is not a true one. Other variables besides income may affect sales. We should attempt to include these variables in the equation. In addition, we may have problems because the variables we think help to explain sales do not in fact do so; that is, the equation is mis-specified. Any apparent degree of explanation would be spurious. In some cases, the variable that we think is most appropriate may not be measurable, in which case we should try to use a reasonable approximation. Estimating procedures used to establish the connection between two variables may be based on the assumption that the errors in the variables are independent of the values that the variables assume. If, in fact, the errors are larger for larger incomes than for smaller ones, heteroscedasticity is present and appropriate methods of estimation will have to be used. Many statistical techniques assume that the observed values of variables are independent, that is, that the choice of one does not affect the other. If this is not the case, serious errors in interpretation may result. The effects of this problem may be reduced by measuring independent variables in the form of changes therein, rather than raw observations. This technique may also be used to remove the problem of serial correlation, which occurs when successive observations of the unexplained variation in the dependent variable are systematically related.

The forecasts that we have been discussing are for internal decision-making purposes. However, the Green Paper, *The Future of Company Reports*, published in 1977, recommended the declaration, in the annual report, of forecasts of the future prospects of the company. The idea was to help outside interested parties to be better informed. But many companies are reluctant to comply with this request, since it may give too much away to competitors and since the uncertain nature of the future may make the forecasts misleading. Many chairman's reports do carry general forecasts about future prospects, but usually they are qualitative rather than quantitative in nature. Even so, there is some evidence[16] to suggest that they are not meaningless, since to a small extent they reduce uncertainty about the future. Pessimistic statements tend to be most powerful in reducing uncertainty.

INFORMATION

We have now discussed a number of aspects of control. From what has been said, it is clear that information plays an important part in control. We shall now examine some of the attributes that information must possess for it to be of use.

The primary need is to ensure that information being passed is transmitted and received in an undistorted manner. Distortions in the flow of information may be caused by the number of relays involved in the transmission process or because one department misunderstands what its counterpart requires. Clarification of the information needs of each department is one way of overcoming this problem.[17]

The second requirement is that information is relevant to the needs of decision-takers. This means that there is a clear distinction to be made between data and information. Data may be observed, for example, in the offices of many managers in the form of unopened piles of computer print-outs gathering dust. This problem frequently occurs when management purchase computer services without being clear about what information is required for the decisions to be made. Some means of reducing the mass of data into a usable form is required. This may be achieved by the careful establishment of a control system with clearly identified information needs. In practice, this may be best achieved by involving decision-takers in the information system design process.

The amount of information required is also related to the predictability of the business environment. The more uncertain it is, the greater amount of relevant information is needed, but the less likely is it to be available. The need, often unfulfilled, is for information systems to adapt to changing circumstances. Often there is resistance to change from management, either because they are not qualified to change the system or because the pressure of day-to-day activities precludes them from doing so.

The decision-taker may or may not be able to obtain more and better information. But more and better information is not without its costs. Theoretically, the optimum net value of information is derived when the marginal cost of additional accuracy equals the marginal benefit of additional accuracy. Thus, the most accurate information does not necessarily confer the maximum net benefit. An example, taken from the author's experience, illustrates the point. A firm wished to improve its information from customers' orders in order to improve order costing, to assess the risk from relying on certain customers and other matters. The company had records of old orders supplied going back a number of years. However, the cost of co-ordinating this information into a usable form outweighed the increased benefit that would be derived. In a small firm such as this was, the need to continue to function as a going concern meant that resources simply could not be spared to undertake the task so that the information would be timely and useful.

Until fairly recently, such problems of cost and timeliness of information have been insurmountable for many small companies, precluding them from using relatively sophisticated techniques of budgetary and production control. Prior to the development of the new generations of information technology there was a clear difference in the usage of management accounting techniques between large and small firms.[18] Small firms could cope with an increasing work load imposed on rudimentary control techniques by growth in output, for example, by employing an extra clerk. This would not significantly increase the costs of the firm, and the benefits of having the extra clerk (improved control) would easily outweigh the costs (increased wages). However, if a firm wished to improve control through the use of computers, the benefits from increased efficiency would have to be very large to outweigh the computer costs, which could be many times the salary of a clerk for even a fairly modest installation. For practical purposes, this meant that a firm had to be a considerable size before computer-based control techniques became cost-effective.

However, the last 20 years have seen the cost of computers fall considerably.[19] Wage costs, on the other hand, have risen, both absolutely and relatively to computer costs, such that a computer can now cost less than the salary of a clerk, over its life. This marked narrowing of the gap between the cost effectiveness of computer-based and manual control techniques would lead one to expect that more of the former will be introduced in small companies. A number of computer techniques have been introduced to perform 'stand-alone' tasks, that is to say, those that do not need to be part of a co-ordinated system – for example, sales invoicing, payroll account-ing, sales and purchase ledger recording, etc. In addition to the stand-alone tasks, 'Tailor-made' software and hardware[20] is being developed to provide access to sophisticated control techniques for smaller companies. For example, the ELVIS system was designed to co-ordinate production and sales control.[21]

While our discussion of the use of computers in the provision of information has indicated that there is some room for optimism, it must be emphasized that their adoption is not a substitute for the manager's judgement in making decisions. To be cost-effective, computers must be used in the context of a properly designed control system. The frequency with which information is required for making decisions is still important; information provided too often may be as bad as that available too infrequently. The company must decide whether it is worthwhile incurring the extra cost of faster processing. But whatever the argument, the importance of the controller's ability to interpret feedback information correctly and make his judgement accordingly cannot be emphasized too strongly.

NOTES

1 These two companies are discussed in detail in D. J. Rhodes, M. Wright and M. Jarrett, 'A simple diagnostic tool for improving the control of manu-facturing systems', *Proceedings of the Institute of Electrical Engineers* (June 1982)..

2 Monopolies and Mergers Commission, *Report on Inner London Letter Post* (London, HMSO, 1980).

3 For a full discussion of standard costing and budgetary control see N.

Dopuch, J. Birnberg and J. Demski, *Cost Accounting* (New York, Harcourt, Brace & Jovanovich, 1974).

4 *Inflation Accounting*, Cmnd 6225 (London, HMSO, 1975).

5 E. Whiting, 'User management research and CCA', *Accountancy*, 91 (1980).

6 C. J. Casey and M. J. Sandretto, 'Internal uses of accounting for inflation', *Harvard Business Review* (November/December 1981).

7 For a full discussion of behavioural aspects of accounting see D. T. Otley, 'Behavioural aspects of budgeting', *Accountants' Digest*, 49 (1977).

8 E. A. Lowe and R. W. Shaw, 'An analysis of managerial biasing: evidence from a company's budgeting process', *Journal of Management Studies* (October 1968).

9 For a full discussion see, for example, M. Firth, *Forecasting Methods in Business and Management* (London, Edward Arnold, 1977).

10 C. Chatfield, 'The Holt–Winters forecasting procedure', *Applied Statistics*, 27 (1978).

11 This example is taken from H. G. Berrisford, 'The relation between gas demand and temperature', *Operational Research Quarterly*, 16 (1965).

12 A. Deaton, *Models and Projections of Demand in Post-War Britain* (London, Chapman & Hall, 1975).

13 For a practical guide to carrying out sample surveys see C. Moser and G. Kalton, *Survey Methods in Social Investigation* (London, Heinemann, 1971).

14 See ibid. for details.

15 Lowe and Shaw, 'An analysis of managerial biasing'.

16 For a detailed discussion of the extent of forecasting disclosure and its value, see A. Steele, 'An investigation into the information contents of chairman's reports', paper presented at the Northern Accounting Group Conference, University of Durham, 1 April 1980.

17 For example see J. L. Machin, 'A contingent methodology for management control', *Journal of Management Studies* (February 1979).

18 See H. Hart and D. F. Prussman, 'Firm size and management accounting techniques', *Scientific Business* (November 1962).

19 For a comprehensive discussion of the effects of the new generations of computers on all aspects of society, see T. Forester (ed.), *The Microelectronics Revolution* (Oxford, Basil Blackwell, 1980). A discussion of the effects in OECD countries is provided in: OECD Information, Computer and Communications Working Party of the Committee for Scientific and Technological Policy, *Information Activities, Electronics and Telecommunications Technologies: Impact on Employment, Growth and Trade* (Paris, OECD, 1981). An excellent introduction to micro-processors for the layman is provided in E. Morgan, *Micro-Processors: A Short Introduction* (London, HMSO, 1981).

20 Software relates to the programmes required to get the computer to perform tasks. Hardware is the computer itself and related accessories such as printers, etc.

21 See D. J. Rhodes and S. Marchant, 'Not a computer: a machine to help production', *Computers and People* (July 1979).

11
Corporate Strategy

Corporate strategy relates to the long-term aims and policies of the organization. It is concerned not with matters of detailed day-to-day administration, but with the overall nature of the business and how it can adapt to changing circumstances. It has been defined as: 'the pattern of objectives, purposes, or goals and major policies or plans for achieving these goals, stated in such a way as to define what business the company is in or is to be in and the kind of company it is or is to be.'[1]

These wider aspects of a company's operations are directly related to the concept of strategic control, which was discussed in chapter 10; and the determination of strategy needs to be based on the existing environment of the organization and its current performance as well as on forecasts about the future. All organizations, whether explicitly or implicitly, do have a corporate strategy, even if it is simply to preserve the status quo. The business that wishes to secure a successful future will seek to anticipate events in both its existing and potential markets and to review the alternatives available. Such anticipation and review builds on information generated as part of the control system, as discussed in chapter 10, covering both past performance and likely future- trends. For instance, based on its assessment of the market for energy, the Shell Oil Company is beginning to move into coal mining overseas (e.g., by the acquisition of American mining companies) and into the bulk transport of coal between countries.

The various dimensions of strategy are drawn together in figure 11.1, which illustrates the 'wheel of corporate strategy'.[2] At the centre of the wheel are the broad aims or objectives of the enterprise, which were discussed in chapter 1. These aims, together with their associated strategies, would, at a more detailed level, lead to the formulation of precise tasks for the systems of tactical and operational control as outlined in chapter 10. The spokes of the wheel are the major policy alternatives that are available to management for

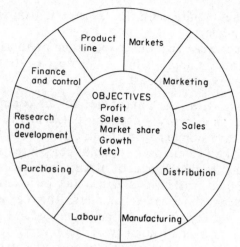

Figure 11.1   *The wheel of corporate strategy.*

achievement of the objectives. Once the policies have been specified, and their relative importance determined, they influence, through strategy, the overall behaviour of the firm. As Porter expresses it, 'Like a wheel, the spokes (policies) must radiate from and reflect the hub (goals), and the spokes must be connected with each other or the wheel will not roll.'[3]

THE IMPORTANCE OF THE COMPETITIVE ENVIRONMENT

The first stage in formulating any long-run strategy for an organization is an assessment of the market environment within which the company is placed. Such an assessment must not only consider the current position but also analyse the future and the relative strengths and weaknesses of the organization in respect of both the likely opportunities and threats in the market as a whole and the likely reaction of competitors. The key questions in this process can be itemized as follows:[4]

(1) What are the essential economic and technical characteristics of the industry in which the company participates?
(2) What trends suggesting future changes in economic and technical characteristics are apparent?
(3) What is the nature of competition both within the industry and across industries?

(4) What are the requirements for success in competition in the company's industry?

(5) Given the technical, economic, social and political developments that most directly apply, what is the range of strategies available to any company in this industry?

Such questions stress the importance of the competitive process within a market, and to many economists the intensity of competition is related to a number of structural features of that particular market. Several key elements are usually considered in this connection. First, there is the degree of rivalry between existing sellers reflected in pricing, marketing and product differentiation policies which were discussed in earlier chapters. This degree of rivalry is influenced by a variety of factors, including custom and convention, but where there is a small number of large firms accounting for a high proportion of the market (oligopoly), the degree of mutual interdependence is greater and aggressive tactics pursued by one company are soon identified and possibly followed by rivals, as illustrated by the cigarette market discussed in chapter 6. It is not only competition from existing sellers that is important, but also that from new producers — either firms of foreign origin, through imports and multinational production, or domestic firms seeking to expand their activities through diversification (discussed below).[5] There is a number of characteristics or policies that can impose barriers against new entry. Thus, for example, in the merger proposed between British Rail Sealink and European Ferries,[6] the Monopolies and Mergers Commission regarded the dominance of particular docks by the proposed new enterprise as a serious barrier to new entry, which was one of the reasons for which they found the merger to be against the public interest.

As was noted in chapter 4, the existence of substitute products is a major determinant of the own-price elasticity of demand. Furthermore, the ease of substitution affects the discretion that an enterprise possesses over many of its activities, and reduces its market power. Similarly, the power of an enterprise within a market cannot be divorced from the bargaining power of both buyers (as we saw in chapter 5) and suppliers of raw materials and other inputs. To be successful a strategy needs to be based on a careful appraisal of these competitive factors in order to identify the relative strengths and weaknesses of the organization and to take account of them in formulating an appropriate course of action. The liquidation of the company producing Gross cash registers, outlined in chapter 3, illustrates clearly the consequences of a failure to adopt a realistic appraisal of market circumstances.

In this context, the concept of the product life-cycle is sometimes a useful starting point for analysis. The product life-cycle hypothesis generally suggests that a product (or industry) will show a path of sales over time that traces out an S-shaped curve as shown in figure 11.2. As illustrated in the diagram, the product is expected to pass through a number of stages — introduction, growth, maturity and decline. The introductory period is one of slow growth as the product seeks to obtain market recognition, and profits will be low or non-existent, since marketing expenditure is likely to be high on product launch. If the product is successful, the introductory phase is followed by one of high growth with a substantial improvement in profits. The market then approaches saturation in terms of acceptance by potential buyers; sales growth slows down and profits are expected to peak, followed by a decline as marketing expenditure, or price reductions, take place to try and preserve market share. Finally, decline sets in as substitute products emerge and profitability sinks.

Although the concept of a product life-cycle has some appeal, there are a number of difficulties associated with its actual application as a planning tool. First, the duration of the whole cycle, and that of the individual stages, will vary greatly from product to product. Second, identification of the separate stages for any particular product may not be easy; and third, not all products move through a four-stage cycle — some, for example, may go straight from growth to decline without an intervening period of maturity.

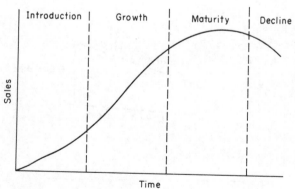

Figure 11.2   The product life-cycle.

The rapid rise and equally rapid fall of revenue earned by Space Invaders machines in 1980/81 in the UK is perhaps a prime illustration of this point as well as an example of a short life-cycle. On the other hand, at the industry level, the bicycle market is one that illustrates a very long life-cycle and, as we saw in chapter 3, one that has shown a marked increase in sales during what might be regarded as its mature or declining phase. Despite these difficulties, the life-cycle approach does alert the company to dangers and is, therefore, a useful preliminary stage in evaluating alternative strategies.[7]

IDENTIFYING THE PROBLEM AND REVIEWING ALL ALTERNATIVES

The product life-cycle concept illustrates one aspect of the rationale for a corporate strategy in that it can forewarn management of a potential problem that might arise in the fulfilment of the objectives. This problem can be examined in more general terms using 'gap analysis'. This simple technique is designed to draw management's attention to possible shortcomings in performance in the future. Taking the objectives set by the company it is possible to envisage the target paths of key variables over time that will achieve the objectives set. These key variables cover sales, profit, investment, employment and many other aspects of a company's operations. For illustrative purposes, we take the case of sales growth as shown in figure 11.3. The original target path for sales growth is plotted in the

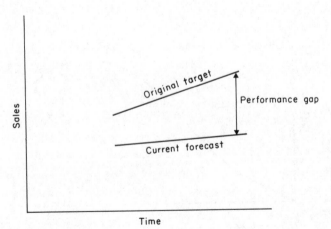

Figure 11.3   Gap analysis.

diagram. An essential part of strategy is to compare the outcome that is currently expected by management with this target. The expected outcome will be derived from the forecasting procedure used by the firm in the manner discussed in chapter 10. As shown in figure 11.3, the forecast is considerably lower than the target, which alerts management to the need for possible action. The difference between target and forecast gives the performance gap. If such a gap is revealed by this process, the management should, first, review its original objectives to assess their feasibility in the light of the organization's current strengths and weaknesses and derive a revised target if appropriate. After this review, the management should seek to assess various alternative courses of action which would close the gap. This aspect of the procedure is known as 'strategic search'. Such search may begin with a reappraisal of the existing business of the organization, paying attention to the particular markets, both for inputs and outputs, in which the company operates and the marketing, pricing and other practices currently in use. At the same time, a review should be undertaken of other alternatives encompassing vertical integration, both backwards and forwards, and diversification as a means of improving company performance.

These reviews are designed to select the appropriate portfolio of products and markets and to assign priority to each — or, to echo the point made in the definition at the beginning of the chapter, to decide in what businesses the company should operate. There are

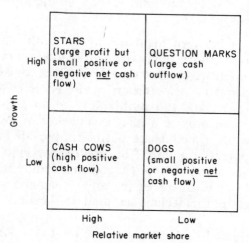

Figure 11.4   Growth-share matrix.

several simple techniques that may help in the process of portfolio selection.[8] For example, construction of a growth/share matrix can reveal a number of interesting features. On to this matrix each of a firm's activities can be plotted, and the matrix itself is usually divided into four quadrants as in figure 11.4. The axes of the chart are growth and relative market share. Into which of the four quadrants the activity falls reveals its fundamental nature with different implications for overall strategy. The quadrants are as follows:

(1) Stars — activities that have a high relative market share in high-growth markets, which will normally require large amounts of cash to sustain growth but, given their strong market position, will provide substantial profits.

(2) Cash cows — activities that have low growth but in which the firm has a high relative market share. Such activities will provide a healthy cash flow which can be used to finance other activities with higher growth potential.

(3) Question marks (or wildcats) — high-growth markets where the firm has a relatively low market share. Cash is required to finance growth but profits are likely to be low since the market share is small. Some of these activities will provide a suitable outlet for the cash generated by 'cash cows' in the search to turn them into 'stars'.

(4) Dogs — activities with low relative shares of low-growth markets. At best, activities in this category do not warrant much attention in the overall strategy, although care has to be taken that they do not become a drain on cash. It may be appropriate to sell off (divest) these activities.

The distinction between 'high' and 'low' in both dimensions is to a large extent rather arbitrary, and the matrix adopts a rather simplistic view of the competitive processes involved. Thus, for example, it may not be true that relative market share accurately reflects the competitive position, cash flow and profitability of an activity. However, market growth can provide a reliable indicator of the necessity for investment and the growth/share matrix can provide some important pointers for potential action. The use of portfolio analysis does require a careful assessment of the existing competitive position of the firm on the lines discussed in earlier chapters, and it can be a useful addition to the techniques used in deriving an appropriate strategy.

Having considered the general background to corporate strategy, it is now time to examine the major alternatives available to a company.

The question of the appropriate strategy cannot be divorced from the need to obtain finance (discussed in chapter 7) and the investment decision (chapter 9). In the discussion that follows it will be presumed that the organization has taken into account the alternative sources and availability of funds and that the necessary investment decisions will be analysed using the appropriate techniques discussed in the earlier chapter.

It is useful to distinguish seven broad policy alternatives that face any organization:

(1) defence of an existing market;
(2) divestment and restructuring;
(3) expansion of existing activities and markets;
(4) vertical integration;
(5) diversification;
(6) innovation;
(7) international operations.

Such a list is designed simply as an aid to exposition and thought. The individual categories are not mutually exclusive, and any company with the necessary finance can pursue a number of different directions. For example, innovation can either relate to existing products and markets or involve the company in diversification. Several aspects of innovation were discussed in chapter 9 and here we shall concentrate on the other dimensions of corporate strategy. Also, many British companies are already international, either in terms of export sales or with production and marketing overseas, so that, for example, defence of an existing market may relate to one in a foreign country and category (7) is, therefore, designed to cover cases where new overseas ventures are concerned.

As discussed earlier, the choice of strategy and the viability of the various alternatives is closely connected with the existing competitive environment in which the company is placed. The relevant factors and issues are, for example, likely to be different in circumstances of declining markets or increased competition in its main activities as compared with a position of dominance in an expanding, profitable market. Porter[9] considers the different strategies appropriate for various market environments covering fragmented industries, emerging industries, industries reaching maturity, declining industries and global industries. It is important, therefore as we stressed earlier, that a careful appraisal of the existing environment is undertaken before embarking on an analysis of the alternatives.

The first two items in the list above seem at first glance most appropriate to cases where the company perceives threats to its existing markets, either because of increased competition or on account of a general decline in the demand for the products, which may be cyclical or long-term in nature. However, the strategy of divestment and restructuring is of wider applicability, since it provides an opportunity for a company to change direction and, furthermore, sales of assets can provide a useful source of finance for investment in alternative processes and products. Items (3)–(7) relate principally to the issue of the growth of the company and the direction in which this growth takes place. Such growth can occur either by investment in new assets or by the acquisition of existing ones through the take-over of another company. The factors influencing the choice between these two avenues are discussed in a later section, but again it needs to be recognized that the two decisions are not independent and the availability of another company on the market at a particular price may be a crucial determinant. This last point merely serves to empha-size the factor that is at the heart of the economics of the decision: the company needs to compare the costs and benefits of the various alternatives, and to the economist the relevant costs are opportunity costs (see chapter 2). Where finance or the managerial ability to handle a large corporation is limited, the cost of following any one long-term strategy such as diversification may be at the expense of, for example, vertical integration. The decision requires information, therefore, on all the relevant costs, including the price that has to be paid for the assets, whether new, second-hand or from the acquisi-tion of another company.

Taking account of this point, the following sections consider the general arguments involved.

DEFENCE OF AN EXISTING POSITION AND RESTRUCTURING

The defence of an existing position and the restructuring of assets are closely related, and it is sensible, therefore, to consider these two strategies together. If the analysis of the competitive environment and performance of the company suggests weaknesses in, and threats to, its long-run survival and profitability, the management has to consider the appropriateness of defending its existing position in the market. It is important to distinguish between weaknesses caused by a decline in competitive ability, probably reflected in falling market share, *vis-à-vis* other domestic producers or imports, and the general decline of a whole market or industry. In the case of the former the source(s) of the competitive decline need to be identified. For example, it could be that the company's products are well established and beginning to be affected by the declining phase of the product life-cycle. In this case, investment in research and development and the introduction of new varieties may halt the decline. Similarly, the problem may rest with inefficiencies in production or marketing, which can be examined using the tools discussed in earlier chapters. In other words, the process of corporate strategy may bring into question the existing mode of operation and policies of the enterprise. The existence of a declining market, on the other hand, raises more direct issues for long-term strategy.

Care needs to be taken to distinguish temporary decline, which might arise from cyclical factors, from that which is likely to take place over a long period. The former raises issues of stock-building, hoarding of skilled labour, etc., through which the company seeks to ride out the slack period and remain well placed to satisfy orders once demand picks up. When growth was relatively steady, if unspectacular in Britain during the 1950s and 1960s, many companies took this route during phases of slower growth. However, as world economic growth has declined during the late 1970s and early 1980s, inflation has increased, the rate of technological change in many areas has been rapid, and the problems of declining markets have become more significant. This has perhaps been most marked in the debate about de-industrialization in the UK.[10] It has become even more relevant, therefore, to consider those strategies that can be adopted by firms in declining markets.

Following the work of Harrigan and Porter,[11] it is possible to identify four main alternative strategies: leadership, niche, harvest and divest-quickly.

A leadership strategy is of relevance to a company that has competitive strengths such that it can expect to achieve above-average profitability in that sector. It seeks, therefore, to remain as one of the few producers in that market. If the market continues to decline it might be expected to shift to one of the alternative strategies.

The niche strategy is suitable if the market has different segments, some of which may either be stable or subject to slower decline. In this case the company can seek to gain a position of dominance in one or more of these sectors. Again, if the decline continues it would be appropriate to switch strategies.

Under a harvest strategy, the firm gives pre-eminence to the cash flow from the business and would follow a policy of curtailing investment, reducing maintenance, reducing the variety of products supplied and generally cutting back on expenditure and service. Such a strategy presumes that the firm has some pre-existing competitive strengths which are not immediately eroded by a cut-back on advertising and other activities.

The divest-quickly strategy involves the company's selling the business or assets at an early stage in the decline. Generally speaking, in these circumstances the earlier the business is sold, the greater the price obtained, but the reward from this strategy has to be compared with the return that could be obtained from running the business for a longer period but receiving a lower ultimate price for the assets.

Any business, whether in declining markets or not, can seek to restructure its assets and change direction not only by acquiring new assets but also by selling some of its existing ones. It can even consider the sale of all its assets, in the sense of seeking to be taken over as a whole by another company. During the last two to three years many companies have undertaken substantial restructuring programmes. The closure of many plants by the British Steel Corporation and the controversial decision in 1982 of British Aluminium to shut its smelter at Invergordon in Scotland serve as simple illustrations. Many of these moves involve the closing down of operations, the sale of plant and equipment to other manufacturers at home or abroad, and the loss of productive capacity. On the other hand it is possible, and indeed quite common, to sell the unit as a going concern. There is, in fact, quite a lot of mobility of subsidiaries from one company to another, much like the transfer market among football clubs. Thus, for example, during the 1970s about 20 per cent of all takeovers involved the acquisition of the subsidiary of another company.[12] In the difficult market circumstances of the 1980s there have also been a number of instances of management buyouts — the acquisition of part of a company from its owners by the management. At the time of writing (22 January 1982) the latest such purchase involved the acquisition of Rotunda, a leading British manufacturer of self-adhesive tapes, by four of its senior managers from BICC.[13]

The reasons for restructuring either through plant closure or divestment are varied. Many of them may stem from unsatisfactory performance and are designed to reduce costs or capacity and/or create an exit from markets that provide poor prospects. Further, market circumstances may create cash flow problems for the company, either because of the poor performance of a particular operation which the company now wishes to cease, or because it needs to protect its primary activities. For example, ACC, the owners of

Central Television (previously ATV), faced cash flow problems as a result of expensive forays into the making of films. Consequently, they sold their Ansaphone (telephone answering equipment) subsidiary (a management buy-out, as it happens). Likewise, EMI at one stage proposed the sale of a 50 per cent share of its record business to Paramount, although the deal was later abandoned.

A company may also wish to reorganize for managerial or technological reasons. Thus, on the basis of the review of markets conducted as part of corporate strategy, it may become apparent that it would be appropriate for the company to concentrate on particular areas of activity and that greater returns could be achieved by the sale of parts of the existing operations. Also, the company may wish to concentrate managerial resources in those markets where it considers that it possesses more specialized knowledge. Again, this would provide an incentive for the sale of the peripheral parts of the business.

As noted in chapter 1, there has been a large amount of merger activity in Britain since the early 1960s; yet there is some evidence that the performance of these mergers has been rather disappointing.[14] Divestment is one way of correcting any past mistakes in previous acquisitions, but companies can also consider the possibility of breaking up a company into two or more separate entities. So far, tax regulations in Britain have made this expensive, but recent changes have eased the problem somewhat. Indeed, the first major de-merger proposal was announced in January 1982 involving the separation of the newspaper interests (primarily the Express Group) from Trafalgar House. Although there may be special issues in this case, increasing consideration in companies seems to be being given to the possibilities of de-merger.

There are many ways, therefore, in which an enterprise can adapt to changing market circumstances and restructure its organization in an attempt to secure its future.

EXPANSION OF EXISTING ACTIVITIES

The expansion of existing activities, or 'horizontal integration', is one way in which a company can grow. If some of a company's products are at an early stage in their life-cycle, there is clear scope for expansion. It is important, therefore, for the company to distinguish between markets that have overall growth potential and those that are static or increasing only slowly. The growth potential of any particular market depends on many factors, including tastes, technological change and the emergence of substitutes, but one important relevant factor is the income elasticity of demand, as discussed in chapter 4, together with expectations about the future course of the economy. The problems of forecasting demand have already been examined in chapter 10.

In growing markets it is generally easier to expand along with the overall trend unless the competitiveness of the products is so bad that product sales decline. In slow-growing or static markets, an increase in the volume of sales can be accomplished only at the expense of rival producers. Thus, for example, Unipart, a successful arm of British Leyland, has recently expanded its interests in the provision of spare parts for all makes of vehicle, and not just those of BL. As part of this expansion it is building a large new warehousing facility in the Midlands. It was recognized by the management that such expansion could take place only if customers could be gained from other suppliers. The car parts market has been static in recent years, and Unipart clearly believe in their ability to compete with rival suppliers. Similarly, the expansion of Sainsburys from its southern base into the Midlands and North could be successful only if it could gain grocery sales from other outlets. Again, such an expansion would depend on the competitive ability of the enterprise. The growth of discount retailers like Comet, Argos and Asda illustrate the same feature, in which success depends on low prices and volume sales.

If a company's sales grow at a faster rate than those of the market as a whole, it follows that its market share must increase. We have noted earlier in this chapter and also in chapter 1 that it is often assumed that there is a relationship between market share and market power. Indeed, the increase in market share, if it leads to market dominance, may be one of the main motives for horizontal expansion. Such a view may be particularly appropriate if the expansion occurs through the acquisition of existing rivals rather than through the purchasing of new assets and the building of new capacity. We look at some aspects of the merger decision at the end of this chapter.

The expansion of existing activities raises little by way of new principles to those discussed in earlier parts of this book. Thus, decisions on pricing, marketing, output and capacity all involve the considerations outlined in the relevant chapters. Expansion into new activities, whether through vertical integration or diversification, does however suggest some special features, and we turn to these next.

A firm may grow or restructure its activities by expanding into new areas (diversification), or by taking on activities that it currently conducts through the market, either as a customer or as a supplier (vertical integration). It can also decide to cut back on its range of activities and curtail the extent of vertical integration or diversification. We shall first look at the issues involved in decisions about vertical integration.

As is clear from the previous statement, vertical integration means that the firm is replacing a market transaction by an internal arrangement. Why should it do this? The issues involved with vertical integration are central to the existence of the firm itself as an economic organization. This important point was recognized in the 1930s by Coase in his classic paper on 'The nature of the firm'.[15] Thus, apart from incentives created by legal and taxation provisions, some activities can be organized almost entirely on the basis of market transactions. For example, some independent record producers operate in just this way, purchasing studio time and facilities such as mixing, mastering and pressing from other organizations. Some publishing can be organized similarly, with copy-editing, typesetting, printing and distribution handled by many separate entities. Thus, even if there are technical links between different processes, it does not necessarily follow that the individual processes have to be in common ownership. Indeed, before *The Times* was acquired by Rupert Murdoch a scheme was being proposed whereby the various parties such as journalists, compositors, etc., should form separate companies and trade with each other to produce the paper.

The success of Marks and Spencer in the retail clothing market illustrates clearly that ownership of textile and clothing production is not necessary to ensure adequate quality and reliability of supplies. Their acquisition of textile products is done entirely on the basis of market transactions, and yet through their contracts they exercise considerable control over their suppliers. This last point emphasizes the crucial role of contracts, which, it is often forgotten, are the key element in market exchange.

In his original discussion, Coase pointed out that market transactions do involve costs, which can take many forms, including the need to obtain the appropriate information about price and quality as well as the problem of uncertainty. He argued that a firm would tend to expand until the costs of organizing an extra transaction within the firm become equal to the costs of carrying out that same transaction by means of exchange on the open market or the costs of organizing it in another firm. If the costs of using markets are low, it can be argued that they will be preferred to internal supply. The extent of vertical integration therefore depends on whether markets work well. Williamson, in an extension of the Coase analysis, provides a succinct definition of a market working well:[16]

An intermediate market will be said to work well if, both presently and prospectively, prices are non-monopolistic and reflect an acceptable risk premium, and if market exchange experiences low transaction costs and permits the realisation of essential economies.

It is important to realize, therefore, that markets and internal supply are alternative means for conducting a set of transactions, and that the choice between them rests on the relative efficiency of each in the particular circumstances facing the organization. These circumstances are likely to change as the firm, and the markets that it serves, adjust over time. Thus, for example, in the early stages of the development of a product there may be no independent suppliers with the equipment and technical know-how to produce the relevant specialized components. At the same time, the costs of these components may be of little significance in that, in the early stages of the life-cycle, demand may not be particularly price-sensitive. Thus the firm may have no alternative but to supply the components itself. If the product is successful, however, as demand for the inputs expands and the market becomes more price-sensitive, with economies of scale and specialization it may be more appropriate for independent firms to take over the necessary component production.[17] Thus, a firm should constantly reappraise the extent of its vertically integrated activities and consider alternative uses of its investment funds.

What are the advantages of vertical integration? These are normally listed under a number of headings and we will provide a brief review of the main factors involved.[18]

Cost savings
Cost savings can arise either because of increased efficiency of combined operations (including the avoidance of transaction costs) or because of a change in prices as a result of the increased bargaining power of the combined unit. Let us examine technical economies first.

Where production processes are technically interdependent, it may be possible to gain substantial economies by integrating the processes at a common site. Thus, handling and transport costs can be reduced; in the commonly cited example of steel, substantial re-heating costs are also avoided. But as we noted above, it does not necessarily follow that the processes have to be under common ownership. If they are, it implies that the costs of co-ordinating within the firm are less than those involved with negotiating and concluding complex contracts. Where such close technical links are involved, one firm will be the dominant supplier, or customer, of the other, and if costs of transport, re-processing, etc., are high there is a necessary interdependence between the firms. The disadvantages of using the market in such cases explain why the occurrence of separate ownership in these circumstances is rare. The real difficulty lies in specifying and negotiating the terms of the appropriate contracts, particularly to cover the many eventualities that might arise. Short-term contracts will increase uncertainty, especially where long-life investment is involved, and long-term contracts raise problems of foreseeing possible changes in circumstances and specifying the relevant action by the parties concerned.

The ability of management to monitor performance and control operations may be enhanced if the processes are under common ownership. Also, managers may reduce the costs of acquiring the necessary information for successful control on the lines discussed in chapter 10. It may be that some market processes can be removed completely. Thus, for example, as was noted earlier, many manufacturers now supply the major retailers directly rather than through wholesalers. One of the main functions of wholesalers had traditionally been to break bulk, i.e., to split up consignments from manufacturers into smaller units for distribution to individual shops. With the growth of larger stores and retail chains, the breaking of bulk is in some cases unnecessary or can be better performed by the retailers themselves through their central distribution depots.

This last point raises a common misconception about the nature of vertical integration. It is frequently argued that by integrating it is possible to cut out the middleman with his corresponding mark-up. This argument can be false and misleading in many circumstances. If the middleman is performing a valuable role by breaking bulk, handling stocks, etc., these functions will still need to be carried out by the integrated firm. If the middleman was operating efficiently and was not earning an excessive profit, there are no obvious savings in taking over the activity. After all, investment funds need to earn some rate of return, and the firm should be concerned with the opportunity cost of these funds as discussed in chapter 9. The relevant issue, therefore, is not the removal of the middleman's profit, but whether the activity can be performed more efficiently by the combined operation or whether 'excessive' profit can be removed.

Attention also needs to be paid to the costs of internal administration. Just as we usually regard market structure as important in determining the efficiency of markets (see chapter 1), so the internal organizational structure of the firm is likely to be important in the success of its own internal co-ordination. It does not follow that internal administration is superior to that exercised by the market, and each case needs to be considered on its merits.

It is clear from the above discussion that transaction costs are central to the decision as to whether the costs of internal supply are greater or less than those of using markets. But, there are other issues involving more strategic elements, which we turn to next.

Strategic implications

It is often argued that vertical integration provides both security of supply and security of markets, implying that in periods of depressed demand the company will have an outlet for its products and in periods of tight demand it will be able to obtain essential raw materials. Of course, no form of organization can provide complete immunity from market forces, but vertical integration may reduce the range of the fluctuations, particularly where changes in market conditions lead to disproportionate changes in stockholding at various productive stages. Such a rationale was used to explain the importance of vertical integration in the textile industry between those spinning the yarn and those weaving it into cloth. A change in demand for cloth led to a large increase or decrease in the stocks of yarn held by weavers. In periods of depressed demand they would reduce their stocks and correspondingly reduce their new orders to the spinners. Vertical integration at least allowed a co-ordinated stock policy, taking account of the relevant implications for costs.

The above issue is really concerned with aspects of risk and uncertainty, but vertical integration may also have implications for the bargaining power of the larger unit. In particular, if there are also cost savings involved, it may make it more difficult for another firm to enter the industry, since to reap economies of both integration and scale it would need to enter at a larger size. Also, the integrated firm may have advantages over the non-integrated firm in terms of higher selling prices, lower costs or lower risk. If there are no serious imperfections in the capital market, this may have no marked consequences for competition. If the firm does have market power at one or more stages of production, however, it may be possible for it to extract higher prices and greater profit at the expense of the consumer. Practices such as predatory pricing and cross-subsidization can be used to enhance market power. Thus, in the former case a firm with, for example, control of an important raw material could attempt to squeeze out rivals at a more competitive stage by raising the price of the raw material and reducing the price of the final product − a price squeeze. Whether such a policy is practicable depends entirely on whether alternative sources of the raw material, or substitute products, are available. Cross-subsidization is a related policy and occurs when a firm with power at one stage can use the profits derived to subsidize other products at more competitive stages. Such a policy can also apply to diversification, which will be discussed shortly.

Vertical integration is not without its problems. It is not true that success at one stage automatically ensures success at another. Thus, for example, attempts by some companies to integrate forward to the retailing stage have sometimes had disastrous consequences, since the problems of retail management may be quite different to those of production management. The failure of the Cyril Lord carpet chain in the 1960s is a good case in point; problems in its management of retail stores forced the operation into liquidation. Further, if vertical integration implies that the company is closely tied to the success of one type of product, its ability to adjust to changing circumstances may be seriously impaired.

The merits of vertical integration as against the use of markets need to be analysed carefully in the light of the specific circumstances of each company and the markets in which it operates. Vertical integration is not necessarily beneficial, and any investment in this area needs to be considered in relation to alternative uses of the capital funds and managerial skills. In addition, the company needs to consider whether it should integrate fully either forwards or backwards or only partly, whereby it would continue to buy some of its supplies of a particular input from other producers, or to sell part of its output to other customers. Some of the advantages of integration can be achieved by the use of appropriate contracts, and there is also the intermediate stage of quasi-integration, where there is some form of vertical integration which falls short of full ownership. Such arrangements could include minority equity shareholdings, loans, interlocking directorships and exclusive dealing arrangements. To illustrate the last point, this particular text was first typed using a microcomputer for which one British company has an exclusive dealing arrangement with the foreign manufacturer. In turn, this company will supply other retailers, but all UK supplies originate from this company. The exchange of technical know-how and market information can take place quite satisfactorily within this type of arrangement.

Vertical integration ties the company to a particular product range; a policy of diversification, on the other hand, allows the firm to spread its interests and reduce the risks of operating in any one market. The diversification strategy of the Imperial Group is a good illustration of this process at work and we consider the Group's views at the end of the chapter. In the next section we consider the broad principles involved.

DIVERSIFICATION

Diversification occurs when the firm moves into new areas of activity which are not vertically related to each other. There may, however, be links between the activities in that they use common inputs or the same distribution channels. It is, therefore, possible to distinguish two broad types of diversification:

(1) narrow spectrum – where the activities have close production or marketing links;
(2) broad spectrum – where the new activity is remote from the main interests of the business.

Where broad spectrum diversification is the common form within the company, the business may be classified as *conglomerate*.

Thus, a diversified company is one that operates in more than one market. Such a definition raises problems of determining exactly when diversification is occurring, as distinct from a simple expansion of the main activity (horizontal integration) or vertical integration. The crux of the answer lies in the definition of a market, and we considered the difficulties involved in chapter 4. To the firm attempting to reach a strategic decision, the distinction is probably of little significance, but its relevance is clear if one wishes to ascertain the nature of firms operating in an economy such as the UK and whether these firms can be classified as diversified or specialized. In a major study, Utton[19] sought to examine the interests of the 200 largest firms in the UK. He used the Standard Industrial Classification to determine the relationship between the various activities of the enterprise. The Standard Industrial Classification distinguishes, among other things, between Orders and Minimum List Headings. Orders represent broad industrial sectors such as Food, Drink and Tobacco, Chemicals or Textiles, while the Minimum List Headings are narrower groupings within the Orders, such as Tobacco, Man-made fibres, etc. Thus, a firm's primary activity was taken as that Minimum List Heading which accounted for the largest amount of its employment. For example, on average, the principal activity for each of the 200 largest firms accounted for about 57 per cent of total employment in that firm. This principal activity was, on average, four times as important as the next largest. Further, each firm operated in about nine of these industries but of these quite a few were quantitatively insignificant for the enterprise.

If the diversification was into a Minimum List Heading that fell within the same Order as the firm's primary activity, Utton viewed this as narrow spectrum diversification, whereas if it was into an industry outside the Order within which the main activity fell it was classified as broad spectrum diversification.

Clearly, the finer the distinction between activities, the greater the degree of diversification that will be revealed. At the same time, a scheme such as Utton's does not distinguish between diversification and vertical integration. Bearing in mind these difficulties, and allowing for the fact that the two Orders covering Engineering and Vehicles respectively are closely related, Utton concluded that about two-thirds of the diversification by large firms in the UK was into activities that were closely related to their main activity. His results suggest that diversification, and particularly broad-spectrum diversification, is perhaps not as widespread as is commonly believed.

Having considered some of the facts, it is now appropriate to examine the possible motives for diversification and how such a strategy can benefit the firm.

The incentive to diversify clearly exists if the firm possesses an asset or assets that provide the capacity to operate in more than one industry. These assets can include management expertise and innovatory ability as well as physical capital. As such, diversification is merely one aspect of the reasons for the emergence of multi-product firms. Thus, technological factors result in multi-product or multi-industry production incurring lower costs than under specialization. The economies involved have recently been classified as 'economies of scope',[20] and they are quite distinct from the notion of economies of scale. Economies of scope occur when joint production of two goods by one firm is less costly than the combined costs of production by two specialized firms. Using this definition, it can be seen that if such economies exist it is cheaper to add an additional product to an existing range (through, e.g., diversification) than to produce the particular product on its own. For economies of scope to exist there must be some inputs that are shared by more than one product; and, further, either the inputs involved must be large and indivisible, so that they cannot be fully utilized by one product alone, or an input bought for the production of one product must be available for use in another. In the latter category, skilled general management is perhaps the prime example.

Most firms are multi-product, which suggests that such economies are almost universal, and their existence creates a clear incentive for diversification if the main product of the firm cannot fully utilize these assets. The degree to which any additional products are diversified depends on the precise factors involved, but the closer the links between the activities, the greater are likely to be the possibilities for economies of scope.

Taking account of these economies of scope, arguments for diversification can be centred around three issues: growth, market power and risk avoidance.

Diversification for growth, or even to preserve the existence of the enterprise, can be linked to the product life-cycle model discussed earlier. Thus, as the company's principal product matures and profit and sales potential decline, it becomes sensible to consider alternative products. Sutton[21] has distinguished two contrasting forms of diversification: cost-push and market-pull. Cost-push diversification occurs when the primary activity is unable to absorb additional investment without a serious decline in profitability. Thus, provided the funds are available for investment and are not required for the defence of an existing market position, the incentive to diversify will increase as the growth rate of the firm's primary activity falls. The Imperial Group, which we discuss later, is perhaps a good example of cost-push diversification at work.

Market-pull diversification, on the other hand, occurs when the firm perceives an opportunity for diversification before it is forced to reappraise its market position by declining profitability. The perception and realization of such opportunities may be greater the higher the importance of research and marketing functions within the organization.

The possible effects of diversification on market power are revealed in a number of directions. If the company already possesses market power in one activity it may be able to extend its power into other markets through a number of different practices. The most common of these are tie-in sales, cross-subsidization and reciprocal dealing.

Tie-in sales (otherwise known as full-line forcing) occur when the intending purchase of a particular product over which the producer has market power is required to buy supplies of other products from the same manufacturer. This practice can enable the diversified firm to operate a form of price discrimination and extract greater profit from the market. A policy of cross-subsidization involves the use of profits in one market to subsidize sales in another market with the intention of driving other producers from the market and achieving greater profit and sales in the long run. Reciprocal dealing arises when two large diversified firms agree to buy from each other rather than from alternative suppliers. It is not clear to what extent these practices are widespread, or even that they are in the interests of the companies concerned, but they may provide some incentive for a diversification strategy where a firm already possesses some market power.

Diversification, by spreading the company's activities, may provide greater long-run security and a more stable cash flow. But such stability is usually obtained at the cost of greater returns that could be earned by the adoption of greater specialization in activities with the largest potential returns. To a large extent, therefore, the decision will be influenced by the attitudes to risk adopted by the managers concerned. Diversification can help to even out cash flow that is affected by seasonal or cyclical factors, where the timing in the two or more activities is complementary. Thus, for example, W. H. Smith diversified in the 1970s into the travel agency business, partly to offset the seasonal pattern in its retail business which peaked with the Christmas sales boom.[22] The problems of seasonal cash flow are perhaps highlighted by the liquidation of Sir Freddie Laker's airline, which was announced in February 1982. One of the immediate problems was poor cash flow, since January and February are very low months for transatlantic travel. Given the fear of liquidation, travel agents held up payment of income received for holiday bookings, and with no other major source of earnings, the company could not continue. This is an example of failure in a high-risk activity.

Shareholders, the ultimate owners of the firm, can spread their risks by buying shares in a number of companies and holding a mixed portfolio. Such risk-spreading is predominant in the growth of unit and investment trusts, which seek to provide a diversified portfolio for the smaller shareholder. Even here, the customer can opt for different degrees of risk since some unit trusts, for example, invest in high-risk activities while others seek a more stable pattern of returns. But, unlike shareholders, the management of a company is, in general, not able to switch the company's portfolio of assets so easily. To return to Laker as an example, although the company had assets that could have been realized, since there is a second-hand market for aircraft, the small print of the initial purchase contract prevented Laker from selling some of them without incurring a penalty in terms of a much higher interest rate on the outstanding loans. It would not have been feasible for the company to sell all the aircraft concerned because of commitments to fly passengers during the busy summer months. Again, the only real course of action was to liquidate the company.

As a final aspect of diversification, we should consider the possibility of a company entering overseas markets. Most of the larger British firms are multinational companies in that they own and operate assets in more than one country. Further, many of the large companies operating in Britain are themselves subsidiaries of overseas firms, such as Ford and General Motors in the car industry, Philips in the electrical goods market and Unilever (50 per cent Dutch) in many consumer goods markets. There are many complex issues involved in the operation and tactics of multinational companies which it would not be appropriate to discuss in detail here.[23] However, since we have referred to the Imperial Group on many occasions in this book, it is worthwhile looking at their reasons for acquiring the Howard Johnson chain in the United States.

In the annual report for 1979, the Imperial Group chairman stated that the company had been diversifying for a number of years in order to lessen its dependence on a single market (tobacco) in which it was the dominant supplier. The acquisition of Howard Johnson, with its motels and other activities in the USA, was designed to provide foreign earnings and a platform for the growth of such earnings in the future. The chairman also noted that, for a large company, Imperial was unusual in being so dependent on one single economy. Thus he stated that the objective of the Group was to acquire new trading assets, adding to the growth prospects of the company and that, in particular, the USA provided a suitable market. The Group was, therefore, clearly seeking to diversify its asset base, not only in terms of its activities but also in terms of the international use of its assets. As a conclusion to this chapter, we consider in further detail the components of the Imperial Group's corporate strategy.

CQUISITION OR INTERNAL EXPANSION?

As we have seen, the growth, or restructuring, of a firm can take place in three principal directions: horizontal integration, vertical integration or diversification. Furthermore, any of these activities can be carried out within the home country of the company or overseas. Each can be achieved in two ways: by the expansion of existing capacity through the installation of new plant and equipment, or by the acquisition of existing assets through takeover or merger. Strictly speaking, an acquisition involves the company's obtaining control of another firm, either through a purchase of shares for cash or through an exchange of shares. A merger, on the other hand, involves two separate firms coming together to form a new combined enterprise, as illustrated, for example, by the merger between the British Motor Corporation and Leyland to form British Leyland. For analytical purposes, the distinction is perhaps of no real significance.

Expansion by acquisition is often called 'external growth', whereas that by the creation of new capacity is termed 'internal growth'. A firm wishing to redirect its activities can, therefore, choose either, or both, of these routes. In addition, it can dispose of some of its existing assets on the lines discussed earlier, which in combination with acquisition or internal expansion will restructure the nature of the business. We need to consider, therefore, the factors that will influence the choice between internal and external growth.

At a simple level, it can be seen that the firm will choose between internal and external growth according to which is the cheapest and most profitable in terms of the objectives of the company. In some cases acquisition may be the only feasible strategy. The relevant circumstances would cover those where the firm wished to change the position of existing producers (reduce competition), or to obtain control of some specialized assets (e.g., raw materials, technical know-how or patents), or where the change needed to be brought about quickly. The construction of new assets, especially if it involves new buildings or large specialized machinery, can take considerable time, whereas if these assets are already owned by another firm, acquisition accomplishes a change of ownership relatively quickly. However, any change in the operation of these assets or improved efficiency and profitability may take time to accomplish. It should not be assumed, therefore, that acquisition produces immediate beneficial results.

Internal growth allows the firm to be more selective about the type of assets it employs and it can tailor the expansion more exactly into its existing activities and needs. On the other hand, acquisition may bring with it a bundle of undesired assets which require time and effort for their disposal, and can involve a substantial jump in the nature of the business, its size and management problems.

A further factor that can be of some significance is the fact that, in the UK and other countries, the government may be adopting a merger policy that involves either the outright banning of certain mergers or the requirement that they may be subject to investigation. As we have noted earlier, in the UK, under the Fair Trading Act 1973, there is power to refer proposed mergers to the Monopolies and Mergers Commission for investigation, which Commission may recommend that they are against the public interest. For example, in recent months the bid of European Ferries for Sealink, the alternative bids by the Standard Chartered and Hongkong and Shanghai banks for the Royal Bank of Scotland, and by Lonrho for the House of Fraser have all been found likely to operate against the public interest by the Monopolies and Mergers Commission and have been prohibited. Horizontal acquisitions or mergers that create a firm with a substantial market share are perhaps likely to be subject to closer scrutiny, although both vertical and diversifying mergers are equally subject to the law.

The firm should make its decision about investment using the criteria discussed in chapter 9. For internal growth, the decision rests on the purchase price and development costs of the new assets in comparison with the expected returns. Where acquisition is concerned, however, the price depends on the value of the potential subsidiary on the stock market if it is an independent company. If a subsidiary is to be acquired as part of the divestment process of another enterprise, or from liquidation, the terms are obviously subject to individual negotiation between the parties concerned, including the Official Receiver where appropriate. The majority of acquisitions however, involve the stock market, and it is therefore necessary to consider the role that it performs.

In essence, the stock market is seen as performing two functions: it allocates capital resources to their most profitable use, and it ensures that existing assets are most profitably utilized. Companies with poor profitability records, and low expectations about future performance, will have low share prices, which will increase the difficulty they face in raising any additional capital and may at the same time make them attractive propositions for a takeover. The share price is presumed to reflect the valuation placed by the stock market on the earning power of the assets of the company under the existing management. The costs of acquisition, therefore, depend on the view taken by the stock market of the likely performance of the company under its present ownership and, since future returns should be discounted as discussed in chapter 9, on the rate of discount adopted by the market. A takeover bid will prove successful to the acquiring company, therefore, only if it can improve the performance of the unit sufficiently to justify the costs of the acquisition. However, the mere fact that a company makes a bid for another indicates that it thinks it can improve the earnings from the assets, a signal that is picked up by shareholders and other traders on the market. The announcement of a bid is, therefore, usually accompanied by a rise in the share price of the company sought, and often a substantial premium has to be paid over the previous share price for the would-be purchaser to obtain control.[24] In considering an acquisition due attention must be paid to these aspects of share price valuation.

In a study of takeovers in the UK between 1972 and 1974 using share price data, Firth[25] found that the acquired firm typically had a poor stock market performance prior to the bid, although the price tended to rise just before the official announcement in the light of leaks and rumours and the build-up of a stake in the firm by the acquirer before announcing a full bid. On the announcement of the bid the share price of the acquired company rose by about 22 per cent on average. Acquiring companies had, on average, slightly better stock market performance prior to the bid, but their share price usually fell on the announcement of the bid. He concluded that, over all, there was no gain or loss associated with takeovers during 1972-74. Thus, the gains to the shareholders in the firms acquired were almost totally cancelled out by losses to shareholders in the acquiring firm. Therefore he suggests that the stock market tends to think that takeovers will not lead to any private economic gains. As he also notes, while the generally poor performance of the firms acquired suggests that there might be room for improvement, the premium paid to acquire the shares was such as to wipe out any potential gains.

The finding that performance of companies after merger is disappointing is not unique to this study. Many other studies, particularly in relation to profitability, have suggested a similar result.[26] Thus, in the major study by Meeks,[27] the profitability of merged firms was lower, on average, than that of the sum of the separate companies prior to the amalgamation for up to seven years after the acquisition. There are many problems of measurement using accounting data, some of which have been discussed in earlier chapters; but bearing all the difficulties in mind, it does not appear that takeovers have been a particularly successful activity for the firms concerned. Thus the recent Green Paper on merger policy[28] concluded:

Notwithstanding [the] limitations it must be acknowledged that a number of independent studies adopting different approaches have arrived at a similar conclusion: a high proportion — at least half or more — of the mergers studied have proved to be unprofitable. Moreover this was not merely a short-run phenomenon, as one study demonstrated that it continued for at least seven years whereas the costs of re-organisation might be expected to arise in the first few years. It also seems that the reduction in profits applies to frequently and infrequently merging companies.

The experience from mergers in the past has not, therefore, been as encouraging as many people might think. Before embarking on an acquisition, the company needs, as part of its strategy, to recognize the limitations and problems that can arise. It cannot be assumed that big is necessarily beautiful. In this context it is relevant to quote from a recent speech by Sir Adrian Cadbury, the chairman of Cadbury Schweppes:[29]

To remain internationally competitive, companies would have to cut costs and become more flexible in the face of less predictable market conditions. To achieve these aims means reversing the trend of the last 20 years towards large centralised organisations. We will want to break these organisations into their separate business units and to give those units freedom to compete in their particular markets. Large companies will become more like federations of small enterprises, not because 'small is beautiful' but because big is expensive and inflexible.

CORPORATE STRATEGY OF THE IMPERIAL GROUP

In many parts of this book we have illustrated the application of some of the principles of business economics by reference to the operations of one of the major companies in Britain — the Imperial Group. As a conclusion to the present chapter, it is therefore appropriate to examine the publicly stated strategy of the Group. The following view of the aims, objectives, strategies and actions of the company is taken directly from the Group Chairman's statement contained in the Report and Accounts, 1980:

For Imperial Group, as for the rest of British industry, the present recession has sharpened the need to look critically at all its operations, to redeploy its assets and to redirect its efforts, so as to build its earning power for the future. We are doing this with thoroughness and resolution, while remaining well aware that we must not base long-term strategic decisions on short-term economic factors and that we must always retain a sensitive regard for the interests and well-being of the employees who look to us for their livelihood and of the communities in which they live. It is also essential to avoid getting lost in a negative world of 'cuts' and to maintain a lively and positive attitude towards the initiation of new activity which will create both jobs and profit. Over the last two years every one of our Divisions has been pursuing these principles with energy and vigour. While we have closed our board mill in Bristol our plastics business has acquired new interests both in this country and in France. While we have reduced our production and distribution facilities in fish, meat, eggs, poultry and the canning of fruit and vegetables, we have responded to changing consumer preferences by investing in new capacity for more profitable and faster growing products – pizza, Pot Noodle and other snacks in the United Kingdom, and pre-packed poultry products and new sauces in the United States. Similarly, the closure of a brewery and a bottling plant must be set against the opening of the Berkshire Brewery, the continuing modernisation of our pubs, hotels and off-licences, and the acquisition of a controlling interest in the Happy Eater restaurant chain.

Yet all this by itself is not enough. Last year we reported our reasons for seeking a substantial overseas trading investment. In June we finally acquired the Howard Johnson Company at a cost of £280 million. The Howard Johnson business is well organised and is staffed by able and strongly motivated people. With them we are already engaged in two detailed studies – one on the motor lodge business and one on the restaurants. We are well aware that part of the restaurant group, which is very big and has much inherent strength, needs some reorientation if it is to make the most of an environment where skilful marketing brings substantial reward. . . . It is a very important extension of Imperial Group's activities – hitherto largely manufacturing and mainly confined to the United Kingdom – to be more deeply involved in service industries and to be more broadly based in terms both of geography and of currency.

Imperial Group has gone for too long without showing a real increase in profit. During the last few years however we have laid the foundations for a very differently shaped Group. Much remains to be done, and much of what has been done will only bear fruit in time. . . . Our objective is, by careful and constructive allocation of our resources and by energetic and enterprising management, to sustain a steady growth in earnings per share, measured in terms of Current Cost Accounting. It is this that will provide the best assurance of dividend growth for shareholders and of security of employment for those who work in the business.

This account is, of course, written in the particular language of an annual report and is designed to impress shareholders with the skill and foresight of the management of the company. Nevertheless, it does indicate something behind the thinking involved in determining the corporate strategy of a major enterprise which, through market circumstances, needs to review its position to ensure future growth and profitability. In the language of the present chapter, a performance gap has clearly been recognized and various alternative strategies reviewed, including a reappraisal of the companies' existing activities and actions to change these through closure and new product introduction. Its long-term view of the nature of the business is also clearly specified in terms of a greater involvement in services and overseas activities.

NOTES

1 C. R. Christensen, K. R. Andrews and J. L. Bower, *Business Policy: Text and Cases*, 3rd edn (Homewood, Ill., Richard D. Irwin, 1973), p. 107.

2 M. E. Porter, *Competitive Strategy: Techniques for Analyzing Industries and Competitors* (London, Free Press, 1980), p. xvii.

3 Ibid., p. xvii.

4 See Christensen, Andrews and Bower, *Business Policy: Text and Cases*, pp. 231–2.

5 Potential competition can also come from the possible establishment of a brand new firm, but in practice the threat is likely to be much more real from firms that already exist.

6 Monopolies and Mergers Commission, *European Ferries Ltd and Sealink Ltd*, HC 65 (London, HMSO, 1981).

7 It has also been used to explain the transfer of production by American companies from the USA to other countries through the multinational enterprise. See, for example, R. Vernon, *Sovereignty at Bay: the Multinational Spread of US Enterprises*, (Harmondsworth, Penguin, 1971), pp. 71–82.

8 See, for example, D. F. Abell and J. S. Hammond, *Strategic Market Planning: Problems and Analytical Approaches* (Englewood Cliffs, NJ, Prentice Hall, 1979).

9 Porter, *Competitive Strategy*.

10 See F. Blackaby (ed.), *De-industrialisation* (London, Heinemann, 1979).

11 K. R. Harrigan, *Strategies for Declining Businesses* (Lexington Books, 1980), and Porter, *Competitive Strategy*, ch. 12.

12 B. Chiplin and M. Wright, 'Divestment and structural change in UK industry', *Nat West Bank Review* (February 1980).

13 For a discussion of management buy-outs, together with some interesting examples, see R. V. Arnfield, B. Chiplin, M. Jarrett and M. Wright (eds), *Proceedings of a National Conference on Management Buyouts: Corporate*

Trend for the 80s (University of Nottingham, Industrial and Business Liaison Office, 1982) and B. Chiplin and M. Wright, 'Management Buyouts — a new lifeline for industry?' *Accountancy*, 82 (1981).

14 See, for example, G. Meeks, *Disappointing Marriage: A Study of Gains from Merger* (Cambridge University Press, 1977).

15 R. H. Coase, 'The nature of the firm', *Economica*, 4 (1937).

16 O. E. Williamson, *Markets and Hierarchies: Analysis and Antitrust Implications* (New York, Free Press, 1975).

17 This view is clearly expressed in G. J. Stigler, 'The division of labour is limited by the extent of the market', *Journal of Political Economy*, 59 (1951).

18 For a more detailed treatment see, e.g., C. J. Sutton, *Economics and Corporate Strategy* (Cambridge University Press, 1980), ch. 3, and Porter, *Competitive Strategy*, ch. 14.

19 M. A. Utton, 'Large firm diversification in British manufacturing industry', *Economic Journal*, 87 (1977).

20 R. D. Willig, 'Multiproduct technology and market structure', *American Economic Review Papers and Proceedings*, 69 (1979).

21 C. J. Sutton, 'Management behaviour and a theory of diversification', *Scottish Journal of Political Economy*, 20 (1972).

22 P. Tisdall, 'Branching out at W. H. Smith and Son', *The Times*, 21 February 1977 (quoted in Sutton, 'Management behaviour', p.61).

23 See, for example, J. H. Dunning, *International Production and the Multinational Enterprise* (London, George Allen & Unwin, 1981).

24 For an analysis of the impact of information on stock market prices, see S. Grossman and D. Hart, 'Takeover bids, the free-rider problem, and the theory of the corporation', *Bell Journal of Economics*, 11 (1979).

25 M. Firth, 'The profitability of takeovers and mergers', *Economic Journal*, 89 (1979).

26 For surveys of the available evidence, see, for example, Meeks, *Disappointing Marriage*, and M. Sawyer, *The Economics of Industries and Firms: Theories, Evidence and Policies* (London, Croom Helm, 1981).

27 Meeks, *Disappointing Marriage*.

28 *A Review of Monopolies and Mergers Policy: A Consultative Document*, Cmnd 7198 (London, HMSO, 1978).

29 See *Financial Times*, 10 February 1982, p. 16.

Further Reading

Chapter 1 THE RULES OF THE GAME

For a review of recent developments in the British economy and economic policy see the latest available edition of A. R. Prest and D. J. Coppock (eds), *The U.K. Economy: A Manual of Applied Economics* (London, Weidenfeld & Nicolson).

For an introduction to quantitative analysis see J. Stewart, *Understanding Econometrics* (London, Hutchinson, 1976).

Chapter 2 PRODUCTION AND COSTS

J. S. Bain, *Barriers to New Competition* (Cambridge, Mass., Harvard University Press, 1956).

J. Johnston, *Statistical Cost Analysis* (New York, McGraw-Hill, 1960).

A. Silberston, 'Economies of scale in theory and practice', *Economic Journal*, 82 (1972).

G. Stigler, *The Theory of Price* (London, Macmillan, 1966).

Chapter 3 PRODUCTION DECISIONS

W. G. Baumol, *Economic Theory and Operations Analysis* (Englewood Cliffs, NJ, Prentice-Hall, 1965).

C. W. Churchman, R. L. Ackoff and E. L. Arnoff, *Introduction to Operations Research* (Chichester, John Wiley, 1958).

R. Dorfman, P. A. Samuelson and R. Solow, *Linear Programming and Economic Analysis* (New York, McGraw-Hill, 1958).

R. Ferber and P. J. Verdoom, *Research Methods in Economics and Business* (London, Macmillan, 1962).

J. F. Magee and D. M. Boodman, *Production Planning and Inventory Control* (New York, McGraw-Hill, 1967).

D. C. Vandermeulen, *Linear Economic Theory* (Englewood Cliffs, NJ, Prentice-Hall, 1971).

Chapter 4 THE MARKET

For a more analytical treatment of the basic economic theory see e.g.

D. Laidler, *Introduction to Microeconomics*, 2nd edn (London, Philip Allan, 1981), chapters 1-4.

J. Hirshleifer, *Price Theory and Applications*, 2nd edn (London, Prentice-Hall, 1980), chapters 1-6.

D. McCloskey, *The Applied Theory of Price* (London, Collier Macmillan, 1982), chapters 1-7.

Chapter 5 MARKETING

For a good introduction to the marketing literature see P. Kotler, *Marketing Management: Analysis, Planning and Control*, 3rd edn (London, Prentice-Hall, 1976).

For a good treatment of marketing research see P. M. Chisnall, *Marketing Research: Analysis and Measurement*, 2nd edn (London, McGraw-Hill, 1981).

On advertising see B. Chiplin and B. Sturgess, *The Economics of Advertising*, 2nd edn (London, Holt, Rinehart & Winston, 1981).

Chapter 6 PRICING

For a more analytical treatment of the basic economic theory see e.g.

D. Laidler, *Introduction to Microeconomics*, 2nd edn (London, Philip Allan, 1981), chapters 12-14.

J. Hirshleifer, *Price Theory and Applications*, 2nd edn (London, Prentice-Hall, 1980), chapters 9-13.

D. McCloskey, *The Applied Theory of Price* (London, Collier Macmillan, 1982), chapters 11-21.

For an analysis of pricing policies in practice see A. Gabor, *Pricing: Principles and Practices* (London, Heinemann, 1977).

Chapter 7 FINANCE

M. W. E. Glautier and B. Underdown, *Accounting Theory and Practice*, 2nd edn (London, Pitman, 1982).

G. A. Lee, *Modern Financial Accounting*, 3rd edn (London, Nelson, 1981).

F. Wood, *Business Accounting*, Vols 1 and 2, 3rd edn (London, Longman, 1980).

318   *Further Reading*

Chapter 8   PERFORMANCE

H. Edey and B. S. Yamey (eds), *Debits, Credits, Finance and Profits* (London, Sweet and Maxwell, 1974).
H. Ingham and L. Taylor Harrington, *Interfirm Comparison* (London, Heinemann, 1980).
T. A. Lee, *Company Financial Reporting: Issues and Analysis* (London, Nelson, 1976).
M. C. Sawyer, *The Economics of Industries and Firms* (London, Croom Helm, 1981).
D. Swann, *Competition and Consumer Protection* (Harmondsworth, Penguin, 1979).

Chapter 9   INVESTMENT

R. A. Brealey and S. C. Myers, *Principles of Corporate Finance* (New York, McGraw-Hill, 1981).
M. Bromwich, *The Economics of Capital Budgeting* (Harmondsworth, Penguin, 1976).
R. Layard (ed), *Cost-Benefit Analysis* (Harmondsworth, Penguin, 1972).
B. M. Mitchell and P. R. Kleindorfer, *Regulated Industries and Public Enterprise* (Lexington Books, 1980).
R. Sugden and A. Williams, *The Principles of Practical Cost-Benefit Analysis* (Oxford University Press, 1978).

Chapter 10   CONTROL

N. Dopuch, J. Birnberg and J. Demski, *Cost Accounting*, 2nd edn (New York, Harcourt Brace Jovanovich, 1974).
M. Firth, *Forecasting Methods in Business and Management* (London, Edward Arnold, 1977).
K. R. Harrigan, *Strategies for Declining Businesses* (Lexington Books, 1980).
T. Horngren, *Cost Accounting: A Managerial Emphasis*, 4th edn (Englewood Cliffs, NJ, Prentice-Hall, 1977).
D. J. Rhodes, D. M. Wright and M. G. Jarrett, *Computers, Information and Manufacturing Systems* (London, Holt-Saunders, 1982, forthcoming).
J. Sizer, *An Insight into Management Accounting* (Harmondsworth, Penguin, 1976).

Chapter 11   CORPORATE STRATEGY

For a general introduction linking economic analysis with the corporate planning literature see C. J. Sutton, *Economics and Corporate Strategy* (Cambridge University Press, 1980).
For a more advanced treatment incorporating the findings of the latest research see M. E. Porter, *Competitive Strategy: Techniques for Analyzing Industries and Competitors* (London, Free Press, 1980).

Index